From Chicago to Vietnam:
A Memoir of War

FROM CHICAGO TO VIETNAM
A MEMOIR OF WAR

By
MICHAEL DUFFY

DEDICATION

This book is dedicated to my deceased brother, Dan Duffy, who served his country in Vietnam with the 82nd Airborne Division, 1967 to 1968. It is also dedicated to the anonymous three Vietnamese women and one young Vietnamese boy who risked their lives by helping me carry a wounded American soldier from a battlefield in the early morning hours of June 7, 1968.

This book is also dedicated to the officers and enlisted men of C Battery 7th Battalion 9th Artillery. These men, some draftees some volunteers and some career Army, served their country in Vietnam. They didn't run to Canada to avoid the draft or go AWOL to avoid Vietnam. They, like me, were unremarkable men who came from every part of the United States and every ethnic background. They performed the job the United States of America asked them to do. They did not deserve the bitter unwelcome reception most of us received upon returning home.

I also wish to dedicate this work to my late wife, Peg Duffy, my human spellcheck. I love you, Peg.

AUTHOR'S NOTE

Some names and identifying details have been changed to protect the privacy of individuals.

CONTENTS

Chapter 1

THE ARRIVAL

My plane arrived at the Cam Ranh Bay Airbase in South Vietnam about 2:00 a.m. The air was muggy and hot. We disembarked and were herded onto olive-green buses; wire mesh and thin metal bars covered the windows. I thought the wire and bars were odd. Why do they have to worry about us escaping from the bus? Where could we go? I was quickly told by the driver that the wire and bars were used to keep hand grenades from being thrown into the bus, not to keep us on the bus. "Oh," I said.

The military base at Cam Ranh Bay sat between two bodies of water, the South China Sea on one side and the bay of Cam Ranh on the other. I scanned the night sky. I saw flares floating down above low mountains just west of the bay. The flares were shot from artillery cannons and fluttered down, hanging from small parachutes. I was scared one moment, then I talked myself into a state of calm the next. No one on the bus said a word; we were tired from the long flight and anxious about fighting in this Asian war.

The bus made a short run and dropped us off at a large building. We walked into a great room, where our green, look-alike duffle bags were being piled. The bags formed a small hill. Men began clawing through the bags, searching for theirs. As the bags were being picked up, we were told to form a line, where, we were informed, bedding and a barracks assignment would be issued. Once in the barracks, we would spend the night in a fitful sleep, filled with fear and a human clock still ticking on U.S.A. time. I stood and watched as each man found then pulled his bag off the pile. The end came when I was alone standing next to the luggage drop without a bag. I mumbled to myself, "The fucking army lost my bag. Now what do I do?"

I asked the private on duty about any other bags that might be arriving.

"Nope, that's it, sir," he said.

"What do I do?" I asked.

"Sir, walk down to the lost bag office, about a block from here. Maybe your bag fell off the luggage cart. If they find it on the tarmac, they send it to the lost bag office."

I made the short walk to the lost-and-found bag office, my small attaché held tightly in my hand. My attaché held the orders directing me to Vietnam and to my new unit in Pleiku. Purchased in a Chicago stationery store, my attaché was made of heavy Kraft paper, and it had two side gussets, a flap, and a brown, shoelace-type string to secure the flap. I used this attaché as my mobile file cabinet. It also held a letter from the Department of the Army appointing me as a reserve commissioned officer, my army vaccination record, a paperback copy of John Steinbeck's *East of Eden*, and a small book filled with the addresses of friends and relatives back home. We were told never to pack one's orders in checked luggage for fear our luggage could get lost. They were right.

"Yes, sir?" said the private on duty at the lost-and-found office.

"My name is Lieutenant Duffy. I got off the flight from McChord Air Force Base in Seattle."

"Yes," he said.

"I have no bag."

"We may have it. They come in at all hours. Do you want to look?"

"Yes."

This green duffle bag had everything I needed for a year in Vietnam. It held two sets of jungle fatigues, a lightweight jacket, two pairs of green combat boots, socks, underwear, a toothbrush, and a green jungle hat, the kind with a floppy brim. These were all issued at McChord Air Force Base. It even held the illegal switchblade knife I purchased in Colón, Panama, during our jungle training. The knife was black with a four-inch steel blade. It had a silver button in the middle, and when pushed, the blade switched out and was held rigid by a locking device. I pictured myself in combat, fighting hand to hand. As the enemy was getting the best of me, I would ask him to wait a minute as I reached into my pocket, pulled out my switchblade, and found and pushed the silver button, and then I'd finish him off, just as they did in those black-and-white war movies my brother, Dan, and I watched on weekend nights. I just hoped that Charlie,[1] would cooperate with my ridiculous fantasy and wait until I was able to find my knife. But now it was gone.

The private at the desk showed me through a set of double doors into a huge metal building the size of a high school gymnasium. The room was filled, wall to wall, floor to ceiling, with lost bags. It was a sea of green duffle bags, and every bag looked the same. "My God," I mumbled. "How do I find my bag?" The private looked at me, smiled, and calmly said, "Sir, no one ever finds his bag."

---

1.   Charlie is short for Victor Charlie, or VC, the Viet Cong insurgents fighting the U.S. forces in Vietnam.

I thought for a moment as I faced the wall of green duffle bags. Then I turned to him and asked, "Can I take someone's bag that didn't get claimed, maybe a bag that has been here a month or two? I need a change of clothes."

"No, sir," he said, then he shook his head back and forth. "What if I give you someone's lost bag tonight and then the owner of that bag shows up tomorrow? I'll lose this job and be out in the field walking in the muck that very day. Sorry, no dice. I can't risk it, sir. This is too good of a job. Plus, I go home in forty-six days and a wake up. Nope, can't risk it, sir, sorry." Then he turned and marched away.

I walked over to get my barracks assignment for the night and thought about the socks and shoes I needed. I was clothed in dress khakis with shiny black oxford shoes. I wore a short-sleeved shirt with a glossy black nametag that read "DUFFY." I couldn't function in Vietnam like this. I needed green fatigues and combat boots like everyone else.

I entered the barracks, found my bunk, hung up my khakis, and fell into a fitful sleep. It was about 4:00 a.m.

The next morning was oppressively hot and humid. I awakened with a throbbing headache, pulled myself out of bed, put on my dirty khakis, and then walked to the headquarters building to report for duty. As was, and still is, military custom, each arriving officer reported to the Officer in Charge, or OIC. The OIC reviewed orders and then arranged transportation to one's new unit. My new unit was the Fourth Infantry Division in Pleiku, Vietnam. An indifferent company clerk glanced at me and told me that the OIC would be at his desk in about an hour. I walked out of the office and toward the front gate of the base. Off in the distance, I saw hills, the same hills that I had seen as dark silhouettes the previous evening. The hills were now a sooth-ing blue-green in the soft, humid morning light.

I watched as three young Vietnamese women pedaled past me on bicycles. They wore straw hats pushed back off their heads. The hats were tied to their necks with broad, colorful ribbons. They wore shiny black waistcoats with fat fabric buttons. Their loose-fitting, black pants flapped in the breeze. I watched their long, black hair fly in the wind. They talked and laughed as they passed me. I wondered to myself, *Who are they?* They were, I found out, Vietnamese civil-ians working on the Cam Ranh Bay Airbase. Employing civilians on the American bases was a common practice. The employees, usually women, because the men were off in the South Vietnam Army, would work on the roads, in the mess halls, or in the laundry. Any job was welcome—it brought a few piasters[2] into their homes.

I glanced at my watch, the watch my parents had given me when I graduated from Officer Candidate School in Oklahoma. It was a Bulova with a black face and a gold-plated back. The watch was engraved "LT. DUFFY, 14 MAR 1967." My hour was up, so I began my walk back to the OIC office. "Welcome to the Republic of Vietnam," a stiff-faced captain said to me. I saluted and handed him my orders. He quickly looked them over, then he told me there was a change. I would not be heading to Pleiku as my orders stated; instead, I had a new assignment to a unit near Saigon.

"Why the change?" I asked.

"They need men down south. There's a lot of enemy activity in and around the Saigon area. The brass think the VC are up to something. You'll be leaving in thirty minutes on that plane."

---

2. The piaster was the currency of the Republic of South Vietnam.

He looked out his window and pointed to a C-130[3] aircraft with its four engines running. Then he asked me why I was still in my khaki-colored shirt and pants.

I told him my lost luggage story. He said to find some green jungle fatigues as soon as possible. "Here are your new orders; get over to the plane now. Wait, before you go, here's a booklet on Vietnam. Read it."

The book was a small, thin paperback. It had Vietnamese phrases and useful words to help with directions or making a purchase. The book discussed the monetary system in Vietnam; it mentioned that the U. S. military needed to keep our "greenback" dollar out of the Vietnamese currency system. It also gave a brief history of the Vietnamese people and their culture. The Vietnamese culture dated back thousands of years, and it read, as visitors to this country, we should respect their culture. After reading a few pages, I stuffed it into my attaché and ran to the waiting plane.

The pilots were peering out their windows, and they looked worried. The flight crew was unfriendly. I boarded quickly. We were headed to Saigon.

About twenty GIs were crowded into a small rear-passenger cabin, along with boxes of military equipment. We sat on webbed nylon benches facing each other. The plane taxied and then took off like a rocket, banking to the left over the South China Sea, then back over land. The flight was wrenching. The plane pitched to the left and right, and soon I became dizzy and lightheaded. The pilots set a course for Saigon's airport, Tan Son Nhut. I glanced at the other men on the plane, and I thought, *They all look so young*. At the age of twenty-two,

---

3. C-130 is a four-engine turboprop military aircraft.

I was probably the oldest on the flight. But all the men on this flight did have one thing in common—they looked frightened.

Soon the pilot's voice welcomed us aboard. "If there is any trouble, there are plenty of spots to land along the way," he said. "Don't worry." I thought, *What does he mean by trouble?*

I turned my head to look out a small window. I watched as we flew over rice paddies, palm trees, and rubber plantations. The country-side was stunning; my eyes were filled with bright, yellow-green foliage and dark, shadowy blue-greens; occasionally, I saw a red-tile roof. Our flight was short, and soon I heard the plane's engines throttle down.

As we began our descent into Saigon, I glanced out the window and noticed thick, black smoke rising from different quarters of the city. Soon the plane plummeted downward, spinning my stomach. The plane's right wheels hit the ground with a slam, then the left wheels banged down, rattling the cabin and the men inside. The pilot began lowering the back door; he made a jarring stop. Brilliant sunlight streamed into our cabin. I watched a young soldier run toward the now open back door. He was waving and shouting frantically. "Get off the plane! *Over there! Over there!* Have your orders out, move, *move!*" I ran off the plane onto the tarmac.

The young private pointed to another soldier with a clipboard. He was glancing at our orders and directing us to different locations on the air field. This place was a madhouse. We were standing on the field with planes, helicopters, jeeps, and trucks everywhere. They had their engines racing, and the noise was earsplitting. A fine red dust began filling my eyes; they began to burn. I could hear the sound of small arms fire. I instinctively ducked; I saw smoke rising over a long earthen wall. After three nights without sleep and the jarring plane ride, I was bewildered and dazed.

The private with the clipboard grabbed the orders from my hand. He quickly looked them over, then using his finger, he pointed to a waiting helicopter. You could not hear voices clearly. Messages were given with the point of a finger, a scream, or a wave. I looked back at our C-130 aircraft as its four engines roared and launched it back into the sky; a cloud of dust blew into our faces. Once again, I was told, but this time with a harsh shout and a pointing finger waving back and forth in my face, "Lieutenant, *run!* Move! The base is under attack, and you need to get the hell out of here."

I turned from the private and began a sprint to the helicopter, only to catch my foot on a block of wood. I fell to the tarmac. My hands were outstretched to break the fall. My attaché went airborne, and my knee caught a corner of the wood block, ripping my khaki pants. The palms of my hands tore and now were bloody and filthy. I got up and collected my attaché and myself and ran to the waiting Huey helicopter.

The helicopter pilot was at his controls, and the blades were pulsing. He watched through a side window as a few others and I ran to his craft. A second anxious GI standing at the helicopter's open door glanced at our orders as we climbed aboard. He yelled to me, "Get off in Bien Hoa. It's the first stop." He looked me over and then asked if I had a weapon. I shook my head and said no. He cocked his head and said, "Well, sir, you better get one, and sir, I would get out of those khakis. You look like a target." He turned and sprinted off.

I quickly took the end seat. The pilot rushed the engine. Our chopper tilted forward, then it began a slow rise over an earthen berm separating the airport from the shanties of Saigon.

As we gained altitude, I heard more explosions, but I couldn't judge where they were coming from. I sat with my head turned toward the open helicopter door; if I vomited, I didn't want to do it inside the cabin. The few hours since leaving Cam Ranh Bay were a mass of confusion, and I was feeling ill. We flew over a thick cloud of black smoke rising from a burning vehicle. The young private's words back on the tarmac resonated in my head. He said I looked like a target.

It was January 31, 1968, the opening day of the Tet Offensive[4] in South Vietnam.

The army had removed the large side doors on the Huey helicopters to lighten the load. I was sitting on a nylon bench with a perfect view of Saigon under attack. I saw men, armored personnel carriers, tanks, and clouds of smoke fade into tiny dots as we flew toward Bien Hoa. It seemed peaceful up there, almost safe. I began to relax a little. I glanced at the palms of my hands—they were a mixture of dirt and blood and sweat. I wiped them against my torn pants. The two other men on the chopper were also going to Bien Hoa, but they had army-issue green fatigues. They also carried M-16 rifles in their hands.

They both glanced at me with worried faces and quickly turned away. Soon we were descending, this time not to a tarmac but to a road just outside the front gate of the Bien Hoa Base Camp. The Bien Hoa airfield was under attack and could not be used.

All three of us jumped from the helicopter. Bags were tossed out the door by the crew chief, and the Huey was off. As we stood there bewildered, we heard a voice from the base shouting, "Get your ass down!"

I fell to my knees, then to the ground in a prone position. I crawled toward the front gate on my stomach while gunmen shot at us from shan-

---

4. The Tet Offensive was a massive attack by more than 80,000 Viet Cong and North Vietnamese combat troops launched against the United States and South Vietnam forces on the eve of the Vietnamese lunar new year, called Tet.

ties across the street. I saw puffs of dust pop around me as bullets hit the crusty, dry earth. Now I was scared, but it was the voice from the bunker that struck fear in me. As we neared the gate, we jumped up and ran to a sandbagged bunker manned by two sentinels. I tumbled into the bunker as a young private fired an M-60 machine gun toward the shanties. Hot brass casings burned my forearm as they spit from the weapon. When he stopped firing, we began pummeling questions at the two GIs. They looked exhausted and filthy. One man never took his eye off the road. He was hunched over the machine gun. "What's going on?" I shouted.

One of the young privates in the bunker began talking rapidly, stopping only to take shallow breaths. He looked at us and said that Charlie had pulled off a major assault that morning, all over the country. He heard the VC had attacked the American embassy in Saigon. They also were fighting in the Cholon neighborhood, near the Saigon Race Track, and they had infiltrated the Tan Son Nhut Airbase—the base we had just passed through. He went on to say that Charlie had gotten into the camp—no one knew how many VC had breached the coils of barbed wire or where they were.

He said that Charlie was still inside the camp. I asked if "the camp" meant this camp. He took a long drag on a cigarette, turned to me, and nodded. "Where do we go from here?" I asked.

"I dunno, sir. If you're new, you need to check into that building over there." He pointed to a dirty wooden building about a block away.

"Is it safe to go?"

"Shit, sir! I dunno, I dunno if it's safe here. I've been in this bunker going on twenty-four hours. Early this morning they tried to come across that road." He pointed to the road we had just landed on.

"We shot the shit out of 'em. It was so dark I dunno if I hit anyone, but I know we got that." He pointed to a dead water buffalo in a ditch just beyond the road. The carcass was beginning to bloat in the sun. "We've been shooting at the snipers across the road," he said. "They're hard to see 'cuz they hide behind the shanties, shoot at us, then they run to another spot and shoot at us again."

He looked at me and said, "Sir, you better get a weapon."

Just then the private hunched over the M-60 machine gun began firing, producing an earsplitting roar. The spent metal cartridges spit out of the machine gun, and the smell of gun powder filled the air. He stopped and shook his head, but he never took his eyes off the road.

A weapon, I thought. I need more than a weapon; I need a place to relax. I was a nervous wreck.

I made a run for the small, wooden building and barreled through the door. Inside the building it seemed eerily calm. A clerk sitting at a gray, metal desk looked up at me almost as if he were in a stateside office. In a quiet voice, he calmly asked, "Can I help you, lieutenant?"

"I'm here to check in."

"Okay, just a minute." He walked into an office behind his desk. Soon, the day officer appeared wearing a steel pot helmet and a flak jacket. He looked at me and then, with a question in his voice, asked, "Lieutenant Duffy?"

"Yes," I answered. He took the orders from my hand, laid them on a desk, then pulled a ballpoint pen from his pocket, and on the margin of my orders wrote Service Battery[5] 7th Battalion[6] 9th Artillery, Bearcat.

---

5. A battery is a unit of the U.S. artillery usually consisting of six guns or cannons and manned with about one hundred men. Service battery refers to the supply-and-support unit, which delivers food and ammunition to the artillery battery in the field.

6. A battalion consists of four batteries with a fighting force of about 500 men.

He pointed at his writing and said, "That's your new unit. They will be in Xuân Lộc tomorrow delivering ammunition. It's a twenty-minute helicopter ride, and you can get a ride in the morning. Nothing is flying out today."

"Where do I sleep?" I asked.

"Over there," he said, pointing to another building out a window.

"You can get something to eat at the mess hall. Sorry, I gotta go." He ran off.

I looked at two signs nailed over the door of his office. One read: War Is Our Business. Business Is Good.

The other sign read: Don't Knock the War. It's the Only One We Have.

The mess hall was closed. I walked over to the barracks and found a bunk. I lay down and began to think about my home, Chicago. I had left almost a week ago in the same khaki uniform I was wearing. It was dirty and torn, and I was filthy.

I thought about my brother, Dan, who was already here in Vietnam, somewhere. I thought it might be Củ Chi, a military base northwest of Saigon. I wondered how he was and if he was okay. I thought of my old girlfriend, who had dumped me. I imagined she was in her dad's enormous Buick with her new boyfriend parked down at some Lake Michigan beach. That thought was depressing. I thought about the old ladies at the draft board, short and fat in dumpy print dresses. I was drafted before the lottery; it was called Selective Service. Those ladies were the ones who had put me here.

When a boy turned eighteen, he was required to report to the draft board for registration. My draft board was on Devon Avenue, just west of Clark Street on Chicago's Far North Side. When the time came for me to register, I walked over to the draft board office then up a long flight of stairs to the second floor. Two women were working behind a long counter. The counter was covered with brown linoleum. The office was sparse, with a couple of wooden chairs and a few lights hanging from the ceiling. One of the women looked me over and then asked, "Are you here to register?"

"Yes," I said.

"I will need a little information, honey. Sit tight."

Soon I was called to the counter, where she filled out a three-by-five card using a ballpoint pen. She asked me a question and I responded. "Name? Height? Weight?" When she finished, I watched her place my three-by-five card in a long, gray metal file cabinet filled with other three-by-five cards. She turned and looked at me and said, "All done. You will receive your draft card in the mail. You can go."

When the War Department needed more men, the dumpy ladies at the draft board opened the file cabinet and pulled my name. President Lyndon Baines Johnson needed 200,000 more troops in Vietnam, and I was one of them.

I received my draft notice on a cool November day in 1965. I read it and then reread it. The notice arrived in a long envelope with red and blue hash markings on each side. There was no metered postage or stamp on the envelope. Printed in the upper right-hand corner were the words "Postage Paid by the United States Government." I was given a date to report to the Polk Street Induction Center in downtown Chicago for a physical exam. As I sat in the comfort of my parents' apartment reading my draft notice, I could not have imagined the crushing responsibilities and wild journey the document I held in my hand would bring my way. My life would change forever, and my nineteen years on this earth would not be enough to prepare me for the events that lay ahead.

I began to worry about what branch of service might draft me. I thought that I better take control. If I enlisted in the army and pre-empted the draft, perhaps I would get some type of specialized training that could lead to a civilian job when I was discharged. I decided to talk to a recruiter.

I took the 'L' train down to the army recruiting office on Wilson Avenue and Broadway in the Chicago neighborhood called Uptown. I knew the draft meant I could end up in the army or the marine corps or the navy. All of those branches were taking draftees to meet the government's insatiable demand for troops in Vietnam. I didn't want to enter either the marine corps or the navy. I didn't like the macho gung-ho crap that went with the marines; I heard all about the marines from my neighborhood friends. They also told me if I joined the army, I would be a dog-face-shit. Furthermore, I didn't want to enter the navy because I had a problem with seasickness. What if I ended up on a ship? I'd spend the best part of each day heaving my guts overboard.

The fellow at the army recruiting office was pleasant. He gave me lots of brochures showing soldiers jumping out of planes, looking at radar screens, and marching in dress green uniforms, all very impressive stuff. The smiling sergeant offered me coffee and a 120-day delay before I had to begin active duty. He said, "Look, Mike, you gotta go anyway. If you decide to join the army, you can pick your job, plus you don't have to enter active service for four months. Remember, if you take your chances with the draft—well, it's potluck."

He pursed his lips and shook his head as he spoke. He was as convincing as a used car salesman, down to the schmooze smile, but he was correct—the draft would be potluck.

If I enlisted in the army, a year would be added to my service. The draftees served two years of active duty; the enlisted men served three. After talking it over with my dad, I felt the aspect of choice and some control over my future was worth the extra year.

The next morning, a Friday, I rose early with the intention of driving to work with my dad. Most days we took the 'L', but sometimes on Fridays we drove. As we walked to the garage in the back of our apartment building, we noticed a large truck leaving the alley. The Lill Coal & Oil Company had just dumped a huge pile of coal in front of our garage door. The coal pile would take all day to move into the basement of our building, one wheelbarrow at a time. My dad and I took the 'L' to work.

I took my draft notice with me to show it to my boss, Charlie Tague. We worked in the offices of the now-defunct New York Central Railroad. Charlie was close to sixty years old; he was African American and had spent time in the military, so I valued his opinion. Charlie came north to Chicago from Texas during the Depression. He told me that he had worked a number of odd jobs after arriving in Chicago. Just after Pearl Harbor was bombed and the United States entered World War II, Charlie was offered a full-time job with the New York Central Railroad. It seems the executives in the upstairs corner offices needed a valet, someone to shine shoes, brush their overcoats, and tidy up their offices. Charlie jumped at the chance to earn a steady paycheck and a railroad retirement pension. Charlie's main duty was sorting and delivering the office mail. When I first started work as the assistant mail boy, I followed Charlie around the office and watched as he cleaned the executive conference table and made sure the ever-present ashtrays were emptied and wiped out. He pushed all the chairs squarely to the table, took one last look at the room, and then closed the door and moved on to his next job.

Charlie was friendly and talkative; his three young grandchildren were his joy. Each day Charlie gave me running accounts of their lives. During a lull in our workday, I pulled out my draft notice, handed it to him, and then said, "Charlie, I just got drafted, and I need some advice."

He slowly read the letter, looked up at me, and said, "Rolling the dice with the draft was a risky business." He told me that he knew a fellow in World War II who had spent the entire war shoveling coal in the boiler room of a ship; it was horrible. He said he would pick a nice, easy profession and enlist in the army.

The word about my draft notice spread quickly through the office; I assumed Charlie told people on his mail round. People I didn't know looked at me and nodded. Everyone knew someone in the service, and most knew someone in Vietnam. Some of my fellow office workers had been to funerals for GIs killed in Vietnam. Hundreds were dying every month.

You couldn't ignore the Vietnam War; it was on TV every night. The news readers offered information on body counts, firefights, new operations, and old operations. Then the pseudo experts would weigh in and give us their two cents—Secretary of Defense Robert McNamara and General Westmoreland. They, in turn, would get their information from the so-called smart guys at the RAND Corporation.[7]

---

7. The RAND Corporation was a civilian firm that employed "war experts." Those experts worked in a think tank for the Defense Department dispensing advice on the war, sometimes good and sometimes bad advice.

Everyone had something to say about the war and the "light at the end of the tunnel," a.k.a., victory.

Charlie's advice helped me make up my mind, and the following Monday, I walked back into the recruiting office. I enlisted and took the 120-day delay. That afternoon the recruiter gave me a general aptitude test. After the test, the friendly sergeant served me coffee and handed me a list of jobs from which I could choose; the available jobs were based on my test score, which he told me was quite high. I selected the position of land surveyor. I thought I would be surveying roads in Germany or France, but it turned out that my skills would be used to survey artillery targets. I finished the coffee, left the office, and took the 'L' home.

As I lay awake in Bien Hoa in pitch darkness, listening to explosions, I thought of my draft letter once again. It read, "Greetings, Your friends and neighbors have selected you to join the armed forces." I thought about those words "friends and neighbors." These were not my friends and neighbors. These were the two ladies at the Devon Avenue draft board. They reached into their file drawer and selected me. I bet they didn't draft their own kids, or their nephews, or their neighbors' kids. I wondered if the other kids my age living on my block had received draft notices: Ira Goldman, Tommy O'Sullivan, or Steve Murphy. Steve lived on the third floor of our apartment building. Probably not. I didn't see any of them down at the Polk Street Induction Center.

I started hearing more explosions. They seemed louder and more frequent and close. I looked at my watch; it was 11:00 p.m. I still had not been issued a weapon. I would be useless if Charlie came through the door with his gun blazing. Useless, I thought. No, I would be dead.

I suspected this might be a very long night, a very long year. As the explosions became louder, they shook my nerves. Even with my artillery training, I couldn't tell if these were incoming or outgoing rounds. I paced the floor; sleep was impossible. Then about 4:00 a.m., I found an empty laundry bag. I took the bag and walked through the barracks. Ever so quietly I began trying on boots at the end of sleeping GIs' cots. I found a pair that fit, then I tried on green combat pants and a green jacket. I took the items back to my bunk and ripped off the name tags. I stuffed my dirty khaki dress clothes and oxford shoes into the laundry bag. Then I put on my new green jungle fatigues and walked over to the mess hall. I was hungry; it was close to 5:00 a.m.

I entered the mess hall in a state of sleep deprivation. I quietly thanked God that the explosions had stopped, and I was feeling some-what safe in the morning light. All the cooks were wearing steel pot helmets. I noticed a stand of M-16 rifles close at hand. I ate some grits (an army favorite) and drank two cups of awful black coffee. Today I would get on another helicopter and take a short hop to Xuân Lộc (pronounced "swan lock"), a provincial capital north of Bien Hoa. There I would hook up with my new unit. After a quick breakfast, I found my way to the base airstrip. I stood and watched as helicopters flew in and out of the base; there was a small dispatch building near the strip. I walked in and handed the clerk my orders. He told me I would have to wait; there wouldn't be a flight to Xuân Lộc until later in the day. I sat down on my new laundry bag and pulled out the Steinbeck book I had started in Chicago. I read it all day until the clerk knocked on his window, pointed, and said, "Sir, that's your ride." I ran to the helicopter; the blades were spinning and kicking up dust.

I jumped on, and we were off. We flew over jungle, tall rubber trees, and French villas. I saw an empty swimming pool and thought that it must be the home of a French rubber baron. We landed on a dirt road in the village of Xuân Lộc. It was late in the day. An army private ran to the ship and yelled my name, "Lieutenant Duffy?"

"That's me."

"You need to get off and report to that guy." He pointed to another army private with a clipboard in his hand.

I jumped off with my belongings and ran to the guy with the clipboard.

"Lieutenant Duffy?"

"Yes?"

"Your unit left Xuân Lộc this morning for Bearcat. You will have to spend the night here then get a ride to Bearcat tomorrow. You need to report to the headquarters building; he pointed to a half-moon, corrugated metal hut. I walked over and entered the building; once inside, I recognized someone from the States. It was Sergeant Long from Fort Sill in Oklahoma.

"Hey, Sergeant Long. How are you?" He glanced at me and nodded. I got nothing more from him; he looked absolutely grave. He turned from me then walked away. I wanted to ask him what I could expect in Vietnam, but he never made eye contact. I felt he had other things on his mind, so I left him alone. There was no joy in this place. A sign hung over the orderly's desk. It read: Don't Knock the War. It's the Only One We Have.

This was the second time I'd seen that stupid sign.

I spent the night on a filthy cot in the rear of the building. Our artillery blasted all night long; I got about two hours of sleep. I awakened to more helicopter blades churning. Soon I was told to board one. I jumped on the ship; no one looked at me or spoke with me. The crew looked exhausted and unfriendly. We flew for twenty minutes then we landed at Bearcat. I jumped off alone and began the short walk to the flight office. It was hot and dry and the fine red dust of Vietnam was blowing in my face.

Bearcat was huge. It was surrounded by a ten-foot-high earth barrier. About fifteen feet in front of the barrier, completely surrounding the base, was barbed wire rolled from coils. All the trees were either cut down or dying. It was, I was told, the result of Agent Orange,[8] a type of herbicide. Bearcat had streets and wooden buildings and a Post Exchange (PX), a type of army convenience store. The base also had showers. I hadn't had a shower in over a week.

I found my way to the headquarters building of Service Battery 7th Battalion 9th Artillery and I reported for duty. It was here that I first met Lieutenant Jack Smith, the executive officer of the unit and my new boss. Jack shook my hand and welcomed me. He had a broad smile on his face.

His smile was the first hint of friendliness I had seen since arriving in Vietnam. Jack stood about five-foot eleven; he had short blond hair and a toothy grin. I guessed he was thirty-five years old. Jack was thin, with a dark tan from the Vietnam sun. He leaned back in his chair and asked where I was from and how I became an officer. He said I looked young for an officer. He offered me a cigarette. I thanked him but declined. Jack began to discuss the position I was about to assume, my duties and responsibilities. Then he asked me if I had any questions. I had only one. What did the name "Bearcat" mean? He told me the base was originally built by the French. The French used

---

8. Agent Orange was an herbicide sprayed by aircraft in Vietnam.

the term "Bearcat" as the base radio call sign. The name stuck with the Americans. Jack told me I would start work the next morning as the OIA, or the officer in charge of ammunition, convoys. The convoys consisted of twelve two-and-a-half-ton trucks, two three-quarter-ton trucks, and a jeep. I would ride in the jeep. Our first stop would be the Long Binh ammunition dump, a short drive from Bearcat. Jack pointed to a large map on the wall and showed me the route to the ammunition dump. At the ammo dump, each truck would be filled with pallets of 105-millimeter artillery shells. After the trucks were loaded, we convoyed out to one of three artillery batteries in the field. On the first trip, Lieutenant Smith would accompany me; from then on, I was on my own.

Our convoy left Bearcat early the next morning after my first good night's sleep in a week. The weather was hot and dry; the road was dusty. The Long Binh ammunition dump was a vast, open-air storage facility filled with high-explosive artillery shells, mortar shells, and other military ordnance. The ammo dump was sectioned off into small lots. Each lot had three earthen walls five or six feet high; there was an opening at one end facing a dirt access road. The earthen walls were designed to prevent an enemy mortar shell from landing in a store of ammunition, exploding, and starting a chain reaction. The walls, although thick and high, did not prevent this. I watched the ammo dump blow up in a white fireball late in February. It was a reminder to us all that the Tet Offensive was not over.

At the ammunition dump I watched drivers on gigantic forklifts drive back and forth, picking up pallets of artillery shells and then pushing them into our two-and-a-half-ton trucks. The drivers on the forklifts were skilled. They would lower the forks as they drove toward the pallet, sliding the two forks perfectly between the two boards that framed the pallet. I watched in awe as they seemed never to miss the opening in the pallets. Later that month I did see a driver miss his mark as we all looked up at a burning engine on a C-130 aircraft. The plane was trying to make it to the airstrip. The forklift driver, his eyes fixed on the smoking airplane, took his foot off the brake. The forklift rolled forward, pinning a man's leg against a pallet of 105-millimeter ammunition. We all heard the leg snap, then came the scream from the young private. He was rushed to the hospital, but we continued loading the ammunition.

Soon our trucks were filled, and we were off. We drove through the village of Bien Hoa and began the fifty-mile trip to Battery C's position in the town of Xuân Lộc. The small villages were crowded with slow-moving ox carts, minicabs, buses, bicycles, and pedestrians. As we drove into the countryside, I noticed an absence of trees and vegetation on each side of the highway. It looked like a desert filled with dying brown shrubbery. Just beyond the dead foliage, the jungle began again. The area between the road and the jungle had been sprayed with Agent Orange. The road just outside of Bien Hoa was newly paved, but after ten minutes of driving, the road changed into broken asphalt and dusty ruts; our convoy slowed to a crawl. Soon we entered a dark forest of rubber trees. They were beautiful—rows and rows of forty- to fifty-foot-tall trees with large, wide, waxy green leaves. There seemed to be no end to those rows. The rubber tree forest was quiet, with no houses and very few people. I was riding in the third vehicle from the front. Ahead of us were two three-quarter-ton trucks. Behind us were the large two-and-a-half-ton trucks filled with artillery shells.

A sandy-haired private drove my vehicle, a jeep. In the back of the jeep, an M-60 machine gun was mounted high and well above our heads. A young private had his finger on the trigger and his shoulder to the stock, he wore a pair of dusty goggles. I was nervous that morning as we pulled out of Bearcat, but the trip went without incident. We rolled into Battery C midafternoon. I was introduced to the executive officer, First Lieutenant Miller. He told us we would spend the night then drive back to Bearcat in the morning. He said the trucks would have to be unloaded by hand; there were no fork lifts in Xuân Lôc. He went on to say that his battery had been attacked just after midnight, and the combat lasted almost until dawn; the VC had tried to cross the earthen wall bordering the village. He pointed to brass shell casings littering the ground. He walked us to the berm and showed us where they had fought the VC. He said his unit suffered no causalities. Jack and I walked to his hooch and drank a few warm beers, then we tried to sleep. But the howitzers fired all night, and sleep was impossible.

After a week or two of delivering ammunition, I settled into my job. Our trucks left Bearcat empty in the morning. We drove to the Long Binh ammo dump, filled the trucks, and drove to one of the batteries in the field to drop our load. One night a major in the battalion called a meeting of all the officers. We were told to meet in the officers' club, a modest wooden building. The club held a few tables and a home-made bar. I walked over to the club and into a crowd of men drinking, talking, and puffing on cigarettes. In the center of the room, the major and his helper were setting up a movie projector. It was a reel-to-reel projector. The projector had two metal spools. The top spool held the film, and after it passed in front of the projector's light, it rolled onto an empty spool just below it. *U.S. Army* was printed in black letters on the side of the projector. The major fidgeted with it for a half-hour while we drank beer and relaxed. Then he shouted, "Lights out!"

We sat down for a surprise. The major barked out, "I slipped into Saigon and purchased a porno movie. It came all the way from Paris, France." He went on to say, "The gook who sold it to me said it was fantastic."

The major was full of himself and proud of his find in Saigon. He wore a large smile on his face. I thought about Major Major, a character in the novel *Catch-22*, a blowhard. They seemed very much alike.

We were all seated at the small card tables around the club. The lights were out, but we continued talking. "Shut up!" the major shouted as he chewed on a cigar. He turned on the projector, which sat on a small stool in front of him. A beam of smoky light passed through the room. The major flipped a switch and the movie started. There were a lot of black-and-white Xs and Os on the screen. Then the film went right to a bedroom scene—no opening credits. It was a black-and-white silent film without subtitles. We found this out when someone asked to have the sound turned up. The movie was made long before talkies, probably in the early 1920s.

On the screen a tall mustachioed man was taking off his clothes. He was puffing on a cigar and walking toward a woman in a Japanese kimono who soon let the kimono fall to the floor revealing her naked body. Their movements on the screen were jerky. Occasionally, we would get a flash of white light on the screen. We all put our hands over our eyes when this happened. Just as the two porn stars were embracing, the film broke and white light flooded the screen. "Shit!" yelled our host. "Turn on the lights!" A few moments later, he had someone run to his office for tape.

"I'll have it fixed in a jiffy," he said.

Everyone started drinking beer again. Twenty minutes passed, and we were told to take our seats and shut up. I thought, *Why couldn't we talk?* The film was silent. When the movie started again, it seemed to have jumped to a completely different scene. The camera was panning a large tapestry on a wall, and in a hokey special effect, a naked woman moved out from the tapestry and began to walk across the floor toward another woman and the man, who was now lying on a sofa staring at the ceiling. The man held his lit cigar in his mouth; it was sticking straight up pointing at the ceiling. Just then something happened with the projector again, and the major yelled, "Shit!" The image stopped, and I heard a loud ticking sound. The sprocket pulling the movie through the projector was stripping the small squares in the aged film. The major began pushing on a button and soon the image on the screen smoothed out. However, not long after the ticking sound episode, the movie became so jerky it looked as if we were viewing a black-and-white slide show at high speed.

Now we were watching images of naked people jerking back and forth in fleshy spasms. People in our small audience began to laugh. "Shut up!" the major yelled. He took his art film seriously, but his words "shut up" made us laugh all the more. The next thing that happened surprised everyone. The major spilled his drink on himself and screamed, "Ah, fuck!" Then he jumped up from his seat and knocked the projector to the floor. The projector, which was sitting on a flimsy, three-legged stool, continued to run, but the reel of film fell off the arm of the projector and the light bulb broke. "Turn on the lights! Ah, shit!" the major yelled. "Shit. Get me a towel."

When the lights went back on, we rubbed our eyes and started drinking beer again and soon forgot about the movie. The major began the job of picking the projector up off the floor. He sent his assistant to find another bulb. He barked, "Fuck, I spent fifteen dollars U.S. for that movie, and I am going to watch it." His efforts were futile, and the club began to empty out. It was late.

The next day I was told to report to the radio room. I had a radio message from my brother, Dan. He found me in Bearcat and wanted to come down for a visit. I hadn't seen or heard from Dan since the previous summer. He had a three-day pass. He was to arrive the next day, if it was okay with Lieutenant Jack, my boss. I told Jack about Dan, and he said it was ok, but I would still have to run the convoy to Xuân Lộc. I kept thinking about Dan all night. How on earth did he find me here in Vietnam?

Dan arrived the next afternoon on the mail shuttle, and I met him at our helicopter pad. He had taken the shuttle from Củ Chi, a large military base twenty-five miles northwest of Saigon. Dan was younger than me, but he had preceded me into the army.

Dan and I spent the afternoon talking about his girlfriend, our new nephew, and Vietnam. Dan told me that his hope was to work for the airlines when he was discharged. The army served him well. He was promoted to corporal. We walked together out to the berm. I set up my camera, put it on the auto setting, then I ran back into the picture. I thought I would give a classic combat pose. I remembered seeing a *Life* magazine black-and-white photograph of an American soldier fighting in Italy during World War II. The soldier in the magazine photo had a week-old growth of beard and a cigarette hanging from his mouth. To me it was the classic World War II combat pose. (The fellow's name was Evangelo; his son Nick runs a bar in Santa Fe, New Mexico. Evangelo's picture is plastered on the walls of the bar. Evangelo was even pictured on a 2002 U.S. postage stamp entitled *The Masters of Photography* series.) Well, I didn't smoke, and I couldn't grow a beard, but I could give that cocky, self-confident, tough-guy look. Later, when I had the pictures developed, Dan displays a fine, broad smile, but I look as if I have a large wad of gum in my mouth.

We went on talking, and I told Dan about my plans to attend Colorado College. That is, if I was accepted. I had applied a few months earlier and was hoping to begin school in the fall of 1969. I would wait months to hear the outcome of my application. I told Dan he could leave Vietnam early now that I was there. The army had a policy of having only one family member in a combat zone. However, this was not a given; you had to fill out paperwork and formally request a transfer out of Vietnam. Dan told me he was going to finish his tour with his unit.

The next day, Dan got into the jeep with me. Together we headed for the Long Binh ammo dump to fill the trucks with ammo and then make the trip to Xuân Lộc. We left late, so we had to spend the night and return the next morning. The roads were too dangerous for night travel. Our trip from the Long Binh ammo dump to Battery C in Xuân Lộc was uneventful. After our evening meal in the mess hall, we began talking with some of the men. They told us that the night before there was another attack on their compound. They were up all night fighting and fending off the assault. While we talked, we heard gunfire from the street outside the compound. An ARVN (Army of the Republic of Vietnam) soldier was in the street firing his weapon. He was drunk. A group of ARVN soldiers followed him. He turned a corner and was out of sight, but the gunfire continued.

The next morning, after very little sleep, Dan and I had a breakfast of black coffee and waterlogged eggs; it was horrible, as usual. We walked to our waiting trucks, now empty. I began the ritual of checking with the drivers to make sure that each truck started. Then I walked around the trucks looking for a flat tire or an open tailgate; I found none. Sergeant Judd ran over to me when all the men were accounted for and the trucks were running. He said, "Sir, we're ready to roll."

The lead truck, a three-quarter-ton, pickup-sized vehicle with a machine gunner in the back, began slowly moving out of the camp past the sentinel, then past the many wood-and-tin-roofed shanties of Xuân Lộc. Women and children looked us over as we snaked through the narrow streets onto Highway 1 and toward our home base, Bearcat. A few of the children waved, but the adults turned away and walked into their huts. Dan and I were together in a jeep just behind the three-quarter-ton truck. We had a driver and a fourth person with us, Lieutenant Smart. He told us that he had some legal business in Bearcat, "papers to sign in front of a lawyer." Lieutenant Miller told me why he was really traveling with us. Lieutenant Smart needed to see a doctor at the Bearcat medical clinic, not a lawyer. He had a common Vietnam ailment that usually went away after a few days, but his case was a bit stubborn. The most bothersome symptom of his ailment was a painful burning sensation when he urinated. It seems that Lieutenant Smart had spent a night out in Saigon a few weeks earlier. He had had a tryst with one of the many bar girls on Tu Do Street, and now he was paying for his night out. He looked awful.

Our convoy picked up speed as we left the city limits and no longer had to worry about ox carts, bicycles, or pedestrians. There was little traffic on the road. The previous night's attack had kept many civilians indoors, not knowing if it was safe to travel. About halfway back to Bearcat, just as we neared the edge of the Binh Son rubber plantation, one of our trucks broke down and stopped the convoy. We were stuck in a low point on the road with a small hill on one side, perfect for an ambush. Sergeant Judd muttered, "We're sitting ducks here." Sergeant Judd asked me in a nervous voice, "Sir, what should we do?" This situation put me on the spot. I didn't want to stop the entire convoy. I thought for a moment, then I foolishly told Sergeant Judd to keep the convoy moving. This was the wrong decision. I realized that after the last truck passed my small jeep. I suddenly had a panicky feeling as I watched our convoy vanish down the road. Sergeant Judd and the mechanic began working on the motionless truck. There were now four vehicles stopped on the road and eight men. My stupid decision left us vulnerable. I walked over to the mechanic, looked him in the eye, and using all the self-control I could muster, I calmly said, "Get it running."

Sergeant Judd looked scared. He was a short-timer with only a few weeks left in Vietnam. He had been through a lot. He knew how dangerous this road could be. His fear triggered more concern in me as I told Dan to watch the rear part of our now very small convoy. Dan ran to the last vehicle. Then he chambered a round in his M-16 rifle. Using his thumb, he pushed the safety to the off position. Sergeant Judd kept telling the mechanic to hurry up. "We need to get out of here." It was eerily quiet. As the mechanic worked on the disabled truck, we all raised our heads to the sound of a small motorcycle coming our way. The sound of the two-cycle engine got louder, and soon we watched a middle-aged Vietnamese man ride by us on a beat-up moped. He slowed as he passed and looked over our situation. His face was expressionless. He looked, I thought, like a young Ho Chi Minh. He had a weathered brown face with deep, wrinkly lines and a long, wispy beard. He gunned the moped then sped off in the direction of Xuân Lộc. Now Sergeant Judd looked frightened. "Sir," he said, "that guy on the moped could tell Charlie we're broken down. We need to get out of here."

I looked at Sergeant Judd and said, "I know that." I glanced at Dan. I now viewed him as my little brother, whom I had just sent into a dangerous situation, to guard the rear of our convoy alone. My concern was for him. We could be attacked if a squad of VC found us. I cursed myself for letting the convoy continue. I was filled with doubt about my reasoning and my decision. I barked at the mechanic, "How long?"

"Sir, I'm working as fast as I can." Thank God he was calm. Sergeant Judd walked over to tell me once again that the guy on the moped was going to tell Charlie we were broken down. He also thought it was important to remind me that I never should have let the convoy go ahead.

I decided not to bother the mechanic again because even the slightest interruption might slow his work. I literally bit my tongue. I pulled my army-issue .45 caliber pistol out of its holster, chambered a round, and then I scanned the small hill next to our position. My heart was pounding. I glanced at Dan with worry then at Sergeant Judd, who was now pacing back and forth along the road. Lieutenant Smart was still in our jeep grimacing in pain. The mechanic finished his work, jumped in the front seat of the truck, and pushed the starter. It turned and began to pop and backfire, then it started! *Oh, thank God.* The sound of it was a breathtaking relief. The motor roared to life as the mechanic gunned it, keeping the rpm's high. He didn't want it to stall again. We jumped into our vehicles and were off. We raced through the open road, past rows of rubber trees. After ten minutes speeding down Highway 1, we caught up with our convoy.

We made it back safely to Bearcat, but I was exhausted from the stress. This was my first test of leadership in Vietnam. It turned out okay, but I know that Sergeant Judd thought the "green lieutenant" had made the wrong decision. He would tell others. I didn't want that; I wanted to be liked by the men and the officers. This need to be liked would get me in trouble later in the year.

My brother, Dan, flew off on the mail shuttle the next day. We both said we would write each other, but we never did. I received a letter from my mother later that year saying that Dan had arrived home. He had purchased a new car, a Pontiac Firebird, and had applied for a job with Continental Airlines. He still had a few months left in his army tour, and he would spend those months in North Carolina at Fort Bragg. I smiled to myself, glad that he was home and happy for him.

A few nights later, I awakened to sirens going off. Our battery commander ran into my room and yelled at me to get into the bunker. The bunker was a four-foot hole in the ground with sandbags piled high on each side. It was just next to our sleeping quarters. The bunker had a metal roof with sandbags stacked three deep on top. We stood in the bunker and heard the sound of incoming rockets or mortars. I was too new in Vietnam to tell the difference, but I would soon learn the difference. After a short while, the captain turned to me and said, "Lieutenant Duffy, go out to the berm with the enlisted men and watch for an attack." I wasn't ready for this. I wanted to stay in the bunker, where I thought it was safe. I looked at our captain and asked, "Outside, sir?"

"Yes, get out to the berm." I left the bunker and ran to the berm. My breath was short. I had a deep fear of the enemy climbing over the berm wall with guns firing. When I arrived, I found the berm filled with troops from our battalion, all lying on the ground. Everyone was pointing his weapon toward the barbed wire. One fellow had a star-light scope, a telescope that gave us grainy ghost images in the dark. "Can you see anything?" I asked him.

"No, sir."

Another volley of rockets flew over our heads and crashed into the compound. They came from the dense jungle in front of the camp, but to determine the point of origin was impossible. I thought, *They could fire all night and we would never be able to get a fix on them.* The VC would set up 122-millimeter rockets, either Russian or Chinese. They would use logs and tree branches as launching pads, a type of sawhorse that propped the rocket up off the ground. The rockets were pointed at our position, then the VC would light the fuse. By the time we figured out where the rockets were coming from, the part-time Viet Cong soldier/part-time farmer was back at home. Even with our high-tech starlight scope, the countryside was too flat and full of dense jungle to find the launching pads. I looked behind me. One of the rockets had hit the camp generator. It was burning. We watched the coils of barbed wire all night. The sky lightened to a sunny morning. The attack never came; neither did sleep.

The next night, our captain said he wanted to teach me pinochle. We sat together at an army-issue green table, and he began the process. While he dealt the cards he began asking me questions, "Where did you go to college?" I told him that I had never gone to college, except for a few hours at Chicago's City Colleges. There was no money in our house for college; after high school I began working. He went on quizzing me. "If you didn't go to college, then how did you become an officer?" I told him the story:

In the 1960s, if an enlisted man serving in the army had a high school diploma (and many did not), a good score on the army's IQ test, and then passed a review board, he was offered a chance to attend Officer Candidate School (OCS). After my ten-week survey course at Fort Sill in Oklahoma, I was asked by my commanding officer if I would be interested in OCS. A quick assessment of an officer's pay scale (much higher than a private's), and the thought of improving my living conditions on base made me quickly accept. The other men in my survey class who were offered OCS turned down the army's invitation, and they were all promptly sent to Germany, where during their off hours they chased girls in the German beer halls. They sent me pictures with beers in their hands and women on their arms. I, on the other hand, sealed my fate. After OCS, I had a direct path to Vietnam.

Our captain was a Dartmouth man. He had gone through the school's ROTC (Reserve Officer Training Corps) program. He told me that he was considering the army as a career, and it was important for a career man to punch his ticket here in Vietnam. His life seemed relatively safe in Bearcat. While on duty in his office, he pushed papers and wrote letters home. He sent the junior officers like me out to run convoys up Highway 1. In the evening he played pinochle, drank beer, and then went to bed. Bearcat was never overrun while I was stationed there, and short of a few rocket attacks, it was a great place to spend your year in Vietnam and, as the captain said, "get your ticket punched."

The captain leaned back in his chair, looked at me, and then asked, "Did you get drafted?"

I told him the story of getting my draft notice, then quickly enlisting in the army's survey school to avoid the marines or the navy. I told him about the 120-day delay before reporting for duty. I mentioned a trip to New Orleans for Mardi Gras.

"Tell me about your trip," he asked.

I began my story:

> I rode the Illinois Central Railroad from Chicago to New Orleans. My dad secured a pass for me from his employer, the New York Central Railroad. When I arrived in New Orleans, I was met by my sister, Irene. She was spending a week in town with her new hus-

band and offered me a few nights of lodging and a chance to see the city and experience Mardi Gras. Early one Monday morning, after two days of wading through drunks and beer cans, I began hitchhiking east to Florida. I wanted to experience the white sandy beaches and lie in the warm Florida sun. I had about fifty dollars in my pocket. Through a series of long and short rides, I ended up in Pensacola, Florida. I checked into the Pensacola YMCA Hotel. It was an aging but well-maintained wooden building painted white with a red roof. From the center of the lobby ran long halls like spokes from a wheel. At the end of each of those long halls were the rooms. The clerk asked me if I wanted a ten-dollar room or a five-dollar room. I took the five-dollar room and headed down the hall with the key. When I opened the door, I saw two beds. One bed was empty; in the other bed a middle-aged man was sitting up reading a newspaper and puffing on a cigar. I excused myself and told him the clerk probably had given me the wrong key. He looked at me and said, "No, no, you must have checked into a five-dollar room."

"I did, but how did you know that?" I asked. He told me the five-dollar rooms were doubles, and he was my roommate for the night. "This mistake happens all the time." He looked harmless, and I was tired, so I got into my bed and fell asleep.

The next morning my luck changed. Just outside of Pensacola, I got my first long-distance ride. A trucker driving a large eighteen-wheeler slowed and stopped. I picked up my small plaid suitcase, the one I had borrowed from my sister, and I ran to the passenger door.

I sat on a long bench seat and looked over at a gearshift lever with a dozen positions etched in white on a black knob. The trucker had the radio blasting country and western music. He asked where I was headed. I told him I was going to enter the army in a few weeks. I assumed he knew going into the army probably meant going to Vietnam. After a half-hour we stopped for breakfast, and I reluctantly paid the bill. Now I had only forty-four dollars in my pocket. From the back of the cab, the driver pulled out a six-pack of Budweiser, tall cans, a half-quart each. He placed the beer between us and offered me one. As we drove east on the two-lane highway, I slowly drank one beer. In the same time, he drank five beers. I told him I was headed to Sarasota to visit some friends. We talked all day; somewhere near the east end of Florida's panhandle, he told me he was heading north into Georgia. He dropped me off in a small town and he gave me the key to a trucker's flophouse. He said I could spend the night. "Just leave the key in the room." The hotel was old, made of wood, and hadn't seen paint in years. The room was on the second floor, and it was filthy. I took a walk around the small town and saw an open-air laundry with two sets of washing machines. A wooden sign over one set of the washing machines read "*Colored*." The other set of washers had a sign that read "*White*." I thought, either the whites in northern Florida didn't want to wash their clothes with the Negroes, or the Negroes didn't want to wash their clothes with the whites.

I put a blanket on the floor and lay down for the night; the mattress looked a bit too gamey for me. The next morning I headed for the highway and Sarasota. After five or six rides, I made it to Palmetto, Florida. I called my friends, and soon they drove to the crossroads and picked me up.

I thought I was talking too much and slowing down my pinochle lesson, so I stopped. The good captain asked me to continue. I thought, *He's a Dartmouth man.* He probably had never hitchhiked, and he liked my story, so I continued.

After a few days in Sarasota, I said my goodbyes and headed to Fort Lauderdale. My first memorable ride was with a young couple in a 1956 Chevy. The car was the pride and joy of the driver. It was painted a deep red; the driver called it "candy apple red." The Chevy had a hole cut through the hood and a large chrome air filter poked through. There were long chrome exhaust pipes running from just under the front wheel wells along the rocker panel to the rear wheel wells. The pipes had a piece of metal bolted to the end, blocking the flow of exhaust. The car was a two-door, and I was invited to sit in the backseat. The driver, a young man in his twenties, peeled off the gravel shoulder, screeching the tires as he shifted into second gear. When he shifted into third, he was speeding down the road at fifty or sixty miles an hour. He settled the speed at eighty miles an hour and passed every car in sight on this two-lane Florida blacktop.

His girlfriend turned and leaned toward me, then asked, "Where ya goin'?" I told her the same story I had been repeating day after day: draft notice, 120-day delay, and warm weather, blah blah blah.

The driver decided to pass a car that was also going eighty miles an hour. He moved into the oncoming lane of traffic pulled up next to the other car, glanced at the driver, and then floored it, taking the car close to a hundred miles an hour. I watched the red needle move ever closer to the end of its arc. He leaned toward the backseat and said to me, "This car is fast, huh?"

"Yeah, it seems real fast to me," I said. I was on the edge of my seat, and I wanted him to slow down, but I dared not ask him for fear he would drive faster.

"See those canals on the side of the road?" He pointed to long drainage canals. "If this car ever blows a tire at this speed and we go into the canal, they'll never find us."

Why would he say something like that? "How are your tires?" I asked him.

"Shit, they're as bald as billiard balls."

"Oh," I said, "maybe you should slow down a little?"

"Naa, it's OK."

We came to a crossroad and he pulled into a service station. I thanked them and said I was going to call my friend to pick me up. I walked into a small diner and waited until they drove away, then I walked back to the highway and put my thumb out. There was another hitchhiker standing on the road. He gave me a stone-faced look. I walked back into the restaurant and waited until he found a ride.

I made it to Fort Lauderdale in one day and checked into a downtown hotel, twelve dollars a night, cash in advance. The weather was warm and breezy. I thought if I could find a job parking cars or working in a kitchen, I could afford to stay a few days. I hitched a ride to the beach. After making some inquiries at restaurants, I found no work and headed back to the hotel. An older man in a huge, white, two-door Cadillac convertible, top down, saw me and made an illegal U-turn. Tires screeching, he pulled over and, with a broad smile, said, "Need a ride?"

"Yes," I said. "I'm going into town."

"Get in. I'll give you a lift." I jumped in the car and glanced at the driver. He looked to be in his mid-seventies, maybe even eighty years old. He had a puffy, sunburned face with a few wisps of white hair on the top of his balding head. His arms were thin, dark brown, and without form; his legs, sticking out from a pair of Bermuda shorts, were hairless and skinny. He looked over at me, took a cigarette from his mouth, then asked, "Where are you from?" I told him my story—draft notice, no work, low on money, and probably leaving for Chicago in the morning. He told me he was a philanthropist down from Boston on holiday. He lived on his boat, which was berthed at a yacht club. He told me there was always work to be done—"Things to be fixed, things to be cleaned and painted." As we pulled up to my hotel, he asked if I would be interested in a few days of work helping him on the boat. He would be leaving for Boston in a week and had to "put things in order."

"Just a couple of days, but it would put a few dollars in your pocket. What do you say?"

He seemed harmless, so I said yes. It was decided that he would pick me up in the morning. I thought, *This is good, I need the money.* "Okay, see you in the morning," I said.

The next day, I walked out of the hotel and noticed his car was parked a block away, and he was waving at me to walk over to him. *That's odd*, I thought, *maybe he doesn't want to be seen by the hotel staff.* Two of the staff were standing on the sidewalk smoking cigarettes. I walked down the block and got into his car, then we drove to his yacht. It was big and it was docked next to other boats off a wooden pier. He showed me around the deck, the bridge, and the other parts of a boat that I knew nothing about. We went below for coffee. He brewed it on a small stove in the galley. I asked him what he wanted me to paint? He hesitated then told me with a faint smile that he wanted me to be his … "special friend."

"Special friend?" With a question in my voice, I repeated his words out loud, "Special friend?" I was trying to figure out what he meant by "special friend."

"Oh," I said. "So does that mean you don't want me to paint your boat?"

"That's right," he said, smiling.

Ahhhhh, shit! I thought. *You fucking idiot, Duffy. You should have known.* I jumped up and started for the small door near the galley, but he was blocking my way. I roared at him, "Let me out of here!" He could see the determination in my face, and he backed off.

Once off his boat, standing on the pier and boiling with anger, I realized that I was still miles from the highway.

He saw my dilemma and suggested that he could drive me to the outskirts of town where I could get a ride. It was awkward for me because I was still smarting from his deceit. I hesitated and then said, "Okay, just get me to the highway."

I hugged the passenger door as he drove, and I didn't say a word. He mentioned during the drive that he thought I was a bit naïve, and I should have known why he had invited me onto his boat. I thought, *Of course, it's my fault because I didn't decipher his cryptic bullshit job offer.* I didn't answer him or look at him. He stopped the car at an intersection, and as I left his white Cadillac, he reached over to put some cash in my hand. I glanced at his hand, then at him. In a voice filled with anger, I said, "I don't want your money." Then I slammed the door and didn't look back. He drove off.

The fact was I didn't *want* his money, but I did *need* his money. And now I had very little of the green cash that I had just refused. I had refused it out of pride, out of my distaste for his lie. All I wanted was work and a little cash. If he had been honest with me the night before, I would have said, "No, thanks." Then today I would be off to Chicago without feeling as if I had just been snookered.

I don't know if I was more pissed off at his lie or at myself for being so stupid in swallowing it. Now I was walking again on the highway with about ten dollars in my pocket. As I walked along the road, I thought of things I should have said to him, "Fuck you, you lying jag-off." Jag-off was a great Chicago slur.

I hitchhiked north to Jacksonville and spent the night in a blue-green fiberglass chair at the Trailways Bus Station. As I sat there trying to fall asleep, I went over the day's events again and again. I was furious with myself for being so gullible. I couldn't sleep.

The captain put his cards down; he was listening intently to my story. "What happened in Jacksonville?" he asked. "Keep going, what happened?" I went on with my story.

The next morning, I purchased a bus ticket to Mobile, Alabama, and I kept a few bucks in my pocket for food. I *wanted* to buy a ticket to New Orleans, but I didn't have the money. All day I rode the bus west, arriving in Mobile about 8:00 p.m. My goal now was to get to the New Orleans Illinois Central train station. I left the bus and soon was back on the highway with my thumb out. A light rain began to fall.

A guy in a gigantic car pulled up and stopped; it was a 1965 Chrysler Imperial. As I jumped into the car, I noticed a large dent in the right rear quarter panel. The driver, a middle-aged business man, wore a brown suit coat with narrow lapels, matching brown pants, and a white shirt. To top it off, he had a skinny black tie and a brown snap-brimmed hat. The hat had a wide, black hatband, folded over on one side. He told me he was a traveling salesman heading home to LaPlace, Louisiana. He had spent a week out selling women's lingerie. He pointed to the boxes of his samples; they filled the long, bench-like rear seat and obstructed his back window. He was proud of his car. He told me it had a new feature—cruise control.

He looked at me then said, "You see, kid, I get it up to the speed I want, push this button, and … let 'er ride." A smile crossed his face as he said, "Let 'er ride." Then he floored it.

I glanced over at his speedometer—it read somewhere between eighty and eighty-five miles an hour. As we flew along the highway, the light rain in Mobile turned to a heavy rain as we crossed Lake Pontchartrain. The salesman kept the Chrysler on cruise control, never slowing down. I looked over at him, watching his small hands on the wheel, his small frame in the large bench seat, and his shiny brown shoes that barely reached the pedals. I thought, *Is this guy driving the car or is the car driving him?* I was worried about the speed. There were no seat belts, and if there were seat belts, no one used them in 1966. At one point along the Lake Pontchartrain causeway, I could feel the car hydroplane, but the driver never slowed. He just kept talking and telling me dirty jokes. "Here's another one, kid."

He barked out his joke, then just before the punch line, he began laughing, throwing his head back and exposing his tobacco-stained teeth. He looked like an aging horse with huge, brown teeth that were pushed away from the gum line. His laugh turned into a phlegm-choked cough. At that point, he pulled a gray handkerchief from his pocket, then he emptied the contents from his mouth into it, folding it and then placing it back in his pocket. It was disgusting. He lit Pall Mall cigarettes one after another. He continuously offered me one each time he lit up. "No, thanks," I said. His jokes were boring, but I listened and laughed. It was the price I paid to arrive in New Orleans dry. I counted the mileposts. With the grace of God, we made it to New Orleans and the Illinois Central train station.

I spent the night on an oak bench. The next morning, I boarded the first train north to Chicago. It was an express train. The first stop was Memphis, Tennessee. Twenty minutes out of New Orleans, the conductor walked by and asked for my ticket. I handed him my railroad pass, the small card my father had given me in Chicago. He looked it over, up one side and down the other. Then he walked away and began consulting with the other conductor. He walked back to me. With an indifferent voice, he told me I would have to get off in Memphis and board a local train to Chicago; the pass I had wasn't valid on express trains.

I protested. I told him the pass worked on the express train coming down from Chicago, *The City of New Orleans*. "Well, they made a mistake. You are getting off in Memphis." He turned and walked away.

I looked around the car. It was half-empty. I should have played up the Vietnam card and my draft notice: "Sir, could you please see your way to let me ride on your train? I need to get back to Chicago before I'm sent to Vietnam." I was too tired to think straight, so I left the train in Memphis and found another oak bench.

I waited five hours in Memphis for the local train. The local made every stop between Memphis and Chicago, every crossroad, every small town, and every grain elevator. It seemed like an eternity. I arrived in Chicago the next morning and took the 'L' train home. I slept for twelve hours straight.

The captain and I were called away from our card game. The Long Binh ammo dump was being mortared. We were just a few miles from the ammo dump, and we could see the mortar rounds flash as they hit the ground. One struck its mark, and the Long Binh ammo dump went up in a white ball of fire. The sky lit up with an enormous flash, and soon the sound filled our ears. A deafening roar that elicited a collective, "Wow!"

Weeks went by at Bearcat. Each day, I would lead the empty trucks to the Long Binh ammo dump, which was quickly rebuilt after the mortar attack. Our trucks were filled with artillery shells, then we drove out to the batteries, unloaded, and headed back to Bearcat. One evening our captain informed me there were orders coming down from headquarters that would send me out into the field. He said it might be weeks before they were issued. He went on to advise me to purchase anything I might need from the PX, because there was no PX out in the field. The orders the captain mentioned would send me out to the bush as the Fire Direction Control (FDC) officer of Battery C. My boss would be Lieutenant Jack Smith, the same man who had greeted me when I arrived at Bearcat; he was now in the bush.

Lieutenant Jack Smith had been a sergeant in the army stationed at Fort Sill, Oklahoma. He told me he was encouraged by his battalion commander to apply to Officer Candidate School. Jack passed the exam and entered OCS at Fort Sill for the six months of excruciating physical and academic training. He was my senior by ten or twelve years. He maintained an imposing dignity that only age and experience can produce. He was sent out to Battery C as its Fire Direction Control officer a few months ahead of me. This position required extreme care; I will explain.

Each day, twenty-five to fifty times, the FDC officer was radioed a set of map coordinates. Those coordinates, a series of numbers, were used to pinpoint a target on a map. After the position on the map was found, a small pin was inserted into a chart representing the target. Then a long metal ruler with hash marks indicating meters was rotated to the pin. Our position was also represented by a push pin; it was at the bottom of the ruler. That accomplished, we could read the distance in meters from our gun position to the target. A metal arc fixed to this ruler gave us the deflection, the position of the gun tube left or right of dead center. Using slide rules, we figured the elevation and powder charge for the 105-millimeter artillery pieces in our battery. Each artillery round had seven powder charges these charges blasted the high explosive shell from the cannon. The powder charges were packaged in small cotton bags and the seven bags were tied onto a long string; if the fire mission called for a charge one, six powder bags were cut from the string and a single bag was left in the brass canister. A charge one would fire the shell out about 2,500 to 3,500 meters. A charge seven sent the shell out almost seven miles. So there were many points from the initial coordinate numbers to the actual firing of the weapon where a mistake might occur. A mistake with artillery could be deadly. A short or a long round could hit and kill your own troops, or civilians. That was referred to as friendly fire, or in our camp as a fuck up. Errors from artillery shells, bombs from airplanes, or small arms fire from the infantry were not uncommon. Our job in the FDC bunker was to make sure there were no mistakes, and no friendly fire casualties.

Jack was a careful man. If there was the slightest doubt about the location of a target, he would call the infantry to confirm the coordinates. Then he double-checked the target locations on our maps, along with each calculation of elevation and deflection. Now for the second time in my Vietnam tour, I would work under Jack Smith. He would train me to be as careful and diligent as he was. Jack did his job well.

Chapter 2

JUNE 7, 1968

In May 1968 the heavens over Vietnam opened up. Humid air rushed in from the South China Sea, forming massive clouds. They were dark gray with pitch-black edges, and they dwarfed our compound. The clouds climbed thousands of feet above us; they moved quickly, and they were threatening. The dark sky took our afternoon sunlight and made an already miserable army camp even more miserable. The air became thick with moisture; our clothes were sticky, our skin clammy, and our boots and socks sodden. The torrential downpour over Southeast Asia began in May; these rains would not end for five months.

The volume of rain was something I had never experienced. It pummeled our tin-roof barracks and turned our dusty roads into a series of thick mud ruts. Palm trees swayed as torrents of rain blew sideways. The monsoon storms turned our slow saunters around the compound into sprints to avoid getting soaked. Trucks and jeeps turned waterlogged, their windows unable to keep out the unceasing rain; their canvas covers bowed with the weight of water. Everything and everyone in Vietnam was wet and would stay wet until the dry season arrived in the fall.

It was during one of those torrential storms that I was handed a set of orders sending me from the relative comfort of Bearcat into the field, the bush. The orders were typed on thick paper copied on a mimeograph machine, and five or six copies were stapled together; the humid air made them damp, and the staple had even begun to rust. There was a series of names above and below my name sending other men to units all over Vietnam. My name had a check next to it. Soon I would take the mail shuttle out to Battery C, 7th Battalion, 9th Artillery and start another chapter in this war. Battery C, commonly called Charlie Battery, was billeted in the village of Xuân Lộc, a provincial capital fifty miles northeast of Saigon. It was located on Highway 1. I had read about Vietnam's Highway 1 in Bernard B. Fall's book *Street Without Joy*.[9] I remember reading how dangerous it was for the French Foreign Legion. I knew this change was coming, and I was anxious about this approaching transfer.

I packed my duffle bag and the small attaché holding my orders and sprinted to a small building overlooking our helipad; I got soaked in the process. As I waited, I thought, *No pilot could take off or land a helicopter in this horrid weather. I bet I have another night in Bearcat.* I ran inside the building and watched as the wind carried sheets of rain sideways against the door. Water began streaming in beneath the threshold, and there was nothing but a blur of wet on the windowpanes. Three of us were waiting for the shuttle. Twenty minutes passed, the rain slowed, and soon our visibility increased; we could now see the small airstrip. As the rain eased and the fog began to lift, we looked at one another in disbelief as the unmistakable sound of helicopter blades filled our ears.

---

9.   Bernard   B.   Fall,   a   war   correspondent   and   historian,   wrote Street   Without   Joy   (Stackpole   Books,   1961),   a   book   about   the French Indochina War.

Out of this tempest came the sight of our olive-drab-colored Huey, the workhorse helicopter of the army. We saw the pilot maneuver his ship ever so gently as he landed on the small tarmac. The door gunner stepped away from his machine gun and waved us on board. He shouted, "Xuân Lộc?" I ran to the chopper.

The flight to Xuân Lộc was short and mercifully rain free. At Xuân Lộc, the pilot hovered over the road, not bothering to land for fear of adding weight to the skids from the sticky mud. Two of us jumped from the helicopter into this muck and began slopping our way toward the entrance to the military compound. We walked through the gate, passing a sleepy GI hunched forward on his M-60 machine gun. Only his head and helmet were visible above a sandbagged wall. I looked at the compound and saw six 105-millimeter artillery pieces placed in six sandbagged parapets, twenty to thirty feet apart.

The guns were silent now after a night of firing. Two of the pieces were being cleaned, their green tubes pointing down. The enlisted men were pushing an oily rag through the tube with a long pole; we called this cleaning process punching the tube. These cannons had a pedigree dating back to World War II, then Korea, and now Vietnam. Each gun had a logbook filled with records listing times, places, and dates of maintenance since their casting in the mid-1940s. Five or six soldiers manned the gun; a crew chief, usually a corporal or a sergeant, was in charge. The battery totaled about ninety to one-hundred men, including six or seven officers. Men were always rotating to and from the States, so on any given day, the number of men in the battery changed.

I walked into the headquarters tent and reported for duty. After a few inquisitive pleasantries, I was sent to the FDC bunker, where Jack Smith, my old boss and now my new boss, gave me a welcoming smile. He told me not to get comfortable because the next day we were leaving for a place called Binh Son. He went on to tell me that it was a villa in the middle of a large rubber plantation. The villa was nicknamed Frenchy's after the plantation's overseer, a Frenchman, reportedly from Paris. Jack told me that the American army had taken over the villa. He smiled and then said, "We will have a red-tile roof over our heads."

The captain to whom I had just reported walked in, and the three of us began discussing the move to Binh Son. Midway through our conversation, the captain pointed to me and said, "You, Lieutenant Duffy, are not making the move with us. You are going to computer school in Củ Chi. We need to send one lieutenant for a weeklong course of instruction. You're the guy."

I didn't say a word, but I was disappointed that I wouldn't make the move with my new unit. "Sir," I asked, "when do I leave for Củ Chi?" He told me to be ready in the morning and that he would see me again in Binh Son a week later. He went on to say that he had something for me. I was curious as he stuck his hand in his pocket and pulled out two silver bars. "Congratulations, you made first lieutenant." He handed me the bars, and I thanked him. Then I mentally computed how much more money I would make. I needed every penny to pay for the tuition, room, and board at Colorado College, that is, if I was accepted. I stuffed the bars into my pocket and smiled to myself with an inner pride.

Just after arriving in Vietnam, I was encouraged by the battalion pay officer to join the army's savings plan. If I deposited my monthly pay into the soldier's Deposit Savings Program, I could earn ten percent on my savings. I quickly said yes to this offer, and thereafter, the army took ninety-five percent of my monthly pay and put it into this high-interest

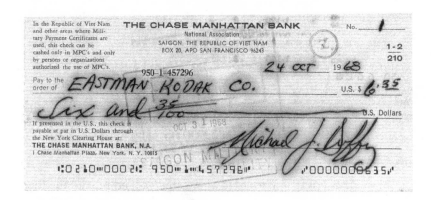

account. I also opened a checking account with The Chase Manhattan Bank, Saigon branch, for any incidentals I needed at the PX.

It was hard to spend money in the bush. We had no retail convenience stores, only local peddlers selling warm beer and Coke. There were, of course, the prostitutes, who quickly appeared near any military base. They took dollars, piasters, or our military funny money—our military payment certificates (MPCs)—but I was told they didn't take checks.

A black bar embroidered on the collar of my field shirt would distinguish my new rank of first lieutenant. The officers usually hired one of the local women to hand-stitch the shape of a bar onto their collars.

✳ ✳ ✳

The next morning, I rolled out of a damp cot, drank black coffee, and ate some watery grits. I passed on the waterlogged eggs. The captain had his driver give me a ride to the airstrip. The sky was cloudy, but there was no rain. I jumped onto a waiting helicopter for the thirty-minute flight to Củ Chi and the FADAC school.

FADAC was an acronym for a bulky 1968 computer that didn't work very well. The letters stood for "Field Artillery" and then some other

words that no one knew or cared about. Later in the year, I found out the full meaning of the acronym—Field Artillery Digital Automatic Computer. The FADAC computer was about the size of a large piece of luggage with garden hose–sized cables protruding from the back. The cables were plugged into a portable generator. When working, we punched in the air temperature, powder temperature, wind speed, and location of the target through a small keyboard. After the data was entered and the compute button pushed, it displayed the elevation and the deflection necessary to hit the target. This computation was normally done by hand using slide rules, but the slide rules did not account for the wind or other meteorological variations. I never trusted the computer, so I always had the targets plotted by hand and the elevation and deflection worked up on the slide rules. If the numbers were close, I used the computer's results; if the numbers were off by a wide margin, I used the numbers worked up by hand on our slide rules. I never made a mistake in computations, either by hand or by computer. A mistake with artillery could put you in a "world of hurt."

My accommodations at FADAC school consisted of a long, wood-framed bunkhouse where twenty-five students lived together for the five days of classes. The classes were boring. Every day we went over exercises using different wind speeds and powder temperatures. By the second day, I had the drill down pat and was ready to move out. After our last day of class, there was a small graduation party at the officers' club. The party was organized by one of the students, a fellow from Texas; of course we nicknamed him "Tex." He was in love with the Texas A&M Aggies. Tex constantly talked football, and when he finished he would give us the Aggies yelp, a sort of war whoop. After a few beers and plenty of Aggie talk from Tex, I left the club, knowing that I needed to get up early for the trip back to Battery C and my new home at Binh Son. I quickly fell asleep.

It was well after midnight when Tex staggered into the barracks and awakened everyone with Aggie talk. Tex was drunk, stumbling around, shouting obscenities, and cursing his ex-girlfriend back in Texas who, he said "was fuckin' unfaithful." Tex ranted about the army, his old girlfriend, and some "fuckin' professor" who gave him a "fuckin' poor grade." Tex slurred his words as he bellowed, "God will punish all them fuckin' fuckers." "Fuck" was the most common word used in Vietnam. By the end of one's tour in Vietnam, even the devout soldiers began their sentences with the word "fuck."

We tried to ignore Tex, but we didn't ignore the camp sirens going off. All of us, except Tex, ran to a bomb shelter and watched through a slit in the sandbags as the camp received volley after volley of mortar rounds. The VC were aiming at the airstrip and hitting it with accuracy. The attack lasted about twenty minutes, then the sirens sounded again and we headed back to the barracks. When we turned on the lights, we saw Tex lying next to his cot. He was on the floor passed out in a large puddle of urine. His pants were soaking wet. Tex was snoring loudly. A few of us rolled him over and pulled him by the arms through the door and out onto the ground, where he spent the night. We washed off his puddle with a few buckets of water, then we went back to sleep.

The next morning I got up early, dressed, and walked outside, past Tex, and over to the airstrip. I was to board another helicopter and make my way to Binh Son via Bearcat. When the shuttle arrived, I piled on with two other GIs and peered out the open door as we lifted off. It was cloudy and humid, but there was no rain. The craft made a quick stop at Xuân Lộc, then we were off to Bearcat. I disembarked at Bearcat and walked over to the Service Battery, 7th of the 9th, my old unit. There was a small mail-supply convoy about to leave for Binh Son. The convoy consisted of a few trucks filled with food, canvas tents, cots, olive-drab paint, and mail. I jumped into a three-quarter-ton truck and waited. Soon the convoy began a slow move out of camp.

We drove through an opening in the earthen berm wall and past the coils of barbed wire that encircled the camp. The convoy turned south on QL 15, a national highway leading to the South China Sea and the beaches of Vũng Tàu. Vũng Tàu was an in-country Rest and Relaxation spot for long weekends on the beach. It was reserved as a treat for a job well done or as a brief exit from the muddy grind in the rice paddies. It was located about sixty miles southeast of Saigon on the Cape St. Jacques Peninsula. I had heard it was absolutely beautiful.

Our convoy turned well before the beaches of Vũng Tàu, onto a dirt road leading into the Binh Son rubber plantation. As we turned off QL 15, we passed a group of boys playing soccer. The boys had fashioned vines into a hollow, semi-round soccer ball. I noticed about seven or eight boys running up and down the field kicking the ball; one boy had a stump where his arm should have been. Civilian casualties were common in Vietnam; mines and booby traps were often the cause.

The poorly maintained dirt road leading to the *ville*[10] of Binh Son was rutted with muddy tire tracks, forcing our convoy to slow. Almost immediately after turning off QL 15, we entered the first rows of rubber trees. Unlike most of Highway 1, the major north-south highway in Vietnam, where the trees were cut back from the road, the rubber trees here were almost touching our vehicles. It was also dark; the leaves of the trees sheltered us from the cloudy sky. Our convoy slowed then moved to the side of the road as one of the many three-wheeled pedicabs passed us. I watched the driver carefully maneuver his vehicle around our trucks. The tiny bus was filled with people sitting on benches. One young boy was standing on the back holding on to a bar and puffing on a cigarette.

Soon we entered the small settlement of Binh Son, I saw a cluster of stucco houses and huts. Facing the main road was a large, one-story stone-and-stucco building set back about 300 feet from the road. It was the largest building in town, and it was encircled with coils of barbed wire. The building itself was inviting, with a wide veranda sweeping down each wall and around each corner. The roof cantilevered out and over the porch providing shelter from the sun and the rain. I thought, *If the ugly military vehicles and rolls of barbed wire surrounding the house were removed, one might think he had arrived at a beautiful hotel in some exotic tropical country.* As our convoy turned off the road into the compound, we passed two sentinels in sandbagged bunkers. Both bunkers

---

10.   "Ville" is a French word for village. The army's 1968 topographical maps used this word.

were positioned close to the veranda, and they were surrounded by rose bushes now in full bloom with beautiful pink flowers.

We stopped in front of the house, and my friend and mentor Jack Smith walked out to greet me. "Welcome to Binh Son," he said.

I looked at him and said, "This place is beautiful."

He nodded and quickly told me the house was part of our FDC group.[11] We would sleep there and work there—no more muddy, sandbagged bunkers. Jack walked me into my new quarters, a small room just off the veranda. I had two roommates—Lieutenant John Ladd from Georgia, a soft-spoken, friendly man with a deep Southern drawl, and Lieutenant Martin Jones from Oklahoma. Lieutenant Jones was a redneck who never held back his opinions.

Lieutenant Smith gave me a tour of the house. The floors were made of red tiles, and the tiles ran from the veranda into and through-out the house. The rooms had doors fashioned of mahogany with a diamond relief shape in each quarter panel. There was no glass in the windows, but all the mahogany frames were still intact.

Our guns were on a small hill behind the house. Jack walked me into the FDC room, where he and I, along with the enlisted men, would spend our days and nights working. We worked in shifts. Someone was on duty twenty-four hours a day, seven days a week. From this room we calculated the figures for elevation and deflection, and then we called them down to the guns via our squawk box. It was like a speakerphone; we could yell out the numbers from the chart tables. Each gun also had a squawk box with a microphone, so every man on the gun could

---

11. An FDC, or Fire Direction Control, group comprised ten to twelve men, both officers and enlisted men, working around the clock to direct the battery's artillery fire.

hear the numbers being called out, thus reducing the chance for error. Back in the FDC room, we also could hear the numbers as the gunner on the artillery piece repeated them to his crew. The real risk with the artillery was a mistake from FDC or the guns sending our high-explosive shells into our own troops. That was always our biggest fear.

Outside of the house and just 50 feet to the north was a company from the 9th Infantry Division. Those men provided security for our compound. Their commanding officer, Captain John Corrigan, was a reserve officer from New York, and he and I got on well. He used me as his forward observer on a number of patrols outside the camp. Captain Corrigan was familiar with the local people: the mayor, the school principal, and the few South Vietnamese dignitaries who came through the small *ville*. I could tell he liked the Vietnamese civilians. He was friendly and unpretentious and gave them a measure of respect rarely demonstrated by our troops.

There was always a cloud of suspicion when it came to the Vietnamese civilians. We never knew if they were working secretly with the Viet Cong or the North Vietnamese Army. We feared they could work as a barber or help in our mess halls, then transfer intelligence about our movements to the Viet Cong. Unlike Captain Corrigan, Jack Smith trusted none of them.

✳✳✳

Life in Binh Son had fewer comforts than Bearcat. There were no showers and no airstrip, so our mail was always slow to get to us. We had no Vietnamese laundry women, so all our wash was done by hand and by us. It was the responsibility of each GI to keep his two pairs of jungle fatigues, underwear, and socks clean and dry.

There was no medical clinic, but we did have a medic, albeit a mediocre one. He had few medical supplies and he seemed to have little interest in his job. He gave me zero confidence. His days were spent playing cards and reading one of the many "fuck books" circulating in the unit. The fuck books were cheesy X-rated novels with dog-eared pages. They were written at a third-grade reading level.

There were no roads inside our compound, only muddy ruts created by the trucks as they came and went. On one side of the villa, we had a grassy area next to a low stone retaining wall. We hung our laundry there and tossed a football on Sunday afternoons. Even though our days melded into one another, we still watched the calendar and worked a seven-day week. There was little time off for lazy Sunday afternoons. We fired our cannons into the jungle every day and night, but when I *was* off duty, I felt a psychological relaxation, especially on the weekends, probably left over from my routine at home. On one of those Sunday afternoons, John Ladd handed his camera to our Thai[12] neighbor and asked him to take a photo.

The photo is black and white, with John Ladd holding a small goat. I'm sitting to the left of John, and our executive officer, Lieutenant Joe Miller, is sitting to the right of him. John had the film developed via our slowpoke mail. He gave me a copy; *I still have the picture in my archives.*

I settled into a routine in Binh Son, working my shift in the FDC room. Late at night and well into the early hours of the morning, we fired Harassment and Interdiction missions. Our intelligence unit in Bien Hoa radioed target coordinates each evening. These coordinates

---

12. "Thai" is short for the Royal Thai Army. A small contingent of Thai troops was stationed at the Binh Son compound.

were not known enemy positions but rather locations where intelligence thought the VC might gather, a stretch of road with evidence of VC activity or a rice paddy where a tunnel was found. Since I was the junior lieutenant, I was given the night shift.

Our unit commander was a jovial fellow; we called him Captain Tom He was in his mid-thirties and married. He was in the army for life, a "lifer." Although Captain Tom was our battery commander, he didn't run the everyday operations of our unit. The executive officer, XO, or second in command, had that job. The executive officer spent most of his time out with the guns, watching them fire, checking for errors, making sure the men were alert. The XO had responsibility for the entire battery. If a mistake was made in the FDC room, the wrong elevation or deflection was sent to the guns, and we blew up a few rubber trees or a road, or in the worst case, caused friendly fire, the XO was sent to headquarters to answer for the error. If a mistake happened on the watch of a lifer and he was written up, it could spell the end of a career. It was the XO's responsibility for the guns to fire each day and night and fire accurately.

Our small compound had a kitchen, or mess, on one side of the villa. Captain Corrigan's infantry company had its own mess next to ours. We cooked separately and, for the most part, ate separately. Our breakfasts consisted of coffee, grits, toast, scrambled eggs, and sometimes bacon. We ate off paper plates. The lieutenants and I usually walked to the veranda with our food and sat on the low stone partition to eat our breakfast. The veranda was a quiet, pleasant place. From the veranda you could look out into the *ville* and see Vietnamese civilians strolling up and down the dirt road. There were women walking their children to school. The women wore their native dress, the *ao dai*.[13] Most of them also wore straw hats with ribbons tied beneath their chins.

Most mornings we saw the village schoolteacher. His house was at one end of town and the school was at the other. We watched him leave his house and greet the children as he marched with purpose to the small, stucco schoolhouse; he always wore a clean white shirt and dark blue pants. We were much too far away to exchange pleasantries. Nonetheless, the civilians on the road made our compound seem less military.

In the evening, between our day and all-night duties, the officers would gather on the veranda. We drank warm beer and talked about home. Sometimes we listened to a small battery-operated radio. Some of the best music in the evening came from Radio Hanoi in North Vietnam.

A sugar-laced voice speaking in perfect English plied the airwaves, playing soul music, rhythm and blues, and American pop. We called her "Hanoi Hannah." Then, in-between the tunes, the soft-spoken DJ would read the American dead for the week. A weekly list of the American dead was published in our *Stars and Stripes* newspaper. The Vietcong would get their hands on a copy and then send it off to Hanoi Hannah in time for her broadcast. It was on a warm, quiet night on the veranda that I had my second pinochle lesson with my teacher, Jack Smith. As we played on a wooden, olive-drab table, Jack told me about his home town of New York City, and his career in the army. He had spent many years as a noncommissioned officer

---

13.   An   ao   dai,   pronounced   "ow-si,"   is   a   traditional   Vietnamese women's   dress   worn   over   pants.   The   dress   runs   the   length   of   the legs and is slit on each side.

(NCO). When the opportunity to attend Officer Candidate School arrived, he took it.

The army had an insatiable appetite for junior officers as President Lyndon Baines Johnson poured another 200,000 troops into Vietnam in 1966 and 1967. Both Jack Smith and I were offered the opportunity to attend OCS, most likely because of this huge buildup. Without the war, in peacetime and with a much smaller army, Jack probably would have remained an NCO, and I probably would not have been drafted.

Jack's experience as an NCO had given him confidence. He was clear-spoken and sure of himself. Ten years as an NCO shouting orders to enlisted men had given him a command voice, one not to be ignored. I was envious of his rapport with the men. They respected and feared him. I listened and learned from him as we worked together in the FDC room.

We drank our warm Pabst Blue Ribbon beer from rusty cans and talked as if we were on a quiet beach. The veranda seemed normal and safe; it was peaceful, and we were dry.

Our mail truck arrived from Bearcat about twice a week. It brought food, supplies, and any new men assigned to our unit or to Captain Corrigan's infantry company. I usually received a letter from home during the twice-weekly mail calls. My father was good about writing in his long, flowing, difficult-to-read hand.

My mother and sister also wrote, as did my boyhood friend Joe Kiefer. I received a box of crushed cookies one day from my cousin. Of all the letters I read on the veranda that hot summer, there was one I treasured. It was addressed to *"Lt. Michael J. Duffy, C Btry. 7th 9th Artillery, APO San Francisco, CA. 96530."* It read:

Dear Mr. Duffy,

We are pleased to offer you admission to Colorado College for our fall 1969 school year.

Congratulations.

My letter of acceptance was signed by the admissions director, Richard Wood. God, how I cherished that letter. It gave me hope and a direction and it gave me a future.

My older sister was accepted at Marquette University. She won a four-year scholarship, tuition, and room and board, but she left after only one semester, to my parents' disappointment. My father, the son of Irish immigrants, was born at home and grew up in an apartment on Pearson Street, on Chicago's Near North Side. He attended Holy Name grade school and then went on to De La Salle High School on Chicago's Near South Side. After the untimely death of his father, he dropped out of high school and began working to bring some money into the family household. I was told, by him, that this was a disappointment to his mother. She wished to see him graduate from high school. My mother attended St. Catherine of Siena High School on Chicago's West Side. She graduated in 1924 and went on to dance with the Chicago Civic Opera Company with our city's famous ballerina, Ruth Page.[14] My mother toured the country with some of the great ballet companies of Europe. My mother loved her life as a dancer. She and my father met on Oak Street Beach and married in 1939. Now

---

14.   Ruth   Page,   an   American   ballerina   and   choreographer,   was considered   a   pioneer   in   creating   works   based   on   American   themes. She   was   the   director   of   the   Chicago   Civic   Opera   Company   from 1934 to 1945.

I had my chance to complete college and break our family mold. I would not disappoint myself.

***

After a month or so in Binh Son, I was called to our headquarters room. Captain Tom handed me a set of orders directing me to Bien Hoa, the sprawling army base just northeast of Saigon. He told me the army was trying to stop the rocket fire from the Viet Cong. The VC were shelling Saigon almost every night and killing many civilians.

My new task as an aerial observer had me riding in a Huey helicopter from 10:00 p.m. to 4:00 a.m. My job was to watch for incoming rockets, locate the gunner's position, pinpoint it on a map, and return fire—a difficult job in daylight and an impossible job in the darkness of Vietnam. I packed my gear and waited for the supply convoy to Bearcat and then a short helicopter ride to Bien Hoa.

Soon after arriving in Bien Hoa, I met with a young major; he was dressed in spotless, starched fatigues and sat at a tidy, gray metal desk. As I stood in his office, he discussed the mission and what was expected of me. He handed me a piece of paper listing the dates and hours I would work and the reports I needed to write after each flight. In a matter-of-fact voice, he instructed me to report for duty at the airstrip that night. He added, "And be on time." It irked me that he added the "be on time." What the hell was I going to do? Of course I would be on time.

On my first night flying as an aerial observer, I climbed into the helicopter and found four other men sitting on one of the long, nylon benches. There were two nylon benches on a Huey; they faced each other in the small cabin just behind the cockpit. I pulled on my radio helmet and then asked the pilot who the other men were. He quickly explained that they were career military men flying each night to earn hours toward an air medal; he said the pilots on base called them medal riders, then he snickered.

After so many hours of combat flight, one was eligible for the army's air medal, even if you sat on your dead ass and did nothing but nod off, as this crowd did. After the required number of flight hours, these armchair warriors sat in their air-conditioned trailers and wrote up one another for their "awards." They seemed harmless—four, five, or six men flying around Saigon and minding their own business. As long as they didn't bother me, I didn't mind them in "my space." The pilot told me the air medal riders would be with me every night of my two-week tour of duty.

On the evening of June 6, 1968, I began my walk to the airstrip. This night we were scheduled to take off at 9:45 p.m. and fly until 4:00 a.m. the next morning. After a week of flying, my head ached from lack of sleep. By 8:00 a.m. the heat in Vietnam awakened me each morning in an uncomfortable sweat.

As I approached the airstrip, I saw my Huey. It was sitting on the tarmac with its blades pulsing. The air medal riders were already assembling. It was a packed house. In the dark they all looked the same, but I think there were two or three officers, a few NCOs, and maybe even a major. These wannabe heroes would surely get in my way tonight. When they filled the long bench seats in the helicopter, I had trouble moving from one side to the other and doing my job. I was becoming intolerant of them. I saw them as excess baggage with zero value. I sat near the open door purposely looking away to show my displeasure. I peered out at the lights on the airfield and waited for the pilot to tell us we were cleared for takeoff.

That night the pilot and copilot were both majors. I soon found out they were gutsy. My radio helmet was secure and working; I checked in as ready, and we were off. We circled the field once and then headed toward the lights of Saigon. We were flying at an altitude of about 2,500 feet; this was low compared with other pilots.

Some pilots would never drop below 5,000 feet, probably out of fear. A rifle shot would never make it 5,000 feet up in altitude. And then there were the pilots who would fly at 3,000 feet or less. We continued flying toward Saigon and soon we were over a branch of the Sông Nhá Bé River, then we flew in a northwestern direction. The sky was cloud free and the moon was full, making the river inviting. About twenty miles upriver, we turned toward Bien Hoa and flew over some small villages. As we neared Bien Hoa, we picked up radio transmissions from a convoy, and I could hear the sound of automatic gunfire and frantic voices through my radio helmet. The convoy was being ambushed by the VC just outside of Bien Hoa. It was a late-night American convoy traveling down Highway 1. Listening to the radio traffic, I heard that the convoy had suffered casualties and needed medical assistance. Our pilot headed straight toward the fighting, and before long, we were over the road watching green and red tracers fly back and forth. To my surprise, the pilot decided to land the helicopter and pick up the wounded.

Two jeeps were parked on the road facing each other with their headlights designating a landing area. The pilot circled the jeeps once and then began a fast and frightening descent. While we dropped in altitude, my stomach spun and the medal riders awakened. They looked to me for an explanation. I was the only one with the radio helmet, and only I could talk to the pilot. I looked into their worried faces as we descended. I confirmed their fear with a thumbs-down signal. This was the worst thing that could happen to a medal rider, being involved in some sort of danger. They just wanted the medal, not the risk.

The landing went off perfectly. Even before we touched down, a frenzied lieutenant ran to the ship, stuck his head through the door, and screamed over the noise from the rotor wash. "I need help." He needed help carrying his wounded man from the battlefield back to our helicopter and then on to the hospital. I pulled my off my helmet jumped to the ground, then turned to see who would follow. Not one of the medal riders made a move. Over the din of the helicopter blades, I screamed, "Isn't anyone going to help?"

As if rehearsed, they put their heads down in a gesture of shame and cowardice. I stared at them, but they would not make eye contact. A moment passed then the lieutenant grabbed my arm and pulled me away from the ship. We ran toward the sound of small arms fire and explosions. As we moved closer to the front line, I thought about the cowards who sat buckled in their seats, unwilling to help the men they sent into battle from their air conditioned offices. My anger gave way to our mission.

Running behind the lieutenant, I felt safer and more secure than the medal riders in the helicopter. The ship seemed so vulnerable, like a sitting duck waiting for a grenade. We ran down a narrow lane past a few open doors, where fear-stricken villagers watched us from their doorways. We soon came upon a group of women and children in a small room; they were huddled around a wounded GI. He was lying on a reed mat. He was still alive. The lieutenant and I struggled with the mat, but it was too heavy to lift. When the Vietnamese women saw our difficulty, they joined us, and we were soon on our way back to the helicopter.

I was holding one corner of the mat. Across from me was a young Vietnamese boy, maybe twelve years old. He was struggling to hold his side. He was much shorter than we were, so his corner of the mat was the lowest. I watched as the wounded GI's blood spilled onto the boy's face and covered his eyes. Yet he never let go of the mat.

In the early hours of June 7, 1968, with the help of three Vietnamese women and one boy, we made our way back to the helicopter, albeit slowly. I will never forget watching the medal riders begging us with their panicky faces to hurry. They could care less about the wounded GI. Their concern was their own skin. As we struggled with this man, inches from the helicopter, they never moved from their seats.

Our helicopter lifted off for the short ride to the Bien Hoa Hospital. I took my jacket and wrapped it around the wounded young man. He kept telling me that he was cold. I tried to reassure him that everything was all right. I lay down next to him, put my body next to his and my arms around him to keep him warm. His blood spilled from an unseen wound and warmed my leg. We were just moments from the medical team. I could see the nurses waiting for their next challenge. They were standing around a gurney. I whispered in his ear that he was okay, that he should just hold on. He didn't respond.

I am not sure if he died in my arms, or on the gurney, or in the surgery room. But I was told the next day that he didn't make it. I never saw the air medal riders again. They left me to fly with someone else. I never knew this young man's name or where he came from, but I heard his last words. On June 7, 1968, my views about human nature, heroes, cowards, and character changed forever. To me the glances of pretentious authority and false bravado from senior-grade officers now seemed meaningless. It was one's actions, not rank or medals, that revealed one's character.

The next morning, I awakened to an oppressive heat. I missed breakfast, I lingered in the barracks, and I wrote a letter to my parents. I tried to explain to them and to myself what had happened the night before. My words made no sense to me. I revised them, and then I revised them again. I ended up mailing a watered-down version of the previous night's events with no real account of what had happened. I didn't even mention the dead soldier; I didn't want to worry my parents. I walked around the post all day thinking to myself that he could have made it, that he still could be alive if we had had some help from the medal riders. I wondered if three minutes or two or one might have kept him alive. He talked to me just before we landed at the field hospital. I was numb. I felt awful.

I still had a few more missions to fly before my short tour was up and I could head back to Binh Son. I reported for duty that evening. My commanding officer, who just a few days before had given me a verbal reprimand for nodding off one night—*I was turned in by one of the medal riders*—now congratulated me for going into the line of fire, as he put it, to save someone's life. I thought about telling him who didn't go into the "line of fire," but I wanted to get out of his office; I kept my mouth shut.

I went through the motions for the rest of my short aerial observer tour, then I packed my bags and left for the Binh Son rubber plantation. I was sure the air medal riders had finished their appropriate number of hours and had received their coveted air medals. I didn't. The day before I left, I was told by the company clerk that I didn't log enough flying time for a medal. "Sorry, sir," he said. I think I missed the medal by a few hours of combat flight time. In fact, because of the medal riders, I didn't want or care for an air medal. I was counting the days until I could return home and start college and forget about this messy war in Vietnam.

I stuffed my blood-stained fatigues into my duffle bag and walked to the helipad for the trip back to Binh Son

Chapter 3

MIDDAY DEEP IN THE JUNGLE

I arrived back in Binh Son to a hard rain, and it fell all day and into the evening. Our compound looked dismal. I was in a terrible mood and still thinking about the soldier who had died in my arms. I was filled with anger and I needed to get my mind off that subject.

The muddy tracks around the villa became slippery ruts, and they were hard to navigate. In spite of this heavy downpour, the villa stayed dry. I walked into my room and saw John Ladd sitting on his cot polishing his boots. John's boots were always shiny and clean; mine were a mess. He asked me about my short tour as an aerial observer. I told him it was impossible to locate the position of the Viet Cong rocket fire flying into Saigon. I went on to say that I had watched helplessly as rockets soared out of the dark jungle then slammed into the civilian neighborhoods in a flash of white light. If I was lucky enough to be pointed in the right direction and witness a launch, trying to find the launch position on a map from a moving helicopter was impossible. I didn't mention the death of the soldier.

John Ladd was from Lyons, Georgia, a small town sixty miles inland from Savannah and near the fruitcake capital of the world—

Claxton, Georgia. When I heard that, I jumped at the chance to tell him that I had eaten the world-famous Claxton fruitcake just last Christmas. John and I now had a bond; we both liked fruitcake. He told me about another famous town near his home called Vidalia, Georgia, home to the famous Vidalia onion. Those are the onions that the Freemasons sold in midsummer. They would set up stands near the highway, put on their funny red fez hats, and sell bags of onions to raise money for their lodge.

I listened as John talked about his boyhood in Lyons, Georgia. We talked about fear. I told him of my deep fear when I arrived in Vietnam at the airbase in Cam Ranh Bay. I told him about the jarring flight to Saigon on the first day of the Tet Offensive. We talked about being kids and how fear seemed to grow inside us and become larger than real life. John continued with stories about his boyhood in Lyons. Soon I had a chance to tell him a story about my boyhood and fear. I told him of the strange fellow my brother and I met one day in Cary, Illinois:

> One hot August day, my kid brother, Dan, nine years old, and I, ten, rode our bikes to the Cary barbershop for long-overdue haircuts. My mother gave us money and told us to get our hair cut short. Long ago, we stopped asking her for a ride in our used 1950 Pontiac sedan complete with an orange Indian head as a hood ornament. The car was painted black and had huge fenders and chrome bumpers. The steering wheel of this Pontiac Super Chief was a cream color with a half-moon piece of chrome in the middle. When this half-moon piece was pushed, the horn sounded. Dan and I found out how the horn worked

and blasted it one morning until our neighbor walked over and told us to stop. The dashboard on the car had a clock and a radio, but neither worked. Crowning the car, the Pontiac designers had added a black metal awning. It hung over the front windshield like a large bill on a baseball cap. My mother was forced to drive this beast, without power steering, after our move from Chicago to Cary, Illinois. She always hated getting behind the wheel. Only under the most urgent conditions would she concede to drive us for our childhood needs. A haircut in August was not one of them.

The Cary barbershop was housed in a long, narrow wooden building and served the town well into the 1990s. We parked our bikes in front of the shop and ran up to the door only to find it locked, with a "*Closed*" sign in the window. We thought about using the haircut money for a sweet roll at Peter's Bakery just across the street, but Dan reminded me that the last time we did something like that Mom was angry with us for a week. We turned our bikes toward home. As we rode alongside the Chicago and North Western Railroad tracks, we noticed a line of wooden boxcars standing idle on a siding. Each car had small windows, a screen door, and steps leading from the car down to the ground. The boxcars were a dirty grey and sorely in need of a paint job. Dan and I peeked into the doorway of one car and saw bunk beds and work cloths hanging from a line then we noticed a man sitting on the steps of another car. We rode over to him and said hi. Not a smile or a gesture of friendliness crossed his face. He looked tired, dirty, and mean. His pants were the color of tree bark. His shirt was buttoned up so that one side was higher than the other. He began to talk to us in an unfamiliar form of speech.

"You boys live 'rounnn' here?" He didn't pronounce the "a" or the "d" in "around," and he held out the "n" sound. I had never heard such speech before.

"Yes," Dan quickly answered. I wished Dan hadn't told him that we lived nearby. The man gave us both the once-over. He was wearing a pair of dusty high-top shoes laced halfway up with the leather tongues folded over the laces. He had a three-day growth of beard, and his hair was a greasy blond color, and uncombed. He was eating peanut butter out of a large tin can. And he used a wide, tarnished dinner knife to scoop out the peanut butter. He would lick the dripping peanut butter off the dull blade, look at us, and then push the knife back into the oily tin can.

"That's a nice bike you have there, boy," he said. He was looking at my new bike and me. It was a gift from a business friend of my father's.

"I'll bet that bike cost your daddy lots of money," he said. I told him that my dad had not bought it. He didn't hear or didn't want to hear what I had just told him. I began to feel uneasy and thought we should move away from this character.

"Let's go," I said to Dan. Before I got Dan's attention, the man looked directly at Dan and asked, "Where you live, boy?" Dan began to answer him, and I yelled, "Dan, let's go." The man gave me a dirty look as I turned my bike toward home, but Dan didn't move. The man asked Dan another question. I yelled again, "Dan, let's go!"

As Dan looked over at me, the man reached out and grabbed the front wheel of Dan's bike. The man held it tight, and Dan couldn't move. "Wait a minute, boy. Where you goin' so faaas'?"

Now I was scared. I looked at this strange man and said, "We have to get home; our mother is expecting us." He looked at me and grimaced. As he did that, I noticed half his teeth were missing. The other half were a dingy yellow. He kept his hand on Dan's bike, then turned to me and said, "Boy, you need to respect your elders. I was talking to your brother here, and you went and interrupted me." He pronounced it "inrupted."

"Your daddy probably got a lot of money, but he never taught you no respect for your elders. You hear me, *boy*?" He raised his voice on "boy." I did not answer, so he said it again. "You hear me, *boy*?" Now his voice was loud and angry.

I began to get panicky as the man continued to hold Dan's front wheel. My brother was frozen on his bike, pleading with his eyes for me to help him. I was hoping someone would walk or drive by so I could wave him over. No one did.

As this angry man lectured me, his hand relaxed a bit. Seeing that, Dan made a quick move back with his bike and pulled it away from the man's hand. As Dan did that, the guy jerked backward and the can of peanut butter fell off the steps and onto the ground. He began to curse at us. Dan sprinted with his bike for a jump-start, but his small legs were slow and his heavy Schwinn bike was huge next to his sixty-five-pound frame. We both began to pedal toward home, but we were slow to pick up speed. The man stumbled, then leaned against the wooden bunk car. He pointed at us and yelled obscenities as we gathered speed and rode toward home.

That night we told the story to our dad. He told us that the boxcars held workers from the railroad called gandy dancers. They were hard men, many without families or education. Some were heavy drinkers, and some had prison records. He told us to stay away from the work trains, and we did.

John Ladd liked my story, and he said that he would think of a good one to tell me. We drifted onto the veranda and drank warm beer.

Captain Corrigan appeared and joined us in a Pabst Blue Ribbon. His can had a rusty top.

When digging through the warm beer bucket, you had to be careful to pick a can without rust. Sometimes if the top was rusty, you could turn the can over and the bottom would be clean and free of rust. Most soldiers didn't like to drink beer with a rusty top, but Captain Corrigan didn't care. We opened the beer cans with a metal can opener.

After some small talk, Captain Corrigan asked me if I would act as his forward observer on a patrol either the next day or the day after. His infantry company was scheduled for a patrol outside our compound. If I was free, he could use me. This was not a duty of mine or an order from him. It was a favor, a request. Captain Corrigan didn't enjoy the luxury of an artillery forward observer attached to his unit, so any help from a visiting artillery officer was welcome. I told him I would be glad to join him, as long as I got back in time for my FDC shift.

I liked Captain Corrigan; he treated me as his equal. He never judged me as green or too young to know the ways of Vietnam and the world, as some other officers in the unit did. It was often difficult for me because I was younger than most officers. Many officers and noncommissioned officers I worked with in Vietnam were my seniors, some by as much as ten or fifteen years. I watched Captain Corrigan guzzle his beer, wave goodbye, and leave the veranda.

I looked up at the sky; it was cloudy. A thin ribbon of sunlight broke through the clouds. I looked over the compound. The rose bushes I had left two weeks before were still in bloom. The roses still had their exquisite pink petals. It seemed as if some caring hand had nurtured them through the dry season, giving them water and pruning them. Next to those beautiful roses were Captain Corrigan's ugly sandbagged bunkers, with wet sandbagged roofs now sagging from two inches of daily rain.

Stationed in each of the bunkers were two of Captain Corrigan's infantrymen. They were scruffy, unshaven, wet, and miserable. Each bunker had an M-60 machine gun mounted on a tripod. The gun was pointing out toward the front gate of our compound. The guards in the bunkers spent their days in wretched heat and boredom. The men usually chain-smoked cigarettes, swore at each other, lied to each other, and dreamed of home or of some long-lost girlfriend.

I focused my eyes back on the roses. I thought of my two-week tour flying over Saigon and the useless medal riders who refused to help carry a dying GI off the battlefield. I thought of the women and young boy who showed more courage than the air medal riders. My emotions swayed between anger and sorrow. I had not told anyone about the death of a man whose name I didn't even know. I heard his last words as he bled to death in my arms. Captain Corrigan walked back onto the veranda and told me the patrol was on for tomorrow. We would leave right after breakfast. I said I would be ready.

The next morning brought something none of us had seen in many weeks—the sun. A brilliant light bathed our compound and changed my mood. I walked to our mess tent and ate grits, coffee, and toast. Then I joined the assembling convoy of Captain Corrigan's infantry company. I didn't have to work our FDC charts until later that night. Captain Corrigan assured me that we would be back for my grave-yard shift. I climbed on top of an armored personnel carrier (APC) then waited for the convoy to move out of camp. Captain Corrigan walked up and down the line of vehicles, then he jumped into a jeep and waved the long line of trucks and APCs forward. We began a slow crawl through our front gate and turned left onto the road toward Long

Thành village. We traveled slowly for about thirty minutes through tall rubber trees. The roads were wet, and the ruts were filled with the previous night's muddy storm water. The earth was steamy with a humid fog just above the surface. Sunlight passed through the rubber trees and reminded me of beams of light from a movie projector. The air was thick and warm and soon would become hot. As we neared the edge of the plantation, a heavy growth of jungle appeared. The military never sprayed Agent Orange near the valuable rubber trees.

Our convoy stopped, and we disembarked, it was quiet. We began a single-file walk on a narrow path that led through the jungle. As our boots crushed the flora, it released an earthy scent. I watched the sunlight disappear; it was obscured by the rain forest canopy. Dark-brown vines twisted their way up tree trunks to form a leafy cover. We continued walking single file, following Captain Corrigan, who was near the front of the line. Our steps were quiet. No one made a sound.

By midday we were deep in the jungle. It was now sweltering. To a man we were covered with beads of sweat. Fatigue was setting in from lugging our heavy equipment. Suddenly, the line of moving men slowed, then it stopped. The man in front of us raised his hand, palm in a fist, signaling the men behind him to halt. Soon a radio operator made his way back to my position. He told me Captain Corrigan wanted me up at the front of the line. I heard his radio squawk, "Send Duffy up. I need him *now*."

I began inching my way forward, passing each man. As I moved forward through the jungle, a fear built in me. I heard no rifle fire or explosion. I thought, *Why does he need me?*

While I moved forward, some men made eye contact and a few gave me a nod. Each man had his rifle cocked and in the ready position looking out through the dense foliage. They were watching for any movement or reflection from the sun off an enemy gun. They were listening for the crack of a branch, a voice, or the scent of boiling fish. The air was still and we were silent. I continued moving forward past more sweaty faces. Some of the men were very young, with pimples and steamy eyeglasses. Some had the downy hair of an attempted mustache. I caught my foot on a "wait-a-minute vine." These were unseen plants growing on the jungle floor that caught on your boot, forcing you to stop and free yourself. I untangled the vine and kept moving. I waded through a narrow but deep, swift-running stream. Then, with the help of an undersized young private, I climbed up on the other side. The private seemed almost too small to be in the army. His M-16 rifle looked huge in his small, delicate hands; he nodded and smiled. Now my clothes and boots were drenched and dripping with muddy water.

As I neared the point of this long line of GIs, I could hear the unmistakable sound of men in pain. Soon I saw GIs on the ground with their hands pressed tight against their midsections. I spotted Captain Corrigan. His face was beet red and full of sweat beads. He seemed calm and determined. He glanced at me and said, "Duffy, I've got fifteen sick men. They ate some bad food this morning; they can't function."

I looked around and saw men moaning in pain. Puzzled, I turned to Captain Corrigan and asked, "How can I help?"

"I need to get these people out of here on a Medevac.[15] There's a clearing over there."

He pointed to a small meadow. The sunlight found its way through the jungle canopy and was shining on a patch of treeless grass near

---

15. Medevac is short for "medical evacuation helicopter."

our position. He continued, "I need to bring a helicopter down in that field; these men need to get back to camp. They can't walk or fight. If Charlie finds us like this, we're up shit creek."

"Okay," I said.

He went on. "You need to pop a smoke round over that clearing so the helicopter can see where we are. And so I can figure out where we are on this map."

Captain Corrigan placed his finger on the map he was holding. The map was as flat as the terrain we were walking through. It was folded in squares and isolated our patrol route. It was made of heavy paper and was colored in light greens and blues. There were long, brownish contour lines twisting through the map. Each line represented five meters above sea level. As I figured it, we were now twenty meters above sea level, but that was a guess. The white spots on the map represented clearings or supposed clearings. I looked at Captain Corrigan and once again said, "Okay." He handed me his map, then walked away to set up a temporary perimeter.

My job now was to find our position on the map. I studied it for a few moments. I could see the spot on the road where we had started our patrol. It was a small trail designated by broken dots. I followed the dots on the map with my finger, but they soon disappeared. We had been walking for hours, well beyond the end of the trail shown on the map. My problem was this: we were in a tunnel of jungle with no reference points, except the sun and the time of day.

I mentally computed our walking time and our direction from the road. I looked back at the map. It was filled with light blue-green marks in the shape of fleur-de-lis representing acres of flat swampland and fields of mangrove. I was worried that a smoke round misdirected by me would come crashing in on our unit, maybe landing on us and killing someone. The smoke itself would not harm anyone, but the empty shell could kill anyone in its path. I thought it best to have the shell explode high over our heads. We could see the smoke, but the shell would travel down the trail. I turned to Captain Corrigan and said, "I think we're here, but I can't be sure. I am going to have the smoke pop about 150 meters over our heads."

I pointed to a small spot on the map. Captain Corrigan said, "Call it in, 'cuz I am not sure where we are either." I glanced to see more men on the ground holding their stomachs.

I called a fire mission in to my unit back at Frenchy's. John Ladd was working the FDC charts and took my radio call. I gave Lieutenant Ladd what I thought were the coordinates of the small clearing and asked for the artillery smoke shell to detonate about 200 meters above the point on the map. I added an extra fifty meters for safety, but I didn't tell Captain Corrigan. A few minutes later, Lieutenant Ladd radioed back, "Round off."

We waited twenty or thirty seconds, and then we heard a pop. I looked around to see the smoke above a spot nowhere near the clearing and so high that I couldn't tell where on the map it was. "Shit," I mumbled to myself. I gave Captain Corrigan a puzzled look.

Captain Corrigan said not to worry, that it was close enough for the helicopters to find us. "When they get close," he said, "we can toss a smoke grenade in the clearing." Captain Corrigan was on the radio calling in the Medevac helicopters.

The white smoke from the artillery shell didn't move. It lingered in the sky and then began to waft slowly toward our position. Soon it was over our heads. The small cloud of smoke began changing shape; it turned into a long, irregular form. We all were quiet and still as we waited and watched the smoke float over our heads. After a while,

Captain Corrigan told the men they could light up, I heard Zippo lighters flip open. Matches were not much good in Vietnam's humid air, so most men who smoked carried lighters. The preferred cigarette lighter in Vietnam was the American-made Zippo. Those were sold at the PX. After the lighter's lid was opened, a quick thumb would spin a small metal wheel that rubbed against a piece of flint, and then a spark would light the flame. The smokers lit up. Most of the men smoked.

We waited for the sound of the Huey helicopters. It seemed like hours, but the unmistakable faint pulsing sound of helicopter blades began and soon the sound grew louder. Through the clearing, I could see two Hueys approaching our position. The helicopters began their hovering dance and then ever so gently landed in the grass-filled clearing. It worked. The choppers came from an airbase miles away, and the pilots used the smoke from the artillery shell as a visual so they could zero in on our position. The smoke rose high in the air and could be seen at great distances.

The sick men holding their stomachs climbed to their feet and slowly moved forward, filling the two ships. The operation took about ten minutes. The helicopters kept their blades turning, and when each craft was full, they slowly moved up and away from our position. Captain Corrigan turned to me and said, "Let's go back to Frenchy's; this patrol is over."

The men were directed to turn back and face the jungle path we had just walked through. The radio man raised his arm and waved it forward; soon, the rear of the line started the slow move back toward the road. The acrid smell of exhaust from the helicopters seemed to follow us. The air was without a breeze and the heat was punishing. I heard a bird call once, then twice. It was a screechy call like a kid yelling, "*Ah wee ah wee ah wee.*" I glanced around, but I couldn't see the bird, or monkey, or whatever it was. The front of the line was now the end of the line, and I began to move back into the dark canopy of the jungle. As I moved forward, I continued glancing behind me, looking for the bird that kept screeching, "*Ah wee.*"

As our column moved I felt vulnerable. After the smoke round popping overhead and the helicopters landing to pick up our sick men, the stealthy VC now knew our location. We were low-hanging fruit for an ambush. I was carrying an M-16 rifle that was on loan from Captain Corrigan's unit. There were two men behind me. We all chambered rounds and held the weapons at waist level, our fingers on the triggers. About fifteen minutes into the walk, I heard a gunshot. We all went down on one knee and held our breath. I remained motionless and waited. Since I heard only one shot, I assumed it was not an ambush. Soon the word came back to continue our walk.

It turned out that one of our men had accidentally fired his weapon. Captain Corrigan was furious with him and would take him to task after we got back to Frenchy's. The risk now was that Charlie knew exactly which way we were moving. He saw the Medevac, and now he heard the shot farther down the path.

I came upon the swift stream I had crossed earlier. I waded in and was pulled out by the man in front of me. I turned to help the last two men out of the water. We continued, and soon I heard Captain Corrigan's voice on the radio say he was back on the road and out of the jungle. I, along with the two men behind me, was the last to arrive at our waiting APCs. We quickly loaded up and moved back to Frenchy's without an encounter with Charlie. Captain Corrigan asked me to ride with him in his jeep.

The army served many purposes in Vietnam. It needed to keep the support of the locals and at the same time fight the Viet Cong insurgency. The support of the civilians provided important information about an impending attack or a stranger in town. The army also helped with public works such as repairing a bridge or painting a school. The most common form of help was providing a medical or dental clinic for the locals. Our doctors would set up a tent near a village and invite anyone with an ailment to come in for treatment. Pregnant women, who otherwise would never see a doctor, soon arrived. One afternoon I saw a farmer with a badly mauled hand wrapped in dirty bandages arrive for treatment. At times, the roadside clinic was mobbed with mothers and their small children: rashes were looked over and treated, fevers tended to, medicine and shots dispensed. This might be the only time a villager saw a doctor. There was never a charge.

One other task the army had was to socialize with the villagers and get to know the locals. Captain Corrigan had accepted an invitation from the schoolteacher to attend a social function. During our ride back to Frenchy's, he asked me to accompany him. He told me it was a small party at the teacher's house and that it would help build a bond with the townsfolk. I told him, "Okay, I'll go."

We ended up back at Frenchy's in the middle of the afternoon. By then the heat was oppressive. Everyone slowed to a crawl, laid on cots, and found a bit of shade. These were the boring times, when we looked for conversation, usually about home. If a GI asked where you were from, he most often wanted to tell you where he was from. A small question would turn into a sermon about home, hunting, cars, girlfriends, anything other than Vietnam. We had only ourselves to turn to. We were on a small island surrounded by barbed wire and isolated by language. We watched life out in the *ville* move around us, ever so slowly. A boy riding a water buffalo sauntered near our compound. We all watched the animal lumber past. The boy rode high on the buffalo's neck. He carried a short, thin whip in his right hand. The water buffalo was so accustomed to the routine that the beast and the boy seemed one and the same. The boy glanced our way. He took an interest in our compound, its occupants and vehicles. Our equipment was always fascinating for a young boy.

We watched the Thai soldiers play kickball all afternoon. They stopped only when the light faded and they could no longer see the ball. We heard the sound of a three-wheeled pedicab. The pedicab could be heard half a mile down the road. Its two-cycle engine screamed in a high-pitched wail, and at top speed, the vehicle moved at maybe twenty miles an hour. It soon came into view. It was painted in colorful yellows, bright greens, and reds, and clouds of blue smoke popped from its exhaust pipe. The small pedicab looked like an oversized tricycle fitted with bench seats. Passengers sat back to back and faced the open air. The passengers had little protection from the elements, but a curved tin roof did offer some shelter from the rain and sun.

We stared at the cab from the veranda and watched it slow to a stop in front of our camp. The driver picked up a few people for the trip to Long Thành, where travelers could board a bus for Bien Hoa or Saigon. A chain-smoking driver tightly held the handlebars of the cab. He guided the passengers toward the open seats. If the cab was crowded, and it usually was, some passengers would hang off the back. After the short stop in the *ville,* the driver raced the engine, engaged the clutch, and sped off down the muddy road, a cloud of blue smoke marking the cab's trail.

Late one afternoon, we heard the sound of a motorbike. We all looked out from the veranda as the sound grew louder. Soon, a strange figure appeared on the road. He was a tall man on a kelly-green motorcycle. He wore khaki pants and a long, open-collared khaki shirt. A fedora crowned his head. We watched as he slowed his bike then stopped at our front gate. He looked European. As his motorbike idled, the guards checked his identity card and let him pass. He revved the engine and pulled up to the veranda. We watched with curiosity as he sauntered up the steps. He glanced our way, and in a heavy French accent, he asked to speak with our captain. He elongated each syllable of the word captain and added extra emphasis on the last syllable—"caapeee*tan.*"

This man's face was long and tan. He had, I thought, one of the largest noses I had ever seen. John Ladd showed him through the front door and toward our battery clerk. We saw Captain Tom appear, and this strange-looking man was ushered into Captain Tom's small office. We began to speculate on the nature of the Frenchman's visit. We knew it was not social. Soon, Captain Tom and our visitor walked back out and onto the veranda. We watched the Frenchman march back to his motorbike. He was wearing a dour look on his face; I watched as he kick-started his bike, engaged the clutch, and rode out of our compound. Captain Tom stood in the doorway with his hands on his waist, watching him leave. We kept our mouths shut and waited until he walked over to us and explained the nature of the man's visit.

The Frenchman was the overseer of the Binh Son rubber plantation. He worked for a large company headquartered in Paris. He told Captain Tom that our artillery fire had blown up four of his trees, and he was requesting reimbursement. There was usually a guide for the destruction of civilian property. In the case of a water buffalo blown to bits by an errant artillery shell, the owner would be reimbursed maybe forty dollars. A healthy rubber tree could produce year after year, and if nurtured, the tree had a long, productive life. Three hundred dollars per tree was what the French overseer was requesting. After looking over our recent fire missions, Captain Tom determined that our guns had not fired anywhere near his trees. And since there were artillery batteries all over the area firing every night and in every direction, it had to be someone else's artillery fire. Captain Tom denied the overseer's request for compensation.

We continued to talk on the veranda. Captain Tom joined us in a warm beer; this was rare; he usually spent most of his time in his hooch. We sometimes wanted for clean water or dry socks, but we never wanted for beer. It was always available, usually delivered in the mail truck. Beer was a pacifier for the troops. John Ladd told us of a time during an operation near Monkey Mountain when a pallet of beer was delivered by helicopter. The pallet hung from straps off the Huey's skids, and in a slow movement, with great care, the pallet of beer was moved from one position to another. Each GI watched the pallet as it was lowered to the ground, its contents still in good order.

To fight boredom in our compound, I usually took a slow walk around camp, greeting the GIs, at least those who were not half-asleep. If they looked up from their paperbacks or opened their eyes, they usually were ready for a bit of conversation, always about home. The most often asked question was, "How short are you?" This phrase referred to the time left in Vietnam. Everyone knew the exact day he was scheduled to leave for home. The GIs would always show you their short-timer calendars, colorful pages with numbers from one to 364 that represented their yearlong tours of duty. The numbers were crossed off their calendars each day. Then the GIs would bark out the number of days he had until the "freedom bird" spirited him home. We all thought going home would be an easy transition, picking up where we left off, moving back into our old, comfortable routines. For me, the routine of home was gone forever, but I didn't yet know that.

Home for me was my parents' modest apartment on Chicago's North Side in the East Rogers Park neighborhood. For me it was a mental paradise. I would daydream about neighborhood girls and sixteen-inch summer softball games at our Lake Michigan beach. I could not wait to get back home. When I left our apartment, I would always run into a friend or the parent of a friend and engage them in conversation. I knew every gangway, alley, and street from our apartment house down to Lake Michigan.

I was luckier than most GIs because I had a plan, a goal. I was going to attend Colorado College after I got home. I was determined to graduate and get my bachelor's degree. I often pulled my letter of acceptance out of my brown attaché and reread it. The letter was confirmation of a future back home.

While I was stationed at Fort Carson in Colorado, my roommate, George Britt, suggested I apply to the small, private liberal arts college nearby in downtown Colorado Springs. George was a university graduate who attained his commission through the ROTC. George and I worked together at Fort Carson, the sprawling army base just south of Colorado Springs. He was my senior by four years, and I took his advice. Colorado Springs was a beautiful town at the base of Pikes Peak, and I fell in love with the Colorado College campus.

Shortly after my talk with George, I made an appointment to visit the admissions director at Colorado College. He invited me into his office, and we had a cordial conversation. I told him of my interest in Colorado College, and he in turn told me how to go through the application process. The first thing I needed to do was take the Scholastic Aptitude Test at a high school in Colorado Springs. I had been out of school for almost three years, and my test-taking skills, never very good, were now rusty. The admissions director encouraged me to walk around the campus and "visit with the students." This was great advice but an impossible task. My short military haircut gave me away as a GI. I was ignored as I walked through the campus. The last straw on my campus visit came that evening at the Colorado College coffeehouse, a kind of folksy music club open to the public on Cache La Poudre Street. As I entered the club, a few of the male students spied me and began a low murmured chant of "How's things at the fort, *the fort, the fort*?" As they did this, they began to laugh. Self-conscious as a stranger on the campus of a college that I did not attend, I left, embarrassed but still determined to apply. There was a huge wall between the CC students and the GIs from nearby Fort Carson. This wall was always present and almost impossible to overcome.

A GI in Vietnam serving in the artillery spent a good deal of time lying in his small space in or near the guns, unlike the footage of Vietnam shown on the nightly news, where units were engaged with the enemy. The firefights and rocket attacks didn't occur every night. In fact, outside of the Tet Offensive, they were uncommon. Granted, the VC attacked and fired rockets almost every day, but usually not at the same target. And although we fired our guns every night, most nights we fired only two guns. That left four other guns to fire the next day, or possibly fire at the same time but at different targets. Our work on the guns became routine. The men knew their jobs and worked as if they were employed as punch-press operators in a Detroit auto factory.

During the off hours, the GIs would read and reread their letters from home. As an officer, I had more responsibilities than the enlisted men, but like everyone else, I had periods during the day when time crawled and daydreams took over. We didn't leave the compound at Binh Son because it was too dangerous. We had our small space, defined by barbed wire, and our fellow soldiers in the battery. That was our life, day after day.

As I sat on my cot reading then rereading my letter of acceptance to Colorado College, I began to think of home. I thought of my neighborhood school, Saint Ignatius Grammar School in Chicago's Rogers Park neighborhood, a Jewish and Irish enclave next to Lake Michigan.

When I was twelve years old, my father moved us from a rented house in Cary, Illinois, to an apartment in Chicago. My father wanted to be closer to his office and shorten his commuting time. I entered Saint Ignatius Grammar School's seventh-grade class in the fall of 1958.

One night in August 1958, not long after our move to Chicago, my mother gathered my brother, Dan, and me, and we boarded the southbound 'L' train at the Loyola Avenue station. We were headed for Chicago's Loop. We got off the train at State and Jackson Streets and walked a block south to a department store called The Bond; it was housed in an art deco building along State Street's retail row. The store had four or five floors and rounded glass blocks facing State Street. My mother pushed my brother and me into the elevator. In those years, there was an elevator attendant, and my mother told the attendant to take us to the men and boys department on the fourth floor.

When the doors opened, we were surprised to see my father waiting for us. We greeted him, but there was no time to waste. Dan and I began to try on sport coats that my mother handed us, one after another. This, she told my father, was the most important part of our uniform, and it had to last at least two years. The store clerk helped us try on the coats. After we put on a coat, he would guide us to a full-length mirror. Then he would stand behind us smiling and nodding at my mother. After many different styles and colors, I tried on a coat made of dark tweed. It was brown and had little nubs in the fabric. I liked it. I looked at my mother and told her this coat was my favorite. My mother took the coat from me and looked at the price. Her face changed, and she said, "I don't know."

The coat I liked was far more money than my mother had budgeted. She consulted with my father, then handed me the coat and said, "Okay, Mike, we'll get this coat for you." It was settled. This would be my suit coat for school. My brother was fitted with a gray suit coat, and then we rushed to find blue shirts and dark blue clip-on ties, along with two pairs of pants. The clip-on ties had small, plastic hooks behind the knots that hooked the ties to your buttoned-up shirt so you didn't have to tie the ties. The store was about to close; it was time to leave.

My dad had driven his aging Pontiac to work that day, and we drove home up Lake Shore Drive to our apartment on Bosworth Avenue. During the drive home, I quizzed my mother about the sport coat. "Mom, do I have to wear the coat every day?" She said yes.

"Do I have to wear a tie every day?"

"Yes," she said.

"Mom, what about the blue shirt?"

She turned to me annoyed and said, "Yes, you must wear the blue shirt with the blue tie and the sport coat every day; now hush."

This was very different from our old school in Cary, Saints Peter and Paul School. Most kids in Cary wore blue jeans and a print shirt. In the 1950s, Cary was still a rural area with many kids living and working on the dairy farms dotting McHenry County. This sport coat business was new to me. I still had no idea what our new school, Saint Ignatius Grammar School, would be like. Dan and I were nervous and very curious.

We were the new kids on the block. We had not yet developed friends in the neighborhood. Our landlady, Mrs. Murphy, lived above us on the second floor.

She saw us in our small backyard one afternoon and told us to go visit Schreiber Park, just a half-block away. She said we would meet lots of new friends at Schreiber Park. One day Dan and I walked over to the park, only to be challenged by a kid our age with a brown paper bag in his hand. The bag was filled with Testors glue. There were empty tubes of glue scattered on the sidewalk. The kid would put the bag to his mouth and take a deep breath. His friends would smile sardonically and nod in approval. After that, they turned to give Dan and me menacing looks. I noticed that most of the kids had very bad teeth graying around the edges. The kid with the bag of glue looked at Dan and me and yelled, "Fuck you, you fucking jag-offs. This is our park." He began to stagger toward us. Dan and I quickly left the park and never returned. I wanted to ask my dad what a jag-off was, but I didn't.

For the next two weeks, Dan and I rode our bikes around our neighborhood, except near Schreiber Park. We would make ever-larger circles with our bikes. We found two World War II tanks on the corner of Clark Street and Devon Avenue. We climbed up on the tanks. From there we could see a tavern called Develanties, a hamburger joint called Dewey's, a bowling alley, a hardware store, the Little Brown Jug restaurant, Gary's cycle shop, and a grocery store. There were four grocery stores on Devon: the IGA grocery store, Bornhofen's grocery and meat market, a Jewish deli, and Kelly's meat market. My mom began to shop at Bornhofen's market. Mr. Bornhofen offered us credit until Dad's payday; the IGA did not.

During our travels, Dan and I met a guy named Tony. He lived in a dank basement room down a gangway off Devon Avenue. I assumed that Tony was retired because we saw him in the alley almost every day. We thought Tony was always thirsty, because he was constantly drinking something out of a paper bag. Later that year, we were told by a neighborhood kid that his name was "Tony the bum," and the paper bag held a bottle of cheap wine.

We also met a guy who hung out in his garage. He would keep the garage door open and survey the alley. As Dan and I walked by one Saturday morning, he made a strange sound with his mouth to get our attention. We became curious and walked over to his garage. He began to ask us strange questions. "Hi, boys, want to call your mommy?"

Then from a shelf in his garage he produced a toy phone. He tried to hand it to us, but we said no thanks. On another occasion he asked if we wanted to see his new car. He then pulled a rusty model car from a shelf and thrust it toward us. He also made an odd sound with his mouth: "Ha cha ... cha ... cha." Dan and I named him Jimmy Ha-cha-cha. He seemed harmless, but we avoided him nonetheless.

It was mid-August and still very hot. Our block was lined with three-flat apartment buildings anchored at the corners with eighteen- or twenty-four-unit buildings.

The alley was where the action was, with delivery trucks and women hanging laundry on clotheslines. Often the women sang as they put out their laundry. I liked listening to them; it seemed peaceful. I also heard different languages; most were European. I recognized German, but there was another language similar to German that I could not place. One day my dad and I heard it together, and he told me it was Yiddish. My dad went on to explain that many Yiddish-speaking European Jews had fled Europe for the United States after World War II. Scores of these people had settled in our neighborhood. They came to East Rogers Park for the same reason we did—the rents were cheap.

One day I saw a man in our alley with blue numbers tattooed on his arm. This was strange to me, but I didn't dare ask him what the numbers meant. Later that summer I found out after watching a TV documentary on World War II. The numbers were identification marks used in the Nazi concentration camps. The man was a survivor of one of those camps.

I saw a kid walk into our yard one day and toss a newspaper up to the third floor. I asked him where I could get a job like his. He told me to go to a storefront near the corner of Devon Avenue and Lakewood Street, the site of the Lewis News Agency. He said they needed delivery boys all the time. I made a mental note.

Dan and I played catch in the alley with our Little League gloves, brought from Cary. The alley became our playground. One hot evening, while our family was eating dinner, we heard music. I ran to the back door and saw a short, skinny man with a brown-brimmed hat, a coat made of stiff fustian, and a dirty tie. He balanced a wooden box on a pole as he turned a crank, and he gave us a smile. Dan and I ran downstairs to see a monkey sitting on this man's shoulder. When we approached him, the monkey held out a dented tin cup. My dad, just behind us, handed us some coins to put in the cup. Soon the man disappeared from our yard down our gangway and into the alley. My dad told us the guy was probably the last of the Italian organ grinders, and most likely we would never see another. He was right.

One of the oddest scenes we saw during our first weeks in Chicago was at the bus stop on Clark Street and Devon Avenue. Waiting for the bus was a guy dressed in a buttoned shirt, suspenders, and baggy pants. He had a white beard and a brimmed hat; on top of the hat was a live chicken. He saw our interest in him, so he quickly turned and began muttering, "I'm Tony, talk of the town, talk of the town, Tony."

Dan and I stopped and watched as the man danced around the bus stop pole with the chicken fluttering its wings still on his head.

"Tony, Tony, talk of the town."

Soon the bus arrived, and the man got on the bus with the chicken still on the top of his head. This made great conversation at our dinner table that night.

Before long, the first day of school was upon us. Dan and I tried on our new school uniforms the night before to make sure things went smoothly the next morning. We hung our shirts, pants, and coats on hangers; we made certain that our ties were near at hand, and then we polished our shoes. We wanted to make a good impression. My mother helped me cut the tags off my new tweed coat. I was worried I would cut the brown fabric. She skillfully used a small pair of sewing scissors then snipped off the price tag and the other labels that the manufacturer had affixed to my new sport coat. Now we were ready for our first day of school.

The next morning we got up early, ate breakfast, and headed off to Saint Ignatius Grammar School, a five-block walk. As we turned the corner at Arthur Avenue and Glenwood Avenue, we heard a kid's voice from behind us. "Hey," the kid yelled.

We turned to see a boy our age in a blue shirt, blue tie, and suit coat.

"Hi," Dan and I said.

We were unprepared for what happened next. The kid jumped me, shoving me on the sidewalk and tearing my pants; then he pushed me onto the grass and held my shoulders to the ground. He began yelling that this was his neighborhood. I said nothing, and soon he let me up. I could not believe this was happening. He walked away laughing. Dan and I continued our walk, but now my pants were torn and my new coat had grass stains on it. I was worried my mother would be angry with me.

Dan and I arrived at the school, worried that some other kid would challenge us on the playground, a patch of concrete and blacktop surrounded by brick buildings and our church. The boys were playing near one building and the girls were near another. The school was housed in two three-story brick structures. One had the word *"Boys"* chiseled in stone and set above the entrance; the other building had *"Girls"* chiseled in stone. A bridge on the second floor connected the buildings. The good nuns figured that boys and girls learning together did not work. This was not the case in our old school back in Cary.

Boys and girls sat together in the classrooms, and we played together on the playground. Dan and I stayed together until a large nun in a black habit came out the side door. She began clanging a brass bell, signaling the start of the school day. Dan and I followed the boys into the school. My class was on the third floor and woe to the boy who talked in line during the trek to the classroom. I walked into a room with large windows facing south. Even at this early hour, the room was stuffy and hot. I was assigned a seat. I quickly found my desk and sat down.

When all the boys were seated and had their hands folded on their desks, our teacher wrote her name on the blackboard. Sister Mary, seventh-grade boys. She turned to the class only to spy one boy with his hands below desk level. She quickly made use of a long, wooden pointer to smash it on his desk. This slapping sound startled all of us. Sister Mary then looked around the room and belted out these words, "Idle hands are the devil's workshop!"

I couldn't figure out what she meant by those words, but I was sure it was something unpleasant. My twelve-year-old mind imagined the devil's workshop as a large room made of red fire brick with windows looking out on huge fire pits. I imagined the devil was busy at his workbench making things like exploding cigars or trick mousetraps that snapped on your fingers when you tried to set them. When I looked at my hands, I couldn't figure out the connection. I thought of asking Sister Mary what she meant, but she was busy smashing her wooden pointer down on another boy's desk. I looked around the room at the other boys in our class. The boy who had jumped me that morning was staring at me with a not-so-friendly eye. I looked away.

Sister Mary began the day by introducing two new boys to the seventh-grade class. She had me stand and tell the class where I came from. I said, "Cary, Illinois," then I sat down. The kid behind me leaned over my shoulder and asked me where Cary was. I turned to tell him it was northwest of Chicago. As I did this, Sister Mary's wooden pointer came crashing down on my desk. That was followed with these words: "Well, Mr. Duffy, it looks as if you are getting off to a poor start in my classroom."

As she said those words, her face came very close to mine. I could see small, white hairs twisting out of her nose. One was so long that it had two curls and almost touched her lip. She had a small mustache of short gray hair. Her face was squished out by a black knotted fabric. It looked as if she had wrapped this black fabric around a door spring, pulled it around her face, and then let it snap tightly, squeezing her face in on itself. Her mouth was curved into an oval. She stared at me with piercing eyes and I stared back, looking at a white hair twisting from her eyebrow. I marveled at its length. Her head snapped away from me in a gesture of displeasure. I thought, *Now she has marked me as a troublemaker.*

By the time the lunch bell rang, our classroom must have been more than eighty degrees. Sister Mary had the boys open the windows, but that didn't help. Finally, the bell rang, and we all marched out of the building. Dan and I ran home to eat a quick lunch and then returned to the playground. It was now filled with boys. A tall priest was standing in the middle of the crowd. He threw a tennis ball high against our school building, and as it fell, the boys scrambled to catch it. The scene was chaos. Boys would elbow, shove, push, and trip one another as they raced for the falling tennis ball. I saw one kid with a bloody nose. He complained to Father that he had been purposely elbowed. Father shouted back, "Life is a big elbow; get used to it."

With his strong arm, Father let go, and the tennis ball flew up against the wall. The mob of kids rushed toward the ball, trying to catch it as it fell. Dan and I wandered around the grounds, exploring this strange new environment. It all seemed so harsh compared with our old school in Cary.

The afternoon bell rang, and we began our trek back to the classroom. By this time of day, the room was unbearably hot. As we moved to our desks, one boy asked Sister Mary if we could take off our jackets. "*No*," she shot back. "Just think of Jesus and how he suffered on the cross." She gave the boy a stern look of displeasure. She would use this phrase often during the school year, reminding us that Jesus had died on the cross for our sins. She told us how great and good Jesus was. I thought that if he was such a good guy, surely he would let us take off our coats on this hot day. Sister Mary began walking the aisles looking at our lessons and keeping a tense control of the class. Our assignment was stultifying repetition. I began to daydream and glance out the window as one lone cloud drifted in the sky. The classroom clock seemed to slow as the hands inched their way toward 3:00 p.m. and the end of the school day.

After a few weeks of classes, I formed friendships with several boys who did not need to throw a punch or thrash me to the ground and shout. "this is my neighborhood!"

It seemed each day I came face to face with a challenge from some bully on the playground. One day I had had my fill of malice and couldn't take it anymore. Two of the most vicious bullies in the school worked together to make my day miserable. One boy spat a wad of phlegm against a door and the other shoved me against it, ensuring that the back of my new tweed jacket got soiled. He then pushed me sideways against the door. I heard my jacket rip on the hinges. He stood in the doorway staring at me, cackling in some twisted pleasure. God, I longed for my school in Cary, where the kids had a mellow life and where I never saw a punch thrown. The harsh tension at Saint Ignatius was overwhelming for me. I began to hate my new school and all its ways. After I heard my jacket rip, I was numb with anxiety. I started for the side door but was stopped by Sister Mary. She told me it was too early to come into her class and go back and play with the other boys. I broke down and told her that I couldn't because all I had experienced on the playground was hate. I told her I wanted to go home, away from this place. After seeing me in this state, she let me in the door. She told me to go up to class and wait.

I was sitting in my seat as the other boys walked in from the lunch hour. Once we were all seated, Sister Mary, with good intentions, addressed the class. She told the class that tormenting a boy was not the Christian thing to do and it had better stop. As she said this, I sat at my desk praying she would not mention my name because that surely would mean a beating on the way home. I was saved; she didn't mention my name, and her words seemed to help because the two good Christian boys slowed their torments. I went home that day ready to leave Chicago and Saint Ignatius and go back to Cary, Illinois.

At the age of twelve, I was absolutely overwhelmed with stress. One night after dinner, I begged my mom to take me out of St. Ignatius School. I told her that at the public school, I would be in class with nonviolent Jewish kids. I pleaded with her, but her no was final. The next day I told my Jewish friend, who lived down our block, that I wouldn't be in his class next year as I had hoped.

John Ladd walked into our room and snapped me out of my day dream. He tossed a letter on my cot. The letter was from Joe Kiefer, a childhood friend who wrote to me regularly while I was in Vietnam. These letters were always welcome. Joe wrote of a party that my old girlfriend and he had attended. She drove her dad's Buick, an enormous battleship-sized car with long bench seats. He went on to tell me of his ROTC experiences and his university graduation date. I loved the letter, but I felt as if it had come from the moon. Everything was so distant, so far away. I wanted to be part of that life again, away from guns, tanks, flak jackets, barbed wire, and mud.

Another night fell on our compound, this one without rain. The officers were on the veranda sipping warm beer when Captain Corrigan walked over and reminded John Ladd and me about the party with the local village leaders: the mayor, the schoolteacher, and others. I had forgotten about the party. Captain Corrigan had mentioned it to me just after our patrol. "Ready to go?" he said. "Sure," I said and joined Captain Corrigan. John Ladd wisely stayed at the compound.

Six of us walked out of Frenchy's toward the party, all of us armed. The night was pitch-black. We took off our helmets and flak jackets, but I carried a .45 caliber pistol in a holster strapped to my leg, as did Captain Corrigan. The other men and a Vietnamese ranger had M-16 rifles. It was a short walk to the home of the schoolteacher. He and his wife and children lived in a modest stucco home built during the French occupation. There were six steps up to a small porch and then a mahogany door, now open. We were greeted by our host and hostess and were ushered into the front room. In attendance were a few town dignitaries, neighbors, and the village prostitute. I found out the village prostitute was in attendance when she offered me a five-dollar "short-time fuckie-suckie."

I felt uncomfortable walking into this home carrying a weapon, but it was too dangerous to leave our small compound without one. I was told by Captain Corrigan that our stay would be short.

The biggest obstacle at the party was the language barrier. No locals spoke English, and none of us spoke Vietnamese. We looked at each other and did a lot of nodding and smiling. The schoolteacher's wife approached me and offered me an hors d'oeuvre. It was a piece of pink meat wrapped in a small leaf. I didn't want to take it, but I didn't want to be impolite. I took the hors d'oeuvre and looked at it a bit puzzled. The schoolteacher's wife began to unwrap the pink meat from the small leaf. She waited for me to take a bite, and I did. After she turned, I found my way out to the front porch and tossed what was left into the bushes. Captain Corrigan glanced at me; it was time to go. We walked back in the dark down the dirt road through the gate, past the security guards, and to our beds.

About three in the morning, I awakened with a wrenching stomachache. This ache was the beginning of my long bout with amoebic dysentery. The morning after the party, I was paying a dear price for eating a bite of the hors d'oeuvre. My stomach was gripped with pain.

It felt as if someone with long fingernails was squeezing my intestines, twisting, and pulling with hatred. I alternated between diarrhea and vomiting. I was sick and facing me was a military operation north of our position. A unit of the 9ᵗʰ Infantry Division was moving out of our artillery range. To ensure our guns would have the range to support the infantry, we were ordered north. For me, moving north meant leaving the comfort of Frenchy's and a dry cot.

I hoped that in a day or two this demon inside me might pass. I rolled from my bunk in a listless stupor and walked to the chow line. Nothing looked appealing. I could not eat. I did drink a cup of coffee, only to rid myself of it in a dash to the latrine. Dehydration set in. I found our medic, but he seemed more concerned with his hand of playing cards than with my illness. I asked him for any medicine he might have for my ailment. He had nothing for me, but he said he would try to bring something in on the next supply convoy. Whatever medicine he requested, if requested at all, never arrived. I was a mess. My friend John Ladd gave me a look of sympathy; it did not help.

That night I was on duty again as the Fire Direction Control officer. This was the graveyard shift, an all-night job with the guns firing at 1:00 a.m., 2:30 a.m., 3:45 a.m., and then again near dawn at 5:00 a.m. I managed to calculate the first fire mission, then I sent the elevation and deflection down to the guns. By the time 2:00 a.m. rolled around, I could barely move. I asked our corporal to figure the calculations and wake me before sending the numbers down to the guns. He did, and the numbers were correct. By 3:00 a.m. he let me sleep, and I was awakened by the blasts of our artillery. I forced myself up and, in a weak, barely audible voice, reminded him to "wake me before sending the calculations down to the guns."

"Sure, sir." I saw him shake his head in a gesture of pity.

Near 5:00 a.m. I heard the guns go off again. He had disobeyed my order. I rolled over in a fit of intestinal spasms, and I ignored the infraction. As the morning dawned, I was stricken by more pain and almost continuous diarrhea. Food was out of the question.

We awakened to a dim gray sky. Nothing was dry. The night's heavy rain turned into a foggy morning drizzle. The men were loading the trucks, preparing for our move. The guns were being cleaned. Our charts and maps were rolled up and wrapped in clear plastic. I did nothing but lay on my narrow cot in a daze of fatigue and pain. I could feel my strength being sucked out of me hour by hour. The day wore on and I knew I would have to rise from my sick bed. Soon the convoy would move from Frenchy's. The drizzle turned into a steady rain, then it poured down in torrents.

I pulled myself up and out of my cot and saw the guns being hooked to the back of the trucks. I watched as they were pulled from the shallow pits one by one. Behind the six guns were two deuce-and-a-half trucks loaded with artillery rounds, a mess truck, a headquarters truck, and a few jeeps. The FDC center was hauled in a three-quarter-ton vehicle the size of a large pickup truck.

I rode in a jeep filled with the charts, maps, and slide rules, the equipment necessary to compute the elevation and deflection to shoot the cannons straight. I was weak and still dealing with a severe intestinal pain. My diet was limited to sips of water, and even that I had a hard time keeping down.

Our trucks were ready to roll. We were to find our position then point the artillery guns then commence three days of fire missions.

Jack Smith leaned out of his jeep, waved his lanky arm, and started the convoy. The trucks belched black smoke, wheels spun in the mud, and we started our move. Our convoy began a slow crawl out of the front gate.

As our convoy gained speed, I gazed up at the clouds; the rain was pouring over my face. Driving through the tall rubber trees offered a view of controlled nature that I always enjoyed. The French had planted and groomed the trees in long, straight rows. The trees had dark green, fat leaves. I looked through the rain to the tops of the trees and wished I could fly away from all this misery.

we drove for about an hour to where the rubber trees opened to a small clearing, and where our guns were quickly set to fire. In front of us, just beyond a low ridge of hills, the infantry was moving through the jungle. Everyone went to work, except me. I was too sick to work; I lay down on the bench seat of a deuce-and-a-half truck.

The FDC bunker was incomplete. The men were building sand-bagged walls next to a lean-to roof; it was half-bunker, half-canvas tent. I forced myself up and out of the truck, then I walked over to the FDC bunker. I began to sway with a lightheaded sickness. I directed the men to start setting up our small field office, but I had to find a latrine. There was none; it was still being dug. I found a clump of foliage and began my dance of vomiting and shitting. I fell to one knee and was close to collapsing. I heard my name called and struggled back on my feet. "Sir, sir, there's a fire mission."

Jack Smith looked at me as I walked back into the FDC tent; it was mess of paper and maps. "We're ready," Jack barked. "Where are the computations for the fire missions?" He looked concerned.

I glanced at the piles of fire missions that needed calculations. I listened to the radio as frantic men were calling for artillery fire. I could hear machine-gun fire from the radio, but I was useless. An angel found me in this plight, a new second lieutenant fresh from the

States. "Can I help?" I looked at him and said, "Yes, take over. I'm sick."
I stumbled back outside through sheets of rain. I lay down on a wall of
sandbags, and in a heavy downpour, I closed my eyes and slept.

The infantry was engaged with the VC not far from our position.
In addition to our artillery fire, the infantry also called in an air strike.
When the two jets arrived, our artillery fire stopped. The risk of an
artillery round hitting a plane was real, although quite remote.

In the absence of exploding cannons, I awakened. I rolled off
my wet sandbag bed and walked toward our six guns, now silent.
Firing had stopped, and we all had our heads up. We were quiet
and listening to the air show above us, I heard fighter jets roaring
somewhere overheard. Although the rain had let up, the cloudy ceiling was still low. In the distance we heard explosions—the jets had
dropped their ordnance. After a short time, I thought the air show
was over and that the pilots were flying back to their base, where
a comfortable bed and a hot meal awaited them. I was wrong. In
a fracture of piercing sound, the two jets screamed over our heads
just below the clouds. This was not a plane in a distant sky; it was a
rupture of sound and energy just above us. Out of instinct, I ducked
for cover. When I looked up, I saw the tails of the planes twisting in
a victory roll.

By this time, the word was out I was too sick to continue working.
There was no place for me to convalesce and we still had three days of
work. Another Angel must have heard my prayer, because at the end
of our first day, we were ordered back to Binh Son and the luxury of
Frenchy's. *Thank God.* We packed up, and in the late afternoon twi-
light, we began our trip back to Frenchy's.

In the weeks following our operation a slow mending process
began in my system. My illness and I struck a truce. I began eating

small bits and pieces of food. My caloric intake was still less than my need, and soon my lost ounces turned to lost pounds. The medic couldn't produce the medicine needed for a cure, so day after day, I saw myself losing weight. But at least I could perform my duties.

After one long night of work in the FDC bunker, just as the sky was beginning to brighten, I crawled onto my cot and fell asleep. I thought I was dreaming as I heard the sound of Captain Tom's voice. My eyes opened to see Captain Tom standing over my cot. He kept repeating, "Lieutenant Duffy, you need to get up."

I sat up, looked at Captain Tom, and asked, "What is it, sir?"

He told me that he had invited a chaplain to Frenchy's. The chaplain, a Catholic priest, was on his way to say Mass. Captain Tom asked me to gather all the Catholics in the battery and assemble them on the veranda. I told him that if it was okay, I'd prefer to spend this Sunday morning on my cot, and asked if he didn't mind, could I miss the service since I was up all last night? He pleaded with me. "No, no we need to have a show of support. I invited Father out for Sunday Mass. Go out to the gun pits and get some men."

I saw the panic in Captain Tom's face and said, "Okay."

As I walked down to the gun pits, exhausted and ill, I cursed the day that I had told Captain Tom I was Catholic.

I walked to each gun pit, stuck my head in, and asked if anyone wanted to attend Catholic Mass, and if so, to meet on the veranda in half an hour. I didn't say it was a mandatory meeting. To my surprise, I gathered about fifteen GIs for the service. The priest flew in on a small light weight helicopter painted olive drab. We watched it land in a small clearing next to the veranda. Father wasted no time; the Mass was quick, no sermon. After the Mass, he asked if any of us wished to talk to him about personal situations. Captain Tom watched as we all shook our heads with a collective no. He quickly boarded the small chopper and flew off.

This was the only time during my one-year tour in Vietnam that I attended Mass. Even in my state of misery, I found it a welcome change. I walked back to my cot and I fell asleep. I didn't wake until that afternoon.

Two new lieutenants joined us later in the week, Lieutenant Peter Hart and Lieutenant Roger Owen. Lieutenant Hart was a friendly twenty-five-year-old from Southern California; he gave me a smile as he shook my hand. Lieutenant Owen was a tall man with a ruddy complexion. I thought he might have a case of psoriasis. He had a sad face and rarely smiled. We quickly shook hands and then parted ways. Lieutenant Owen was also from Southern California.

Hart and Owen became instant friends, and they spent a great deal of time together discussing their lives in California—surfing, boating, and the Southern California lifestyle. It seemed to me that their conversation was a continuous loop. After talking about the merits of living in The Golden State, they would stop, take a breath, and then start all over again. "Beaches, boats, surfing, on and on." It soon bored me.

The army's rumor mill cranked up one morning at breakfast. It began with a young private just back from Bearcat. He told the men in his gun pit about a move. He had a friend who had a friend who had overheard a colonel talking about our unit, Battery C, moving very soon.

The rumor mill in the army was legend. Once started, the rumors could grow to herculean size. This army buzz could take a small cut on a man's finger and turn it into a multi-limb amputation. It could push and shove and expand any story to absurd size and myth. I was asked by the enlisted men about the pending move. Men walked by me, stopped, and asked, "Is it true, sir? Are we moving?" I told them I didn't know a thing. But the men thought I was hiding information. I couldn't convince them that I had zero knowledge of any move. Private Burgess stopped me one day near the latrine. "Sir," he said, "it's true, isn't it—we're moving?"

I had had enough of these questions. "Burgess," I said, "we are not moving. anything you heard in the gun pits is bullshit." He thanked me then walked away. Now he was sure to impress the men on his gun crew when he told them that he had spoken with Lieutenant Duffy, and Lieutenant Duffy had told him the truth.

That night at our evening officers' meeting, I was told we would be moving. So I thought, *The rumor is true!* Our move this time was to a place called Nhá Bé; it was just south of Saigon on the banks of the Sông Nhá Bé River.

I walked into the FDC room and asked John Ladd if he knew that our unit was moving. He said, "Yes." He told me that he had heard about it from the private just back from Bearcat, more than a week ago. John couldn't believe that I had not heard about the move. I told him that I had heard about it but that I didn't believe the rumor. I asked John when he thought Captain Tom would tell the enlisted men. He told me there was to be a large assembly in the morning and Captain Tom would make the announcement.

Chapter 4

THE MOVE

The next day, during a morning assembly, Captain Tom officially put an end to the rumor mill. He stood on the veranda and announced to our unit the impending move. He told us the dry accommodations at Frenchy's would soon end. Our battery was ordered to a new location on the Sông Nhá Bé River. We didn't know why we were moving, and none of us wanted to leave the comfort of Frenchy's.

To be accurate, our unit was ordered to the Nhá Bé tank farm, a large petroleum storage facility just north of the Nhá Bé Peninsula. Captain Tom told us to begin preparations for the trip down the narrow, dangerous road to Long Thành and then north toward Bien Hoa. At Bien Hoa, we would turn southwest onto Highway 1 and travel toward Saigon, the capital city of South Vietnam. Our convoy would pass directly through the center of Saigon. Once through the city, we would travel over a series of canals built during the French colonial days and then head south toward the Nhá Bé peninsula. Our path would take us to the edge of the Sông Nhá Bé River, where we would set up our howitzers.

I walked back into the FDC room and scanned the maps, I was very curious about our new position, where it was and what it would be like. I found the Nhá Bé Naval Base south of Saigon and moved my finger up to a series of black dots labeled in small black print Tanks. I looked up from the map and asked Jack Smith what he thought.

Jack said that the area we were moving into was a vast departure from our comfort here at Frenchy's. He had visited Nhá Bé and said it was muddy, dirty, and industrial. He went on to tell me that large tanker ships docked at an inlet just off the Sông Nhá Bé River and unloaded their liquid cargo. Fuel for the U.S. Army's war machine was pumped into huge storage tanks. Those tanks lined the river's edge and numbered in the dozens. The round tanks were three stories tall and held thousands of gallons of fuel. Jack looked at me, smiled, and said, "This should be my last move. I go home in ten weeks."

Later in the year he would recommend me for the executive officer position that he now held. Little did I know that I was headed for a position with crushing responsibility.

The narrow dirt road from Binh Son to Long Thành was perilous. Our mail truck had been attacked with grenades and small arms fire just a few weeks earlier. The truck was destroyed, and we suffered two casualties. After the mail truck attack, it was determined that our supplies should be flown into our camp to avoid risking another incident. That said we still needed to traverse the Long Thanh road to get out of the rubber plantation. Our preparations began.

I was feeling a little better, not cured from my bout of dysentery, but better. One morning, a few days before our move, I was eating a piece of burned toast when I heard an explosion just outside the wire. The deafening roar sent some GIs running into the bunkers. Others began looking out onto the road, where a cloud of black smoke was rising. Shortly after the explosion, while we were all peering at the road, I heard a faint screech. Soon, the screech turned into a howling scream. We watched a small Vietnamese woman running with outstretched arms. She was sobbing and screaming words in Vietnamese. When she arrived at the explosion site, she flung herself into the mess of burned human tissue, blood, and shattered bones. She wished to help her husband in any way she could. But it was much too late.

Her husband, the local schoolteacher, was gone. He was a victim of justice from the Viet Cong. The teacher had dared to teach a curriculum that differed from the pillar of righteousness in Hanoi. For this infidel teacher, it was agreed by the Viet Cong that summary execution, without trial, was necessary. This was a common form of VC justice. If the civilian leaders did not fall in line, then murder them. I watched from the veranda as the schoolteacher's wife sobbed in uneven gasps. I thought of the night we were invited to her home for the party. It was she who had smiled and introduced me to her husband. He was a petite man and very gracious, almost formal, when he used his halting English to greet us.

This is how the Viet Cong accomplished the assassination:

With stealth and patience, working silently in the night, the Viet Cong dug a narrow trench large enough to hold one artillery shell. The ditch was a few feet in front of a small concrete building, just outside our coils of barbed wire and outside our view. The shell was placed in the ditch, and a blasting cap with two wires was then pushed into the high-explosive bomb. The two thin wires were also buried, and after a tedious early-morning excavation, the death sentence landscape was nearly complete. At the end of the wires sat a VC comrade whose sole purpose was to watch and wait. This VC operative focused on a battery with two metal posts sticking from the top. One of the wires, stripped of its insulation, was taped securely to the negative post. The second wire, also stripped of insulation, was held in the assassin's hand.

As the schoolteacher approached, the assassin touched the wire to the positive post, then in a deafening roar, the shell exploded. The schoolteacher's wife, standing on the front porch of their small stucco house, watched in horror as the blast shattered the teacher's small frame.

The VC used this method against town officials and teachers who collaborated with the South Vietnamese government or the U.S. Army. As the South Vietnamese officials dealt with the morning's assassination, a few of us walked out to the veranda and watched as the cloud of black smoke slowly drifted over our heads. Soon our interest passed, and we turned to the work of packing our gear, loading trucks, and preparing for the drive down the narrow road out of the Binh Son rubber plantation.

John Ladd walked into our room at Frenchy's with new orders from headquarters. He was to join an artillery unit fresh from the States. It was a 155-millimeter artillery unit, and he would become its executive officer. He would make the trip with us down to the Nhá Bé tank farm, then head off to his new assignment. I lamented his transfer. I found him easy to talk with, and interesting and engaging.

Our two new lieutenants, Owen and Hart, would take his place.

I found it was always hard to get a word in edgewise with our new lieutenants; they seemed joined at the hip. Owen was witty and adept with language. He was quick with a joke and often had a piercing tongue. One did not want to be on the receiving end of his pointed, demeaning comments. Unfortunately, as the year wore on, I would become his favorite target.

Captain Tom called the officers into his small office to discuss our trip out of Frenchy's. After the rocket attack on the mail truck, the road to Long Thành was considered "red," or very dangerous. It was thought that the best way to travel the road was with guns blazing.

Most of us would walk on the side of the road with our weapons out and ready, while farther into the rubber trees and just ahead of us, a squad of men would work as our forward security. It was doubtful that any Viet Cong unit in the area would try to attack us during the move. We would be ready for them, and with the help of their spies in Binh Son, they would know that.

Finally, the day of the move arrived. Our unit was packed up, and the trucks hauling the artillery were idling in a line that snaked around the veranda. Soon the convoy began its slow move past the coils of barbed wire and onto the road. After just a short distance from Frenchy's, traveling less than a quarter of a mile out of town, everyone in the unit, including me, began shooting into the woods. If the VC did have an attack planned, we were making sure they knew we had the fire power to stop them. The sound was deafening. Behind us, with the local pedicab in the lead, a long line of Vietnamese pedestrians followed. They stayed far back from our convoy. We moved slowly, all the while shooting our way down the road and into Long Thành village without incident, except for the bullet holes left in the rubber trees.

Our convoy lumbered onto Highway QL 15 for the journey to Bien Hoa, then Saigon. As we accelerated, plumes of belching black smoke poured from the diesel trucks, and we sped off toward our new home. Nearing the village of Bien Hoa, our convoy slowed as pedestrians, bicycles, and livestock began crowding the road. I glanced from my jeep and saw four South Vietnamese Army soldiers walking together. There were two in front and two in back; they had their rifles at the ready. Between the soldiers were five men dressed in dirty print camp shirts, shorts, and flip-flops. Each man had a rope around his neck and an empty sandbag over his head. Like a daisy chain, they were all tied together at the neck. I assumed they were Viet Cong captured by the South Vietnamese Army. Our convoy passed vegetable vendors and a large cage filled with clucking chickens. Soon we turned onto Highway 1 and began our trip to Saigon.

Between Bien Hoa and Saigon, Highway 1 turned to a four-lane road. It was paved and congested, with aging Citroëns, motorcycles, and pedicabs speeding between our trucks. What amazed me was the lack of accidents. It seemed that all traffic rules were ignored and yet no one collided! The motorbikes were the worst offenders, racing past us and weaving between the trucks in our convoy. They passed us on the left and crossed the double-yellow line in a game of brinkmanship with the oncoming traffic. I could not believe how skillfully they avoided being crushed. I did notice a few remnants of accidents, including a black Citroën demolished so thoroughly that anyone inside would have been flattened. Our convoy slowed again, then we crept past an old man with a wispy white beard. He was sitting on top of three huge teakwood logs. The logs were tied together with two rusty chains, one at each end. The logs formed a triangle, with the largest log resting on top of the other two. I worried that the chains might snap and send the driver flying. The old man held a pair of reins in his hands. In front of him and pulling the cargo of teakwood were two water buffaloes; they were fitted with an ancient wooden yoke weathered to a light gray. The logs sat atop an old car or truck frame with four pneumatic tires. It was a wonder to me how it stayed together.

I saw a set of railroad tracks and a small, rusting, blue engine sitting immobilized near a grade crossing. We passed a few more wrecks and a broken-down pedicab with distraught passengers talking to and waving their arms at the driver. He looked concerned as he nodded his head.

Soon our convoy approached the city of Saigon, and we arrived at a convergence of roads. Traffic all but stopped and we found ourselves in a monumental traffic jam, Saigon style. Horns were blaring in an earsplitting roar, and from the side of the road, stray dogs barked at us. The drivers of the small motorbikes and pedicabs raced their two-cycled engines as they moved only inches into the fray. The air was blue with exhaust smoke. The Saigon police in their white shirts with epaulets on each shoulder were directing traffic, but no one was paying them much attention. Our convoy inched forward.

I watched men and women on bicycles squeeze in front and on each side of our trucks. Pushcarts and pedestrians crowded the sidewalks and the streets. I saw an ox pulling a medieval jaunting car. The driver was almost completely buried in canvas bundles. There was even a bundle on his lap. For a moment, I thought there wasn't a driver, then I saw his outstretched arms holding the reins and a puff of smoke from his cigarette. As I watched this throng, I thought, *This is the most amazing blend of traffic I have ever seen.*

As our convoy moved deeper into Saigon, vendors rushed into the street. They began shouting and thrusting their wares at us. Bottles of warm Coke and beer, playing cards adorned with pictures of naked women in suggestive poses, lighters, and black market cigarettes; anything the GIs wanted was here. The women vendors were dressed in the traditional clothing of baggy, black, silk pants and colorful blouses with fabric buttons. They wore large, round straw hats pointed at the top and tied around their chins with ribbons. The older women screamed at us and showed their teeth, blackened by years of chewing betel nut, a local delicacy. I kept saying no thanks to the vendors, but they kept coming. I soon stopped saying no thanks. I just said no and shook my head.

Standing on the sidewalks of Saigon, leaning against buildings, smoking cigarettes and eyeing our every move, were the Saigon cowboys. These were groups of young men either too young for the Vietnamese army draft or perhaps just coy enough to avoid military service. They watched for any opportunity to make money. If a shovel dropped off one of our trucks, they rushed into the street, picked it up, and then vanished into the crowd. If a GI needed to change his greenback U.S. dollar for military currency, the Saigon cowboys would gladly oblige. They were smart, agile, and could produce just about anything an American GI needed or wanted at a moment's notice.

Our military money, the military paper money exchanged for our greenback dollars when we arrived in Vietnam, was nicknamed "funny money." It was brightly colored with green or red images. Numbers were engraved to distinguish the amount—one dollar, five dollars, ten dollars. The army even handed out paper ten-cent bills. This money, we were told, was only good at the American Post Exchanges, or the post office. The military's idea was to keep the greenback dollars out of the Vietnamese economy. This was a grand idea, but it didn't work. Every barkeep, prostitute, and street vendor took the military funny money. Then they used the Saigon moneychangers to exchange it for piasters.

The currency most coveted by the Vietnamese was the American greenback dollar. If a GI was skilled at negotiations, he could exchange one U.S. greenback dollar for three funny-money dollars on the streets of Saigon. We had all heard stories about a GI who had a friend from home mail him $200 in U.S cash. Then the GI would find a moneychanger in Saigon and exchange the U.S. currency for 600 funny-money dollars. He would rush to the American Post Office located inside the Post Exchange and purchase a $600 money order with his funny money dollars. The money order was quickly sent back home to his friend, who would cash it and send more U.S. dollars back to his buddy in Vietnam. On and on this exchange would continue, making the GI a fortune. At least that was the story told in our gun pits. I never did meet a rich GI.

The Saigon traffic continued to be painfully slow. We crept through the center of the city, and I had my first good look at the metropolis the French had built. The buildings were covered in smooth stucco or concrete, and they were brightly painted; most were two stories high. There were a few tall newer buildings, but most of those were hotels. Colorful signs adorned the stores with the shop owner's wares spilling out onto the sidewalk. It seemed that everything imaginable was for sale. I saw army-issue combat boots, bicycle tires, cloth chevrons next to bags of rice, carts full of vegetables, used tools, wooden doors, and on and on. The street looked like a continuous, narrow flea market.

At one point, near the center of the city, we were stopped at an intersection by the Saigon police. My driver turned to me with a worried look and said, "Sir, they are cutting our convoy in half."

I told him to stop and wait. The police held us at the intersection as a polished, olive-green jeep with a Vietnamese driver passed in front of us. Next to the driver was a young woman with long black hair. She wore the traditional Vietnamese clothing, a white *ao dai*. The front window of the jeep was shattered with bullet holes, and the young woman was slumped over. Her white dress was covered with blood. It was shocking for me as I viewed the vehicle and its contents. I assumed that the driver was racing to the hospital. A thousand thoughts passed through my mind. Did the VC fire at the jeep or was this an accident or the work of a jealous boyfriend? Would she be okay? She looked so young.

The Saigon police motioned us forward, and our trucks jerked ahead into the traffic. We soon caught up with our split convoy. The image of such a beautiful young girl soaked in blood was frozen in my mind. Throughout our move, I worried about her, and the image stayed with me. I couldn't erase it.

The blue exhaust haze filling the streets of Saigon seemed to thicken, and I wished we were out of this crowded chaos. After crawling through town, we crossed a fetid canal filled with dark brown water. I held my breath as my jeep crossed the narrow bridge. I looked down at the canal. On the banks of the canal were long wooden boats called sampans; they looked like tugboats without the smokestacks. These tenders served as apartments, housing Vietnamese families. On the decks of the vessels I saw women washing clothes and cooking over charcoal fires. There were chickens squawking, ducks quacking, and children running back and forth from boat to boat. We slowed as our long convoy crossed another narrow bridge. Soon we gained speed and made our way down a newly paved highway toward the *ville* of Nhá Bé.

The drive from Saigon to our turnoff was short, only five or six miles. A few minutes out of Saigon, we passed a gigantic junk pile, where I viewed groups of people combing through the garbage looking for anything of value. There were men, women, and children on this squalid heap; they all had their heads down looking for treasure. We continued on through a series of rice paddies. Farmers were bent over at the waist working their fields. I saw an occasional water buffalo munching in the flooded fields.

Soon our convoy slowed, and our trucks carefully turned onto a narrow, dirt access road. It was unpaved, with ruts and muddy puddles. We passed a small Vietnamese guard post manned by a South Vietnamese Army sentential. He watched us drive past, all the while gripping a .30 caliber machine gun sitting atop a tripod. The guard post was made of ammunition crates filled with dirt. We slowly crossed a narrow estuary, and one by one, our trucks entered our new home of Nhá Bé. I looked it over from my jeep; it was a muddy mess. There were a few small stucco buildings, but for the most part, we would be housed in wooden shanties and sandbagged parapets.

As we entered the compound, I noticed two 105-millimeter howitzers manned by Vietnamese army troops. The Vietnamese enlisted men were dressed in American boxer shorts, flip-flops, and T-shirts. I saw one officer in a green South Vietnamese Army uniform. He was watching us as we passed. Just behind the Vietnamese howitzers was a two-story stucco building. It looked like a poorly maintained 1950s Florida hotel. It held the families of the South Vietnamese soldiers. It was not uncommon for the families of the soldiers to reside in a tent or a lean-to near their husbands. Sometimes these poor accommodations were better than the homes they inhabited in their poverty-stricken villages.

Our convoy circled the gun parapets, now empty; we were replacing another battery that had moved out earlier in the day. I jumped from the jeep and found the FDC bunker. It was a boxlike workplace made of stacked sandbags with a leaky roof and a dirt floor. We began to set up our charts. Our new FDC home was a primitive, waterlogged mess compared with Frenchy's villa. Replacing the red-tile roof and plaster walls at Binh Son were dripping sandbag walls oozing mud. The roof was made of sandbags stacked over wooden beams and empty ammo crates. There were no lovely roses or inviting veranda to soothe the eye. The camp was barren, treeless, and ugly.

Outside and next to our FDC bunker was a small, wooden shed, which Captain Tom claimed.

I watched as he ordered three men to begin building sandbagged walls around his new hooch. They covered the sole window with sandbags and left only a small opening for Captain Tom to enter and exit. He had to duck to fit into his new home. After the walls were built, the men fitted long six-by-six-inch pieces of lumber across the top of the walls. Then they positioned sandbags on top of the long boards to form the roof. This was Captain Tom's new mortar-proof hooch. He would make further "improvements" as time went on.

The officers' accommodations were a combination of bunkers and a few quickly built temporary wooden buildings with tin roofs. There was a noticeable lack of vegetation. Probably the result of an Agent Orange bath. Surrounding our small peninsula was a muck-filled moat. Half the day it was filled with brackish tidal water from the South China Sea; the other half it was a muddy mess. Our new home sat adjacent to the Sông Nhá Bé River; we were midway between Saigon and the South China Sea. The river twisted and turned about ten miles beyond our camp before it emptied into the ocean.

Dogs ran freely throughout the compound. They were all a rust color and they had short, stubby legs. Back in Binh Son there were no dogs. I thought it could have been the Thai or Korean Armies' palates that kept dogs from overpopulating Binh Son. I knew their palates included goat; maybe they also included dog. One day our friendly pet goat went missing. That afternoon the goat was spotted on the skewer of a Thai barbecue.

The other curious thing about life in Nhá Bé was the many Vietnamese civilians coming and going from our base. Men, women, and children roamed among us. There was even a small, wooden building on our base with a sign that read Hot Toc. Translated into English, it read, "Haircut." We also had a generator humming away providing us with electricity. I thought maybe we could drink cold beer.

In-between each gun pit and running throughout our compound was a continuous boardwalk. Empty ammunition crates were used as risers, then long two-by-eight-inch planks were nailed on top of the boxes. We were so close to the South China Sea that the Sông Nhá Bé River was affected by the daily tides. At times the river flowed over the bank and flooded our small base with a few inches of water.

Jack Smith wasted no time setting up the guns and pointing the howitzers for the night's fire missions. In the FDC bunker, we set up our charts, put colorful maps of our area of operation on the wall, and waited for headquarters to contact us on the radio with coordinates for the night's fire missions. We didn't have to wait long; starting that first night the targets were radioed to us one at a time.

As evening approached, Captain Tom had the officers assemble in our mess hall. We now had a wooden building with tables and chairs, almost formal compared with Frenchy's paper plates and sit-any-where-to-eat atmosphere.

Captain Tom introduced us to our neighbors—two officers from the small contingent of the South Vietnamese Army positioned just next to us. Lieutenant Bo was a short, clean-shaven thirty-year-old with a round face; he was portly by Vietnamese standards. Lieutenant Nguyen was a thin man with a long, tan face. Both officers greeted us and began practicing their English. They had a much better command of English than any of us had of Vietnamese. They also were fluent in French.

Captain Tom had us compare our fire missions for the night. Coffee was served by two Vietnamese women. They seemed to appear from nowhere. Captain Tom told us that here at Nhá Bé we would

employ six or seven women in the kitchen to help with the enlisted men's duties. This accomplished three things. First, it put some
needed cash into the pockets of the local women. Second, it kept the
enlisted men's morale up because now they didn't have to wash dirty
pots and pans. And third, it kept the local VC commanders abreast of
all that went on in our compound, where our guns were positioned,
and the exact location of the oil tanks and any new tanker ship that
may have arrived during the night. Jack Smith told us that he thought
some of the women were probably married to VC. He said that as long
as the women were on the base, we wouldn't get rocketed. It turned
out he was right.

A few days later, I had a chance to survey our new home. I walked
to the port facility just north of our guns. The port at Nhá Bé was
everything that Frenchy's was not. Replacing the tall, graceful rubber
trees were the huge oil storage tanks that were represented as small
black dots on our maps. The docking facility on the river was filthy;
oil was dripping from pipes here and there. I saw rundown shacks,
sandbagged fortifications, and a few stucco buildings left from the
French colonial days. The stucco buildings were all in disrepair
with chipped tiles on the roofs and rusty metal steps leading to sec-
ond-floor apartments. The narrow channel near our guns continued
north and emptied into the river just beyond the docks. The channel
was a perfect breeding ground for the ever-present mosquitoes. I also
walked by the Nhá Bé public latrine, an elevated wooden outhouse
with a wooden plank set on an incline. The latrine sat over the tidal
inlet. The public latrine used the tides of the Sông Nhá Bé to cleanse
itself. It never worked.

And so began our routine at Nhá Bé. We fired our howitzers all
night, and then in the morning, exhausted, we walked to the mess

hall to drink black coffee and eat grits. I began to converse with the women in the mess hall. They were friendly and tried to please us. Jack trusted none of them, he told me they probably had mortar tubes hidden at home ready to fire at our position.

As time went on, we saw less and less of Captain Tom. He stayed buried in his sandbagged bunker. He popped out for our nightly meetings, but then he quickly vanished into his small house of sand-bags. Captain Tom was now a short-timer.

The biggest fear of a short-timer was getting hurt just before he left for home. It was the "I am almost done with Vietnam, and I am not going to risk getting wounded" syndrome. At times, I could hear Captain Tom pecking away on a typewriter. At night a dim light came from his bunker.

In the FDC bunker, Owen, Hart, and I worked out an operational truce. I was the senior officer. They knew it, and I didn't push for any unnecessary authority. We all had Lieutenant Smith, our executive officer. Jack Smith's presence was enough to keep personal grievances out of the workplace. I began spending more time with Jack, walking the guns, drinking beer with him on Sunday afternoons, and listen-ing to his stories about the army and his hometown of New York. With Jack as the XO, Captain Tom was all but out of the picture. I watched Jack check every detail of our operation; he missed noth-ing. Were the guns cleaned today? When was the next shipment of ammunition due into our camp? And, most importantly, Jack made sure that the guns shot straight. He told me the men knew their jobs well, but they had their minds on only two things—getting laid and getting out of Vietnam. They were awake almost every night and could not sleep in the daytime. They became overtired, and that's when mistakes were made. Jack looked at me one night and said, "If you ever become the executive officer of this artillery battery, never let these guns fire without supervision. *Never.* And that includes supervision of the FDC operation." This was the first indication I had that he would recommend me for the XO slot.

✳ ✳ ✳

One morning in the FDC bunker, I radioed the small naval base at the tip of the Nhá Bé Peninsula. I told them of my problem with dysentery and asked if I could see a doctor. A moment later, the radio operator told me, if I could get to the base that afternoon, I could be seen. I arranged for a jeep and driver, then I made the short trip south to the Nhá Bé Naval Base.

Compared with our camp's muddy disorder, the naval base was clean and tidy. The buildings were new, and the enlisted men and officers were well dressed in clean clothes. I found the medical building, checked in, and waited to be called into the doctor's office. Soon a young doctor with a stethoscope arrived and motioned me into a room. I told him of my bout with dysentery and how I got the bug. He looked me over and said it was probably a case of amoebic dysentery. He said that it was too late for antibiotics, but I did need fluids. He handed me two large cans of grapefruit juice and said, "Drink both cans and keep drinking water. You are very dehydrated, and it looks as if you have lost a lot of weight."

I sat on the examination table in a clean room holding two quart cans of grapefruit juice. I didn't want to leave this place. It was clean and dry, and the few people I encountered were polite and competent. As I was about to leave, I asked the doctor how he ended up in Vietnam. He told me that he received his draft notice while still in medical school. "They need doctors in Vietnam, and the only way to get them is to draft them." He told me to start eating and gain weight. I left his office already feeling better.

On the way back to our fire base, I scanned the countryside and saw the ever-present water buffaloes grazing in the rice paddies. I saw a group of Vietnamese men and women bent over in the water-filled field, their arms pulling feverishly. I assumed they were pulling weeds. They didn't look up. During my time in Vietnam, I never saw a mechanized piece of farm equipment. Every agricultural job was done either by human hand or by a beast. Even moving fresh water up to a higher-level rice paddy was done with human labor.

As we pulled into our base at Nhá Bé, I saw some enlisted men stretching a bed sheet over our volleyball net. I was told that our ever-cunning first sergeant had arranged to get a movie from Saigon. It was the 1966 black-and-white film with Richard Burton and Elizabeth Taylor, *Who's Afraid of Virginia Woolf?* The movie projector was set up, and all we needed was darkness. I walked into the FDC room and looked over our fire missions for the night. We had just a few, and our guns would not fire until after 2:00 a.m. It was my night off, so I could watch the movie.

As daylight faded, a large group of Vietnamese civilians began collecting around the stretched-out bedsheet. Soon people were everywhere. They were sitting on top of our trucks creating a type of loge balcony. People stacked empty ammunition crates together to form tiered seating. A mass of Vietnamese children collected near the front of this crowd. Most of the children were shoeless, and the little ones were naked. I saw one kid wearing a single flip-flop. It was common for the toddlers to be clothed in only a top and run around without pants. I never saw diapers on children in Vietnam. Kids sat on overturned buckets and flat boards. I saw

Lieutenants Bo and Nguyen puffing away on cigarettes, waiting for the movie to begin. Our GIs and a group of GIs from our neighboring infantry company were milling about, talking and puffing away on Marlboros. They were the favored cigarettes of the American GIs. This had a lot to do with the cowboy image of the Marlboro man. It also helped that each pack of our C-rations held four Marlboro cigarettes in a small cardboard box. GIs would eat the C-rations and then start smoking. I learned my smoking lesson at the age of twelve. I purchased a pack of Salem cigarettes, then I walked over to a Chicago vacant lot and lit up. After inhaling a drag off the cigarette, I became dizzy, lightheaded, and nauseous. I then started a five-minute coughing jag. I threw the pack of cigarettes on the ground and cursed myself for wasting my money. I thought, *Why would anyone spend money to get sick? I never smoked after that.*

As darkness descended on our compound, the projector was turned on, and a hush came over the crowd. The movie began, and soon the screen was filled with a hard-drinking Elizabeth Taylor screaming at her college professor husband, Richard Burton. The movie was a verbal war zone of insults and foul language. I looked at the Vietnamese crowd. They were fixated on the screen. I thought, *Only a few of these people can understand the English dialogue,* yet they never seemed to get bored. When the movie was over, Lieutenant Nguyen approached me. I asked him why so many people would come to a movie they couldn't understand. He said that for most of them, this was the first movie they had seen. That night I drank my first can of grapefruit juice and felt better than I had in ten weeks.

✳ ✳ ✳

The weekends at Nhá Bé were different from those at Binh Son. We were so close to Saigon, those who could get a three-day pass or had enough rank to jump in a jeep and head into the city would disappear. I watched our conniving first sergeant find different ways to visit Saigon. He told us he had to go to Saigon to pick up a can of paint and a length of wire. We all knew he was bullshitting. He would spend his time in the Saigon bars. I viewed him as a narcissistic blowhard. His job in the army usually came in second to his Saigon social life.

The first sergeant hailed from the South, and at times, I thought he resented all Northerners. When he talked about the Civil War, he called it the War Between the States. There was a cadre of people he didn't care for, and just about anyone who was not from the South was on his B list. It seemed to me his mission in Vietnam was about himself. He organized card games with less experienced GIs and then bragged about how much money he had won. One day he exchanged a case of liquor for a broken-down air conditioner. The junior officers financed this hot deal. A week later a civilian from Saigon showed up in our camp and demanded it back. Someone had stolen the air conditioner from his office on the Saigon docks. There was a short standoff over the air conditioner but no one wanted to make a scene, so we handed it over to the civilian. It didn't work very well anyway.

The heat and sun of Vietnam left our first sergeant's face with a type of rosacea. His pointed teeth were tobacco stained and looked near the end of their useful life. I never saw him without a cigarette in his mouth. His banter never ended, and it was always about him; he was a bore.

Almost every Sunday morning the first sergeant would head to Saigon. By Sunday afternoon, he had a belly full of beer and then he would invite strangers to our gun position so they could see what a real combat unit looked like. Saigon was filled with American civilians.

They worked at the embassy, on the docks, at the airport, and at the hospitals. They came over from the States to earn big money as civilian contractors. These contractors built and maintained the many military bases and the large Saigon seaport where supplies were unloaded.

One Sunday, the first sergeant invited a Saigon restaurateur down for a visit. The restaurant owner, originally from Punjab in India, spoke very good English. He was raised in the colonial caste tradition. I met him in our small club, where warm beer was served and a pinball machine kept us entertained. After the Japanese invaded French Indochina during World War II and kicked the French out, Mr. Maan, our Indian guest, closed his French restaurant and opened a place catering to the Japanese. Now, twenty-five years later, he was serving the Americans in his Saigon bistro, and business was good. When Mr. Maan saw me enter the club, he jumped to his feet and offered me his seat. "You, sir, are an officer, take my seat," he exclaimed.

I thanked him then I said, "I can stand at the bar."

"*No, no,* you are an officer—take my seat," he bellowed forcefully.

Now I was embarrassed. Mr. Maan was twice my age, and this situation was becoming awkward. "Okay, I'll sit," I said. Mr. Maan kept his eyes glued on me and asked if I needed anything. I nodded to him and said, "No, thanks, I am fine."

After a moment, I found an excuse to leave the club. I walked out to a sunny afternoon. It was late in the summer of 1968, and our rainy days were giving way to a few partly cloudy days and sunshine. The rainy season was nearing its end. I ran into Jack Smith and John Ladd. They asked me to join them on a walk. They were headed to the dock to look over a ship that had arrived the night before.

We walked along the shallow channel and watched as the brown river water flowed out toward the sea. As we approached the oil terminal, a newly arrived ship came into our view. We walked closer. I looked up at a towering sight; the ship was five stories high and it was painted black, white, and a deep red; here and there were blots of rust. From the railing high above us dangled a rope ladder that ended on the wharf. The smoke stack on the vessel was oval and stood high on the ship. It had a slight tilt toward the stern. In large letters the word TEXACO was painted in bright red and it ran through the middle of the stack. I watched a ribbon of light blue smoke drift from this flue.

We began a conversation with a few of the ship's officers as they stood on the dock surveying the unloading process. One of the men told us that the ship had docked before dawn and was filled with jet fuel. They were midway through the unloading process, and by mid-morning the next day, they would be off to a new port. The long journey from the Middle East made the ship's officers hungry for company. They invited us onboard for a tour. We eagerly agreed. The three of us carefully made our way up the rope ladder.

At the top we, climbed over the railing and onto the deck. More of the ship's officers greeted us. The officers came from the United Kingdom. I was fascinated by their unfamiliar accents. They wore clean white uniforms with gold markings on their lapels. We, on the other hand, wore soiled green fatigues with scruffy boots; except John Ladd, his boots were always polished. Introductions were made, and we all shook hands and began our tour. We roamed in and out of rooms, galleys, sleeping quarters, and the bridge. Our tour ended low in the ship near the engine room. We began to climb a tall metal ladder. At one point while climbing, the rungs became so warm from the boiler room they were close to hot. I pulled my sleeves over my palms to protect my hands from the heat. Here at the ladder's hottest point, we came upon a metal loft where five crew members were relaxing. The loft was so small that they could not stand. They looked as if they were of Indian or Pakistani descent. They smiled and nodded as we passed. I couldn't believe the working conditions. The heat was oppressive, and there was no ventilation other than the ladder shaft we were climbing through. The tour ended at the captain's quarters, where the fine men of the Texaco tanker broke out the good stuff—ten-year-old Scotch whisky.

The captain was quartered in a well-lit room with a row of large windows. The room sat high in the vessel near the bridge. Handsome mahogany furniture adorned his cabin. It looked like a fine hotel suite. The ship's officers took out charts and pointed to a port in the Persian Gulf where they had loaded their cargo. They all had a friendly demeanor. Soon we toasted to home with Scotch and water. The ship's officers kept on pouring, and we kept toasting. The Sunday afternoon in the captain's quarters became a party. They didn't stop drinking, but I did. Although I stopped, it was much too late for me. Just a few glasses of the powerful liquor sent me into a speech-slurring state of intoxication. I hadn't tasted liquor since a toast in Chicago the previous Christmas, in 1967. I couldn't understand how these men could function with so much whisky intake. We said our goodbyes and began our descent on the wobbly rope ladder. Someone in our group, I don't know who, dropped a rifle. It fell to the edge of the dock, narrowly missing the water. We made our way back to the guns in pitch dark, past the small infantry detachment, past the public latrine, and into our compound to sleep it off.

The next morning I awakened to a pleasant surprise. I was called to our small office to pick up an envelope approving my request for a week in Australia. The army called it R&R (Rest & Relaxation), and every GI in Vietnam was entitled to one week during his yearlong tour. Our choices were many—Hong Kong, Taipei, Thailand, and Australia.

I had had enough of the heat in Vietnam, and I knew it was near springtime in Sydney; that was my choice. I was given a departure date and a voucher and was told to arrive at the Tan Son Nhut Airbase the night before my departure. I would make sure I was on time.

Lieutenant Hart, Lieutenant Owen, and I scheduled overlapping shifts in the FDC bunker, making sure that one of us was on duty every hour of the day. My status as the senior officer in the FDC room annoyed Owen. Tension began to build between us. Little things I did in the bunker upset him. He especially resented my checking the enlisted men's work or, even worse, checking his calculations. I would get a quick snap of an answer, "Yeah, I know, go ahead and check it." Then he would turn away in an obvious display of irritation.

It became difficult to maintain a harmonious working relationship with Lieutenant Owen. He was certain that the enlisted men knew their duties well and needed little if any supervision. I, on the other hand, checked their work, and then I had them check my work. Owen resented my authority, however subtle it was.

I had learned my lesson well from Jack Smith. He often said, "It doesn't matter who finds a mistake with artillery; egos in this room are your enemy." Jack was correct on that point—an errant artillery round had no mercy.

Chapter 5

SAIGON TEA TIME

By September of 1968, the monsoon rains were leaving us. Replacing the constant rain and mud was a fine, red dust. This dust blew across our compound and found its way into everything—our trucks, our guns, and even our letters from home, carefully wrapped in plastic and placed in our personal stash boxes, or in my precious attaché.

I spent my days and nights plotting targets in the FDC bunker. Headquarters radioed each night's targets in mid-afternoon. I worked up the elevation and deflection calculations early, then I double-checked them later that evening. I also had Lieutenant Owen or Lieutenant Hart proof my work. Owen thought this was unnecessary, but I had him do it anyway.

The FDC bunker, my bunker, was built of sandbags, three bags thick. It was about seven feet high on one side and eight feet high on the other. The roof was tilted to let the monsoon rains run off and drain toward the ditch surrounding our camp. The bunker had one small doorway, and it faced the huge computer called FADAC. Beyond the computer were two wooden chart tables. The tables had large sheets of translucent velum grid paper tacked to them. We plotted our fire missions on those tables. With just a small pushpin in our chart, we could determine the angle necessary to blow up a series of enemy bunkers or a squad of enemy troops. If the pushpin was in the right place, Charlie was out of business.

Large, colored topographical maps of our area of operations hung on the wall next to our charts. The maps showed most of the terrain near our position as mangrove swamp, with the Sông Nhá Bé River meandering south down to a blue wash of color. The words South China Sea were printed in a large, black, sans-serif font. Our low-lying position on the river's edge was always prone to flooding. Narrow printed lines on our maps indicated dirt roads leading to the main highway—the two-lane road numbered LTL15, or Inter-Provincial Highway 15. The highway began near a bend in the Sông Nhá Bé River just south of our position and near the Nhá Bé Naval Base.

I remember the highway south of us as mostly paved, with a few rutted dirt sections. The ever-present pedicabs were the most common vehicles traveling Highway LTL15, stopping for passengers heading to and from Saigon. The Americans thought the tiny cabs looked like smoke-belching toys. Their two-cycle engines consistently coughed clouds of blue smoke. There was always a chain-smoking driver packing as many passengers inside as possible and having some hang off the back; he made money only when his cab was full. Sometimes the passengers' belongings were stacked and tied to the roof. The pedicabs were wobbly and top heavy and slow.

One afternoon, Wilbur, a classmate of mine from Officer Candidate School in Fort Sill, walked through the opening of my FDC bunker. He came in as I was trying to figure out a meteorological report on the computer. I had entered the day's weather information into the FADAC computer—wind speed, temperature, and humidity.

Loaded with those figures, the computer spat out an elevation and deflection for the night's fire missions. If the figures were entered correctly, the artillery round would hit the middle of a target. Anyone near the target would be blown to smithereens. With or without the computer, the rounds were launched every day and night. Although we would spend hours feeding the information into the computer, we never did get it to work correctly. It constantly started and stopped because of power surges and dusty cable connections. I hated it.

My friend Wilbur was traveling from Bien Hoa back to his unit; he had the battalion payroll—$35,000 in MPCs, a lot of money in 1968. The money was stuffed into a canvas satchel then tossed in the back of his jeep. Wilbur was going to make a slight detour from his route and spend a night in Saigon. He asked if I wanted to join him and Sergeant Mathews for a few beers and a night out in the capital city. I hesitated for a moment. Just then, Lieutenant Smith walked into the bunker. When I introduced Lieutenant Smith to Wilbur and mentioned that he was my boss, Wilbur immediately began working him over. "Why don't you let Duffy come with us to Saigon? I'll have him back in the morning."

I was sure Jack would say no, but his response to Wilbur surprised me: "Sure, go ahead take Duffy to Saigon."

I thought, *Do I want to go to Saigon?* Jack looked at me and said, "It's okay, you can go."

Wilbur spoke, "Duffy, get your stuff." He was loud and firm.

I was still seated at the computer. Wilbur and Jack were standing over me; now they were talking baseball. Jack was a Cincinnati Reds fan, and Wilbur was in love with his New York Yankees. I kept thinking to myself, *I have a job to do here; what will happen without me? Do I really want to go to Saigon?*

"Okay," I said.

I jumped from the computer, ran and grabbed a toothbrush, and we were off to Saigon.

There were four of us in Wilbur's jeep. Sergeant Mathews was driving, Wilbur was riding shotgun, and I was in the back with a young corporal. We sped down LTL15 toward Saigon, passing oxcarts, mopeds, and pedicabs. Sergeant Mathews passed a mama-san riding a bike, a little too close. I turned to look back as she wobbled off the road into a ditch, her belongings spilling everywhere. Mathews was out of control. I yelled at him, "Slow down, Sarge!" He ignored me, then he glanced at his boss, Wilbur, who had a grin on his face and an open beer in his hand.

Sergeant Mathews could not ignore the next thing that happened. A jeep pulled up behind us with red lights blazing and a siren wailing. The jeep carried two men, and they both motioned us over. It was the army's CID. We had heard of these guys—they were rumored to be the army's secret police. No one knew what the letters "CID" meant, but we knew the guys were connected. Later I found out that CID stood for Criminal Investigation Division. They were important people who could put a GI in a world of hurt. Sergeant Mathews stopped the jeep, and we waited as two sober-looking GIs walked up to us. They wore clean, starched fatigues, and both of them had .45 caliber pistols strapped to their sides. "You fellows out for a night in Saigon?" they asked.

"Yeah!" Wilbur shouted loudly.

The men were polite. "Okay, okay, slow down, get to Saigon, park the jeep, and then have fun." Mathews nodded. "We *mean* it fellows— take it easy and slow it down." They let us go. Mathews drove slowly for the rest of the trip.

Our first stop was the officers' club, located in an upscale Saigon neighborhood. The wealthy French merchants—rubber plantation owners and French colonial bureaucrats—built houses and clubs in this highbrow quarter of Saigon. The French were long gone. Their world of luxury in Vietnam crumbled not once but twice. The first was World War II. When the Japanese expanded military operations from China into French Indochina and sent the French packing. The second time was after the disastrous Battle of Dien Bien Phu in 1954. Ho Chi Minh crushed 15,000 French troops and ended colonial rule in Vietnam. By 1968 this part of Saigon was inhabited by free-spending American contractors, diplomats, and high-end call girls. Rumors swirled that senior-level officers from the CIA also lived there. Stern-faced men with mirrored sunglasses would come to spend a few days in town and then disappear for weeks at a time on some secret mission. At least, that's what I thought.

This part of town also quartered pilots for Air America, a private U.S. airline operating in Vietnam. The rumor was that Air America was the CIA's secret airline. I would catch glances of Air America aircraft at airbases or flying overhead. We never knew for sure who they answered to or what they did. The Air America pilots also wore stern faces, mirrored sunglasses, clean clothes, and shiny shoes, and I never saw them smile.

Wilbur, Sergeant Mathews, the corporal, and I walked through the beautiful teakwood portal of the Saigon officers' club. Tropical plants adorned the entrance, and a brilliant tile floor was polished to a high-gloss finish. We were stopped by the well-dressed gate keeper of the club.

"Sir, sir, *excuse* me, *sir,*" he shouted.

Wilbur stopped and stared straight ahead, his head cocked high in the air. He made the greeter walk around to face him. The club, we were informed by the maître d', could not or rather would not serve us.

"Oh, yeah, why?" Wilbur barked.

"First," we were told by the maître d', "you are wearing field fatigues and combat boots." Wearing fatigues and combat boots was a big no-no in the Saigon officers' club. Nothing but tidy starched khakis and shiny black oxford shoes were allowed.

Then we were reminded that Sergeant Mathews and the corporal were enlisted men, and enlisted men were not welcome in the officers' club, at least not in the grand Saigon officers' club.

While in the bush, the officers and enlisted men spent a lot of time together in close quarters, drinking warm Pabst Blue Ribbon beer from rusty cans, playing cards, talking about home, cars, girlfriends, and getting to know one another. In the field, there was no officers' club; maybe a small hut, where beer was served over a card table. In Saigon things were formal and pretentious. Officers fraternizing with enlisted men was taboo, and you had better dress up.

"Shit," Wilbur muttered as he turned. "What a fucking asshole. Let's go."

We walked outside, got back in the jeep, and talked about what we would do next. Wilbur had an idea. He directed the driver down the streets of Saigon to another less luxurious neighborhood. Wilbur turned to me and said, "Don't worry, Duffy, I know another joint. It's better than that dump, and there are women."

Wilbur guided the driver to the door of a hotel that catered to both enlisted men and officers. The hotel was on a side street with narrow, cracked sidewalks and a large tree growing near the front door. Two young Saigon cowboys were hanging out in front of the hotel looking us over. They wore flip-flops, shorts, and short-sleeved shirts; they chain-smoked. Their job was to find a hole in our wallets. Wilbur looked the two fellows over then told his driver to wrap a chain around the radio, locking it to the frame of the jeep, and to disable the jeep by pulling its distributor cap and rotor. The Saigon cowboys watched with interest. As Wilbur's driver removed the distributor cap and rotor, the cowboys lit another cigarette, their eyes fixed on the jeep. A less experienced man than Wilbur might have parked the jeep, waved to the Saigon cowboys, and then later in the day found his military radio missing or, worse yet, the jeep. It was also fair game.

We walked into the hotel. We were quickly told that we had to leave our weapons in a storage cage before we could get a room. I didn't like the thought of that, but the hotel clerk was firm. "You must check *waupons*," he said in a deep Vietnamese accent.

I turned to Wilbur and gave him a questioning look. He said, "Duffy, it's okay. I've been here before; it keeps the GIs from shooting one another."

I handed my Colt .45 caliber pistol in its black, army-issued leather holster to the check boy, actually a middle-aged man with a cigarette hanging from his mouth. His skin was the color of a worn, dark brown saddle, with wrinkles crisscrossing his face. He smiled and gave me a receipt. I peered into the checkroom—M-16 rifles and M-60 machine guns were stuffed in racks along the wall. As I turned away, I noticed a metal gate on the front door with a sign overhead: Curfew 10 p.m., No Entry or Exit After 10 p.m. I thought, *Not to worry. Wilbur and I will be tipping cold beers at the bar.* I hadn't enjoyed a cold beer in nine months.

We rode an antique elevator to our rooms. Wilbur, Mathews, and his driver got off on a lower floor, and I continued up. The elevator cage had rusty, black, wrought-iron bars. I watched each floor pass as the car moved up the shaft. The elevator operator was dressed in a dusty red coat with dull brass buttons. I guessed he was fifty-five or sixty years old. His uniform was left over from the more prosperous French colonial days. He, too, was puffing on a cigarette. It seemed to me that everyone in Vietnam was puffing on a cigarette. The elevator operator's hand never left a handle anchored to a circular brass lever. The lever was the size of a dinner plate, with a wooden handle protruding at a right angle. The operator would fine-tune the cage as it moved, rotating the lever back and forth to make sure that the car was even with the floor requested. He made sure that his car was dead on. No small lip for a patron to trip on as he exited. He said to me, "Waa-your-tep," (watch your step) as I walked off his car.

I found my room, turned the key in the door, and entered. The room was hot and stuffy; it was painted a light pea green. A tropical fan swooshed overhead. I looked for the air conditioner, but there was none. The room had one window overlooking the city of Saigon and another facing an air shaft; both were closed. I opened them and let the humid air from the South China Sea fill the room. The single narrow bed had a mosquito net suspended from a metal frame. There was a small table, a chair, and a tiny bathroom with a sink and a shower. No Gideon's Bible in the desk drawer. I checked. Bibles in this hotel were bad for business. Hotel stationery and envelopes were neatly positioned on top of a small desk; there was a ballpoint pen next to the stationery, but it didn't work. Working on each floor was a towel boy. He was positioned in a small room where personal supplies, such as towels, toilet paper, and soap, were stacked to the ceiling. He also handled communications. On the wall in his small supply office was a telephone with a direct line to the front desk; there were no phones in the rooms. The towel boy was an important link in the hotel's service staff. Your every want or need would be provided by the ever-attentive towel boy. He made his money by keeping the guests happy.

I stripped out of my filthy clothes, grabbed the bar of soap, and jumped in the shower. In Vietnam, showers were rare and memorable. It had been months since I had taken a real shower. We took a type of faux shower in the field. A canvas bag filled with water was hung on a tree branch, and the bag had a large brass showerhead. When turned counterclockwise, it would let water dribble out. Those showers were short and cold. During the monsoon season, we would strip naked and let the warm rain water run across our faces, our shoulders, and our bodies. Those showers were fun; they were new to us and so different from those back home. I would close my eyes and lift my head to enjoy the warm pouring rain. I could never do that in Chicago, but it was okay in Vietnam. No one gave it a second thought.

As I took my shower, I thought back months to a shower I had taken in Bien Hoa. It was in a large room with ten or fifteen showerheads. When I entered the room, it was empty. As I began my shower the clouds opened up and a monsoon storm began. Soon, eight or nine Vietnamese girls ran into the shower room. They needed shelter from the rain. I gave them a look of disapproval, a look that said they were intruding on my space. I was naked, vulnerable, and now I shared the shower with eight young women. They stood there, watching me, and after a few glances and looks, they began giggling. I held my ground and tried to ignore them. They talked in Vietnamese and then giggled some more. One of them pointed at me, then she laughed. I tried to stare them down, but now they were all smiling and laughing. I didn't win this standoff. I quickly ended my shower, grabbed my towel, and left, only to get soaked in the monsoon rain on the way back to the barracks.

The shower in my Saigon hotel room was special. I turned the antique faucets, and although the water never got beyond warm and the water pressure was weak, it was wonderful. I spent the good part of a half hour in the shower with the clean water running down my face. I dried off, put my fatigues and boots back on, and headed for the bar.

The long, narrow pub room had been built during the French colonial days. On one side, running the length of the room, was a beautiful bar made of Southeast Asian teakwood. Behind the bar hung a large mirror. Opposite the bar on the other side of the room, wooden tables with built-in benches extended down the wall to a passageway. At the end of this passageway was an outdoor latrine with a corrugated tin roof and a small, three-inch hole in the concrete floor. The GIs aimed at the hole and then peed. They usually missed.

The benches along the wall had high backs designed to block the view of your neighbor. The bar floor was constructed of small, white octagonal tiles. Tropical fans slowly turned overhead; they were a bit too high to offer a breeze or relief from the heat. The room was painted green with cool fluorescent lighting on the ceiling and running along the edges of the mirror behind the bar. It looked as if the electricity had been added after the room was built, because all the wiring ran along the outside of the wall to a rusty metal box. The room was filled with cigarette smoke. (Later, in the 1980s, I painted two pictures of this bar; the paintings are now in the collection of the National Veterans Art Museum in Chicago.)

The barroom was filling up. Most of the men were enlisted. Wilbur and I were the only officers. Men began pushing their way toward the bar and toward the women seated at the bar. I noticed that Wilbur was without his canvas satchel. The satchel with the $35,000 was tossed in his closet and forgotten, along with his dirty shoes and the military orders that instructed him to deliver the satchel to battalion headquarters with care and haste.

We were served by a young Vietnamese teenage girl who approached our table and in a high-pitched voice said, "What you wann?"

She spoke broken English, unable to pronounce the "t." We ordered a round of Ba Moui Ba, or 33 Beer, a French beer brewed in downtown Saigon. We raised our glasses and we gave a toast to home, a.k.a., the world, then we talked about how many days we had left in Vietnam. Time in Vietnam was always measured in days, never months. Wilbur was a short-timer, only thirty-seven days and a wake-up call, then the flight home on a freedom bird. Sergeant Mathews was next, with forty-four days left in county. He talked about the car he was going to buy once he made it home. It was going to be a fast car, maybe a Dodge or a GTO, a muscle car for sure, painted candy-apple red.

The music on the jukebox was Motown, Sam & Dave, Sam Cooke, the Four Tops, and Martha and the Vandellas. I never heard the Beatles in Vietnam. The military radio station broadcasting out of Saigon played country and western and some soul. The music in the bar was loud and would soon get louder. Women in bright-colored dresses began flirting and hanging on the lonesome GIs. Red dresses, pink dresses, all tight and form-fitting. The women wore spiked heels that matched their dresses. They all had long black hair, falling to their shoulders, crimson red lips, and painted nails. You couldn't take your eyes off them.

They were Saigon B-girls.[16] They slowly moved down the bar from GI to GI, smiling, flirting, and asking each one in broken English if he would buy them a Saigon tea. It was a game—if the GI said no, the

---

16. A Saigon B-girl was a woman employed by the bar to encourage the customers to spend money.

B-girl would move on to the next fellow. If the GI said yes, he would get about ten minutes of time to make small talk. The girl would flirt with the GI in pigeon English, and the GI would do his best to rub up against her and fondle the goods.

The Saigon tea was served in a shot glass with a small, brightly colored paper umbrella and a cherry. Saigon tea was just that—tea. These were working girls who could not afford to get intoxicated. They were professionals; they needed their wits to speak broken English, however poor, and fulfill their role—that of psychiatrist, counselor, and physical joy provider. The cost of a Saigon tea was five dollars in U.S. greenbacks, or 500 piasters, the all-but-worthless Vietnamese currency. The girls would also take funny money—MPCs. This was risky because the military changed the color of the money on occasion, and overnight the old MPC bills would become worthless. However, if the girls were quick, they could change them for greenbacks the next day on the street. This exchange usually took place at one of the black market money operations in Saigon. These street money-changing operations, it was rumored, were all run by the Chinese mob. I envisioned the Chinese mob as groups of cigar-chomping middle-aged men hanging out on corners and counting money all day.

The B-girl, if she was good, could work the bar and get the GIs to purchase thirty-five or forty Saigon teas a night. She would split the five dollars with the house. She could make up to fifty or sixty dollars a night, a fortune in Vietnam. Some girls also worked as prostitutes and picked up another twenty or twenty-five dollars at the end of their B-girl shift.

This was strictly business; romance was never part of this job. The B-girls had only one mission, to separate GIs from their money. Some of the girls lived the highlife away from the slums, from which most came.

They drove pastel-colored motorbikes, mopeds, and Italian Vespas fresh off the boat from the factories of Europe. They wore the best clothes money could buy. They lived in the best new apartments tucked away from the busy polluted streets of Saigon, off Tu Do Street. Their money fed their children, their parents, their young brothers and sisters, their grandparents, and sometimes their war-crippled husbands.

A few women only worked the late shift as prostitutes. They stayed away from the bar because their English was too poor and they couldn't understand or talk to the GIs. Others didn't have the looks or confidence to sell Saigon tea all night. These girls waited in the hotel laundry room for a call from the towel boy. This was another function of the towel boy, to keep the wheels of commerce turning. The towel boys handled all the money arrangements with the GIs, so their English had to be good. In the morning the towel boys paid the prostitutes, a fifty/fifty split. If the GI was not too hungover and had a few dollars and his wits, he would tip the girl, but this tip was never a sure thing. The towel boy also settled the occasional financial dispute with the working girls and their GI customers. The towel boy was all business.

Another Motown song was playing on the barroom jukebox; it was Sam & Dave's "Soul Man." The music was blaring full blast when a scream from the troops got our attention. We turned to see four beauties mounting the bar and beginning a version of a bump-and-grind go-go dance, Saigon style. The barroom went nuts. GIs were shouting for more, pushing and shoving to get closer to the girls. The girls didn't strip. They didn't need to; they just played to the crowd and kept dancing. The tired and dirty GIs dressed in their army-issued green fatigues all had smiles on their faces. We were all in a state of intoxicated bliss, away from the war in Vietnam, if only for one night.

Every day a new group of GIs filtered into Saigon, some on three-day passes. They were given a few days out of the field for a job well done. Here in Saigon they could, if they wanted, change into civilian clothes, walk the streets, and shop for their girls back home. Most headed to the hotel bar, got drunk, and then if they were not too drunk, they negotiated with a willing partner in the bar and got laid. Prices were discussed and arrangements of time and expectations would be spelled out. Nothing was left to chance; as in all businesses, time was money. When the business side was settled, the girl made the walk to the GI's room

Every day on the army bases the men were reminded of the diseases that flourished in Saigon. Some of the diseases were so bad that they were talked about in low whispers late into the night, in a gun pit or a bunker. The talk was of a venereal disease so powerful that there was no cure. Men who got it would scream with pain while urinating. They said it was like razor blades slicing through your penis.

In the worst cases, it was said your pecker would turn black. The story did not end there. Your testicles would turn the color of burnt umber and never stop aching. Yellow pus would drip all day from your deformed penis and then it would fall off! The men's eyes would get large and then you would hear a collective, "Oooohhh."

There was no cure for this Saigon VD. It was said that some GIs would spend months in hospitals; they would be pumped with penicillin, but in the end, the VD would win out. The infected GIs were unable to perform, unable to return home to their wives or girlfriends for fear of passing it on. Of course, they could never have children. This talk passed from bunker to bunker, and stories turned to legend. No one was sure if this horrible VD was real or rumor, but it was always on one's mind, especially if you were about to shack up with a

Saigon whore. But for the GI in the hotel barroom, the drinks blurred his eyes and his judgment; condoms were forgotten, and the fear of VD gave way to lust.

There was another risk during these trysts. This risk was real, not rumor. The risk was shouldered by the Vietnamese working girl sharing the GI's bed. Working to earn money to feed her family or keep her newfound lifestyle, the girl could come face to face with her worst nightmare, an out-of-control drunk and angry GI. A GI who beat his girlfriend or wife back home. Shit, what did he care about a gook whore in a Saigon hotel room? In fact, he cared very little, and if provoked or challenged in any small way, he would erupt and pummel the young girl out of a drunken rage. When the screams of the working girl was heard by the towel boy, he acted on his first mission, to protect the income-producing asset of the hotel. His job was to stop the GI from beating the girl. First, he would call the front desk for help. Then he would run to the room and bang on the door screaming, "MPs coming!" If that did not help, he would use his passkey and try to free the girl. Sometimes the MPs would have to be called to calm a drunken monster. The hotel would much rather handle the situation itself. The management's wish was to keep their hotel off the MPs' watch list. But if the situation got out of hand, a call to the American MPs would be made.

Back down in the barroom, the GI just fresh out of the field was flush with cash. He carried $200, $300, or more in his pocket. The bartenders would watch the cash as it was pulled from the GI's fatigue pants. If the bartenders were good, they would nod to the B-girls, who would take notice of a rich GI and make their way over to him. Why waste time with a broke GI when just down the bar was one flush with cash? With the help of alcohol and pleasure, the GI's money began its journey from the soldier's pocket to the bartender. The B-girls sold everything—their voice, their touch, their scent, their smile. It was all there, and it all had a price.

Wilbur and I ordered another round. Wilbur's corporal was now at the bar buying his new friend a Saigon tea. Sergeant Mathews was talking to another sergeant at the far end of the bar, the two of them puffing on cigars.

Wilbur and I talked about our Officer Candidate class at Fort Sill, in Oklahoma. Who, if anyone, we wondered, might have been killed here in Vietnam? We had heard rumors about some. We wondered who from our class was sent to Vietnam and who was lucky enough to be stationed in Germany. It was getting late, and the smoke in the bar was burning my eyes. We ordered another round. I made my way to the outside bathroom. The dimly lit room was filled with the stench of urine. Heated all day by the Saigon sun, the stench was now unbearable. As I stood over the three-inch hole in the floor, breathing through my mouth, I watched a rat scurry along the wall.

When I walked back to our table, I noticed that the girl with the bright-red dress, one of those who had been dancing on the bar, was now sitting on Wilbur's lap. There were two Saigon teas at our table, and she had a big smile on her face. Wilbur and his new friend ignored me.

I picked up my beer and headed to the bar as the Four Tops song "I'll Be There" began playing. The bar was littered with empty beer bottles, shot glasses, and ashtrays filled with cigarette butts. One drunk GI, his head resting on the bar, looked to be dead, except for a line of saliva seeping from his mouth. The GI's drool looked like the last remnant of a maple syrup bottle forming a puddle on the bar. The bartender was picking up the pieces from another good night of business—the broken glasses, paper umbrellas, and green army-issue jungle hats that littered the floor. I watched the scene as theater, fully aware that I would never see this again. The bar thinned out. It was 2:00 a.m., closing time for the bar, but the night was not over.

On the way out of the bar, we all heard a gunshot. It came from the entrance of the hotel. Quickly, a large doorman—he looked Chinese—blocked our exit. There was a commotion in the hall, punctuated with yelling. I saw a few GIs rush past the doorway. Soon we were ushered out of the bar and up to our rooms. By this time, I was alone. I rode the elevator to my floor and walked to my room. As the elevator door opened, the towel boy greeted me with a smile and asked if I needed anything.

About 4:00 a.m. there was a loud banging on my door. I stumbled over and opened it to find four army MPs in uniform with billy clubs and weapons drawn. One of them barked, "We need to search your room." I told them to go ahead. Two MPs walked in and began looking under the bed, in the closet, and all over my room. As they did this, I heard another commotion outside in the hall. The GI who had fired the weapon earlier that night was hiding under a bed on my floor. The MPs put him in shackles and started for the elevator. I was told that he had shot someone in the arm. They were arresting him. His next stop would be the stockade and an arraignment the following day. The other GIs on the floor and I walked back to our rooms.

A few hours later, Wilbur banged on my door. "Duffy, we need to go now," he yelled. "I'm gonna be late." I pulled on my green fatigues and took the elevator down to the first floor and met Wilbur, his driver, and Sergeant Mathews. Wilbur's driver was holding the canvas bag with the $35,000. Wilbur and I walked out to a bright, sunny day in Saigon. I handed my camera to a Saigon cowboy, and he took a picture of us. The picture came out, but the sun was behind us so our faces were darkened. I titled the photo "Wilbur and Me, Hungover in Saigon." Sadly, years later, I lost the photo, along with others from Vietnam, after a flood in my basement.

On the drive back to Nhá Bé, I had the driver pull over to a Saigon street vendor. I saw a red veneer guitar with metal strings. After a bit of bargaining, I purchased it for ten dollars, MPC. I thought I could teach myself to play during my off hours. We arrived at camp and I went back to work.

A few weeks later, I decided to follow up with Wilbur to find out how things were going. Wilbur was about to leave for the States, so I probably would not see him again. I radioed his unit and asked for him. After a short wait, I was told that Wilbur was at the medical clinic in Bien Hoa. I asked if he was okay. Was he hurt during an attack? The radio operator hesitated, then said, "No, it's Victor Delta." I asked what he meant by Victor Delta. He said that Wilbur needed to go to the clinic because it had become very painful when Wilbur urinated. "Sir, he went to see a doctor. Got it? Over and out." Victor Delta stood for VD, a.k.a., venereal disease.

Wilbur made it back to the States, and mercifully he had not contracted the horrid Saigon VD. He had a curable version that the GIs called the clap. He fared well in life; he started a successful construction business. We met one day in St. Louis many years after our tour in Vietnam. We laughed and talked, and for a brief moment, I even choked up. But I quickly regained my composure, shook Wilbur's hand, and said goodbye.

Chapter 6

THE TOWEL

Just when I thought the monsoon season was ending, we were handed an epic storm. The night sky exploded in thunder, lightning, and a driving wind. During this downpour, a bolt of lightning hit the generator, and our feeble lighting system failed.

My little hooch had one low-wattage light bulb that gave off a weak yellow glow. The light was rigged with exposed wire along the wall, and I had to twist the bulb in the socket to turn it on. I watched as my light bulb flickered, and then a moment later it died. We all lit candles and watched as the monsoon rain found kinks in our faulty roof system. Water began to drip from every location in my tiny bunker. Soon, my second pair of dry socks and the few dry items I had hanging high above my ammunition-crate floor began to get wet. Dry socks were important in Vietnam, but I was a poor judge of dry locations. My roof always seemed to drip on anything I was trying to keep dry. I didn't have to worry about my boots. I was now down to one pair, and I rarely took them off; my feet were constantly damp. One night I gave them a good look, then I put my boots back on and laced them up. My feet looked mangled with a gray-white tint to the waterlogged flesh.

The rain went on for hours, accompanied by ferocious booms and flashes of lightning. Early in the morning, just before dawn, the rain stopped, but my roof continued to drip. I sat up all night watching my small candle get smaller. There was no sleep. Every time I lay down and closed my eyes, a new drip from above landed either on me or on my nylon poncho liner.

I was groggy the next morning; I walked over to the mess hall. A rat scurried past me. I watched it run from the back of our mess facility. It darted toward the canal and disappeared beneath a piece of rusty sheet metal. It probably got rained out of its burrow. The tides were in, and the narrow canal surrounding our compound was close to overflowing with brackish river water.

I drank black coffee, which was especially bad that day. Our coffee was made from water trucked in from Long Binh. Already of poor quality, the water was treated with chemicals designed to kill bacteria. By the time it reached our unit, it was warm from the Vietnam sun and close to undrinkable. Our options were metallic-tasting water, bitter-tasting coffee, or warm beer. We usually drank coffee until the evening, then we switched to warm beer.

I sat with John Ladd in our small mess hall and talked. This was his last day in our unit. He was scheduled to leave on the mail truck later in the morning. We laughed together. John said that he had recommended me for the position he held as casual pay officer. I asked him what the casual pay officer did. He took a deep breath, smiled, and then began to explain the job.

"Well," he said, "at the end of each month, on payday, the first sergeant will hand you a stack of Vietnamese currency." The money was collected from the enlisted men to avoid the hated KP (kitchen police) duty. Local Vietnamese women were hired to clean the mess hall and scrub the pots and pans. As John continued, he smiled then said, "Your job is to dispense the money to the women."

I looked at John and said, "It sounds like a piece of cake."

In his slow Southern drawl, John said, "It is a piece of cake, and now the job is all yours."

We walked outside and gathered for a black-and-white photo with our South Vietnamese Army friends. At the last moment, just before the picture was taken, John Ladd saw Lieutenant Owen and invited him to join the picture. The black-and-white photo is still in my collection of Vietnam pictures buried in a storage locker. Pictured in the print is a cloudy sky, soggy sandbagged bunkers and huge mud puddles from the previous night's ferocious storm and the five of us. After the photo was taken, we all walked with John to the departing mail truck; he climbed in, shook my hand, and drove off.

Now that John Ladd was gone, my isolation would grow. Jack Smith was still here in Nhá Bé, but he too would leave soon. The loss of Lieutenant Ladd left a hole in my pool of friends. I also moved out of our small officers' quarters, where there was always some conversation and a bit of companionship. I moved my belongings closer to the gun pits. There wasn't much to move: my toilet kit, my olive-green bath towel, and my letters from home stuffed in my attaché. Jack Smith changed my job title from the FDC-OIC, (Fire Direction Control-Officer in Charge) to his XO assistant. I assumed I would take over his job as executive officer when he rotated back to the States, but this was never a sure thing.

My new hooch was a large, wooden box the size of a small closet. The room was next to our squawking microphone-type contraption that alerted us to fire missions. The squawk box was on twenty-four hours a day, seven days a week. There was no escape from its loud, scratchy speaker. A small, undersized doorway was the entrance into my hooch. The room held a narrow cot that filled most of the floor space. The doorway was just under four feet high. I needed to bend down and then shuffle into the room backward. Once in the room, I could not stand up. The hooch was built with our discarded ammunition crates filled with sand and dirt. The words 105-mm Howitzer Shell High Explosive were printed all over the wall. This was my least favorite quarters during my tour in Vietnam.

Jack and I walked the guns late one afternoon. He was good with the enlisted men. He greeted every man and knew each by name. He could do this without looking at their sewn name badges; I could not. They smiled and returned his greeting. It was evident the enlisted men liked and respected him. I was a bit envious of Jack's deportment with the men. I wasn't green anymore, and I knew the mechanics of my job well. I was good around the howitzers, and I made sure there were no firing mistakes. The guns didn't fire unless Jack or I stood behind them. I listened for every command that barked out of the squawk box. When a charge was called, I carefully watched the tired crew pull the powder bags from the canister. Then I monitored the GIs as the charge was cut all the while counting each bag to myself, ensuring the crew cut the correct charge. A wrong charge would send a projectile miles off the target. I remained steadfast in my decision to *never* let the guns fire without supervision.

As we walked back to our small bunker, Jack turned to me and said, "Duffy, keep gun number four from firing tonight; the lanyard isn't working. Tell the crew on guns five and six to fire again tonight." Our guns fired in pairs. If gun four was not going to fire, then its companion gun three would not fire.

Jack's request put me in a difficult situation. I had a fault in my personality. I knew what it was, but I didn't know how to correct it or change my behavior. My fault was this, I wished to be liked—not an unreasonable request, but this wish got in my way on more than one occasion. As an officer in an artillery battery in a war zone, being liked was not an option—it was impossible. All my training at Officer Candidate School went against this need. But I still held it, and at times, it affected my decisions.

I acknowledged Jack's request. He walked away to our small club, transferring the night's duties to me. I started my solo walk around the guns, greeting the men and asking if all was well.

The task that Jack had left in my hands was more than telling the men on guns five and six to fire two nights in a row. I knew the troops on guns five and six didn't want to fire again; they had been up the night before. I had watched as they punched and cleaned the tube. The men looked exhausted; they were overdue for a rest. Last night was busy, and we had fired more than the normal number of fire missions. If I asked them to fire again, I would be subject to their looks and murmurs. The old fear rose up within me, and I wanted to avoid a confrontation. I walked over to gun four and talked to the crew chief, a young sergeant. "So, what's the problem with the gun?" I asked.

"Well, sir, the pulley that trips the trigger broke—look here," the sergeant explained as he showed me the problem. "Sir, we can still fire. All we do is trip the trigger without the lanyard. I've done it before in the States and here in Vietnam, and it's not a big deal."

The sergeant showed me the quick fix, the easy way to avoid repairing the gun. This was a solution for me. If I had gun four fire tonight, then I didn't have to ask guns five and six to fire again. My desire not to rock the boat overrode common sense and Jack's directive. "Okay, fire the gun," I said.

The next morning, when Jack found out I had gun four fire, he confronted me in a deserved state of rage. I don't think I have ever seen anyone as angry as he was that morning. At one point, I thought he might take a swing at me, but he didn't. Although, I did get a thorough tongue-lashing.

It was mid-morning, and I drifted over to the mess hall to lick my wounds. I was curious if my new position as the casual pay officer would get me a cup of coffee even if the mess hall was closed. I walked into an empty dining room and noticed all the women were busy in the kitchen; they barely glanced at me. I sat alone listening as they talked and laughed. At one point I stood up and moved my chair, lifting it from the floor then back down again trying to get their attention. It didn't work. I continued to wait, loudly clearing my throat. Finally, all the women marched out of the kitchen. As they passed me the senior employee we called Mama-san Mop said, "Kitten cosed."

I thought maybe John Ladd forgot to tell them I was the new pay officer. Surely they would open the kitchen for a cup of coffee if they knew I was the new pay officer. "Hey," I yelled, "do you know I am the new pay officer?" Mama-san Mop repeated in broken English, "Kitten cosed."

Seven women worked in our mess hall. We gave them all Pidgin English names. Mama-san Mop was the leader. "Mop" phonetically means "fat" in Vietnamese. She was a portly five-foot two, with short black hair cut in a pageboy style. One of her biggest joys in our camp came one morning while I was driving to Saigon. My driver had just turned off the dusty access road onto the blacktop highway. I glanced and saw four people on the corner waiting for a pedicab. I spotted Mama-san Mop. She smiled at me. I told my driver to pull over, and then I asked her where she was headed. She said, "Saigon."

I motioned for her to get into my jeep. Her eyes widened, and a grin crossed her face. She was filled with pride that an American officer would do such a thing. I knew this was a first for her. The other people standing on the corner began feverishly talking to one another. I often wondered if this small act of kindness turned into a prison term for her after the fall of Saigon. If the people standing with her were VC sympathizers, they would surely remember this event. But for now, Mama-san Mop was in heaven. Today was her day off, she was dressed in her best *ao dai* and straw hat, and she was going to the market in Saigon.

In the mess hall pecking order, under Mama-san Mop was a tall woman we named Mama-san Lurch. We called her that because she looked a little like Lurch on the TV hit *The Addams Family*. The youngest of the seven women was a petite girl, maybe seventeen years of age. We named her Baby-san. She served the officers their food, and over the months, I got to know her well. During mealtimes she would practice her English on me, and I would try my limited Vietnamese on her. I also liked it when she brushed against me while clearing our trays from the table. During our idle afternoon hours, I would walk to the dining room for a cup of coffee. My schmoozing with her paid off because now she served it to me whether the mess hall was open or closed.

Baby-san and Mama-san Mop were roommates. They lived together in a makeshift hut built out of wood from our discarded ammunition crates. Their house had a tin roof and one ten-by-ten-foot room. Four women lived in this tiny dwelling. The shack sat next to our tidal basin, the foul channel that drained into the Sông Nhá Bé River. One electrical wire ran from a utility pole into their hut. A lone cord and light bulb hung from the tin roof into their small room. The light bulb was turned on and off by screwing it in and out of the socket. This light bulb was a luxury; most Vietnamese did not have electricity. The dwelling was a short walk from our base, just across the tidal basin.

Payday for these women came once a month. They were paid in piasters. For their labor, six days a week, eight to ten hours a day, they were paid the equivalent of thirty U.S. dollars each month. Even though Mama-san Mop was the head of the work crew, she was paid the same amount as the others.

When the end of the month arrived, our first sergeant handed me a stack of piasters and I walked over to the mess hall. I was a little nervous since this was my first time dispensing the pay. I didn't want to screw up and either overpay or short pay anyone. I soon found out this was the least of my worries.

The women were milling about. I smiled and nodded at them, and then I began to count stack after stack of thirty piasters. I glanced up from counting and noticed that Mama-san Mop was absent. As I counted, the women watched me from afar, talking and waiting. When I finished my counting, I arranged the bills into neat piles across the table. I looked up and motioned that I was ready. I called each woman to my table and handed them their pay, one woman at a time.

Mama-san Mop arrived just after I had paid Mama-san Lurch. She looked flustered and upset; she began to cry. She ran to the group of women and began screaming in Vietnamese and throwing her hands in the air. I was bewildered. I thought perhaps someone in her family had died or had been injured by the VC. I looked at her from my table puzzled, and then I asked, "What's wrong?"

She ignored me and retreated to a table across the room; she sat down, and continued to sob. The group of women I had just paid surrounded her. Some of them put their hands on Mama-san Mop's shoulder in a gesture of sympathy, as if a dear loved one had passed away. A few of the women gave me darting, unfriendly glances. One of the women looked at me and shouted something in Vietnamese. I didn't understand what she said, but it sounded unpleasant.

I watched this scene, mystified, trying to figure out if I had done something wrong. I thought of John Ladd and our conversation before he left. He had said, "Paying the women is a piece of cake."

I decided to approach their table. I stood and slowly walked toward Mama-san Mop. A faint smile crossed my face. By this time, Mama-san Mop was sobbing uncontrollably. She looked up at me with tears running down her face. Between sobs, she began to speak in broken English. Gradually, I realized what I had done.

Since she was the senior worker and the figurehead of the kitchen crew, John Ladd had always paid her first. I was about to pay her dead last. To me, this was of little consequence; to her, I had just lowered her stature in the mess hall to the bottom rung.

I walked back to my pay table silently cursing John Ladd for not telling me about this pay procedure. I was trying to figure out how to correct my error. I motioned Mama-san Mop to my table. She slowly walked over, stood near me, and placed one hand on a chair; she wore a bitter look on her tear-stained face. She began to speak, "You pay Mama-san Lurch before me. John Ladd always pay me firrs."

I decided that any explanation in English would not be under-stood, and even if I could speak Vietnamese, it wouldn't help—the damage was done. But I did have the purse. I figured an extra five dollars would help lessen her grief, so I counted out thirty-five dollars in piasters. She looked at the amount sitting on the table. I watched as she picked up the wrinkled bills. She stopped crying, and then smiled at me. I felt I was finally out of the woods, and it had cost me only five bucks. Mama-san Mop was now overjoyed, grinning and nodding. The extra five piasters represented three days of extra wages for her.

She looked at me and repeated in broken English, "Sir, sir, sir, thank you, thank you, you come my house ... tea?" I quickly accepted her invitation, nodding my head, thinking any more breaches in etiquette and I might lose her to another unit. After a series of hand gestures and pointing at our wall clock, I figured out that she wanted me to arrive for tea at eight o'clock that evening, after the kitchen closed.

That night, after my march around the gun pits, I left our compound and made the short walk to Mama-san's hut. I told myself I would stay no longer than fifteen minutes. Although we could see their small hut from our camp, it was outside of our defense perimeter and I was a little nervous. I arrived and knocked on the wall—there was no door. Mama-san Mop and Baby-san greeted me.

Before my eyes was poverty unmatched in the Western world. There were four women living in this hut; they slept on the ground with a reed mat between them and the earth. All four of the women were barefoot. They each owned one pair of flip-flops. The flip-flops were stacked neatly in a corner. They wore the flip-flops only when they left their home. They heated tea water in a blackened pot outside on a charcoal fire. Everything was prepared for me; the water was hot, and they were all smiles. My tea was served in a cracked cup. I asked them where their tea was. They smiled and nodded their heads. They watched me sip my tea. It took me a moment to realize there was only one teacup in their house.

We all talked as best we could. After a few minutes and almost rehearsed, Mama-san Mop and the other women laid down on their reed mats. Baby-san and I were now alone sitting on the ground just outside her dwelling. She began asking me questions about America. She was smart and she knew her geography. She asked me what city I lived in and where it was. I drew a crude map in the dirt. I showed her the West Coast of the United States, San Francisco, then east to Denver and on to Chicago and New York. She asked if it was cold in Chicago. I nodded and motioned with my hand how deep the snow could get. She continued to talk and soon posed a question that surprised me. She paused and then in her gentle voice asked, "You give me baby?"

I was speechless. Her request was so out of context. I looked at her face; it was almost perfectly oval and her expression was serious. I kept looking at her. Unlike the other women on the kitchen crew, she was petite, almost fragile. Her skin was perfectly smooth and without blemish. Her long black hair covered her shoulders. Her hair was clean; she may have washed it for my visit. She wore a white blouse and black silk pajamas. They were wrinkled but spotless.

As we sat on the ground next to her ammunition-crate house, she watched me and waited for my answer. It took a moment for the weight of her request to register in my head. I hesitated, looked her in the eyes, and said, "No." I was flattered by her request, but again I said, "No baby."

Maybe she believed that with an American officer's baby, she could escape this desperate poverty and make her way to the United States. Opportunities for women in Vietnam were few. There was no industry. The Vietnamese economy was built on agriculture and war. Marriage was difficult for the women because so many men were fighting in the South Vietnamese Army. I don't know why she asked, but I was sure of one thing—I did not want to leave offspring in Vietnam.

She paused, and then she continued to talk. She had one more request. She asked me if I could get her a towel, the type of towel we all had. Those towels were olive-green bath towels, lightweight and common.

"Yes, yes," I said. "I can get you a towel the next time I go to the PX in Saigon."

A towel and a baby were her two requests. I never got to the PX, and I never purchased a towel for Baby-san. I could have given her mine, but I didn't. She never reminded me or asked me again. Time passed, and later in the year, we packed up and moved on to another base. I remembered the towel as our convoy passed her small hut. I grimaced as I thought of her request. Shit, I forgot the towel. For a moment I felt bad. Then that feeling slipped away, smothered by responsibility and war.

There are not many things in life I regret, but that unfulfilled request is near the top.

Chapter 7

R&R

Each GI serving in Vietnam received one week of vacation during his yearlong tour of duty. The Army labeled it R&R or Rest and Relaxation.

One morning I climbed into the mail truck for the trip to Tan Son Nhut, Saigon's huge civilian and military airfield. I had a voucher that would get me on a plane for the long flight to Sydney, Australia, and I had $400 in my pocket. The plane would make one stop to refuel on the north coast of Australia in the town of Darwin. Just before dark, a cabin full of GIs and Australians gave a roar of approval as we lifted off the tarmac for our trip south. I was sitting in the window seat. As we flew over the Mekong Delta, I looked out and saw a landscape with one bomb crater after another. It looked like the face of the moon. I thought, *Half the annual steel production from Pittsburgh is down there, buried in the mud.*

We flew south under a full moon, with the captain announcing each landmass we flew over. When he announced that we were about to fly over the coast of Borneo, I looked out my small window and saw the edge of a dark beach and the reflection of the moon light off the ocean waves. I saw no lights on the landmass. I dozed off, and then awoke as we began our descent into the city of Darwin.

When we landed, I saw Western-style buildings and up-to-date equipment on the tarmac. The captain said we could disembark for an hour. I approached the door of the cabin and felt a blast of hot, humid air. I thought, *What is this? It's still hot.* Darwin sits on the far northern coast of Australia. It is as close to the equator as Vietnam, only in the Southern Hemisphere. After our refueling, we were off again, this time to Sydney.

It was a sunny morning when our plane touched down at the Sydney airport. We walked off the plane and were greeted by a well organized staff. They had us board buses, and then we were driven to the Sydney reception center, just off Kings Cross. The reception center was like a mini travel show set up in a large ballroom of our hotel. There were representatives from entertainment spots, theaters, and a boat tour company that promised a beautiful two-hour trip in the harbor. One booth caught my attention. Two women were sitting at a card table with a sign that read Visit a Working Australian Sheep Ranch. I walked over to them and made an inquiry. They told me that arrangements had been made with families outside of Sydney to host American GIs. There were different spots, all in rural New South Wales. I made a mental note and moved on to the next table.

The first necessary task at our hotel was a fitting for civilian clothes. Each GI rented, with an option to buy, a pair of pants, two or three shirts, and a pair of shoes. We tried on shirts and pants until we found our correct sizes. Then we stuffed our military clothes into our duffle bags. The clothes were the latest styles—paisley-print, short-sleeved shirts, high-waisted, cuff-less pants, no belt necessary, and pointy shoes, the kind the Beatles wore. I searched through the shoes and found one pair that didn't have pointy toes. I thought, *Only the Beatles and the greasers in Chicago wore pointy-toed shoes.*

I watched as a well-dressed woman walked up to a microphone. She hushed the group of GIs and then made a short speech offering us tips on visiting Sydney. Color brochures were handed out with maps showing us the different sights. The zoo was mentioned, and a big fuss was made over the new Sydney Opera House, then still under construction. After the clothes fitting, we were assigned roommates and given keys to our hotel rooms. The hotel was a short walk to Kings Cross, where all the action was. We checked into our rooms, took long showers, and then walked over to a Kings Cross pub.

There was a night of drinking ahead, but I was so tired that I bowed out early and headed back to my room. The next morning, our small officer group had a quick breakfast then headed back to the bar. I protested, "Let's at least spend the morning sightseeing."

It was decided we would go to the bay and look over the new opera house then walk through the shopping district. All this was accomplished in less than two hours, and then we headed back to the Kings Cross bar scene. By four o'clock in the afternoon, my eyes were burning from the barroom cigarette smoke, and I had had enough to drink. I thought about the desk that offered GIs a chance to visit a host Australian family. I looked at my watch; the reception center would close at five. I excused myself from the crowd and ran over to the center. The two women were still sitting at the card table. I walked over to them and told them I would like to get out of Sydney. I asked if there was still time to plan a visit with a host family. They immediately got on the phone and made arrangements with a family in Goulburn, New South Wales, for a five day visit. They told me the town of Goulburn was in the Southern Tablelands of New South Wales. It was about 2,500 feet above sea level, so it would be cool. "Do you have a jacket?" one of the women asked. I answered no.

"Well, you can get one when you arrive," she said and went on to describe the town. "Goulburn is a lovely country town, and it sits in a lush, pastoral valley. It's filled with apple orchards and stations. I asked her what she meant by stations; she told me the American's used the word ranch.

The polite woman at the card table handed me a small map of Sidney and circled the train station with a blue ballpoint pen. The next day, Sunday, I was to catch a morning train to Goulburn. My host family would meet me at the station. The woman handed me a three-by-five card with my contact in Goulburn.

"Just in case anything goes awry," she said.

"What could go awry?" I asked. I glanced at the card. It read, Mrs. Hall, followed by an address and phone number.

The women assured me that every American GI placed by them had had a delightful visit, and they were sure I would too. My concern was my precious few days of R&R and the thought of wasting one of them. I had only seven days in Australia, and I coveted each one. I thought, *Each day was a day I did not have to spend in the muddy gun pits in Vietnam.*

I walked back to the hotel, packed up for the morning trip, and placed a phone call to my parents in Chicago. My call was handled by a Sydney telephone operator. She told me to hang up and wait in the hotel room for a return call announcing the connection with my parents. The operator informed me the call would cost twenty-nine Australian dollars for three minutes. I was told to pay the hotel cashier after the call. I pulled my money from my pocket and counted out twenty-nine dollars. That was my budget for the call—no more.

Forty minutes passed before I got the return call. When I began talking with my parents, the connection was so poor I could hardly hear them. They, on the other hand, told me my voice was loud and clear. We chatted as I kept one eye on my watch. They went on to tell me my brother Dan had returned home from Vietnam, but he still had a few months to finish his stint in the army. He was stationed in North Carolina. My sister, Irene, was doing well, and my nephew, Matt, was now one year old. I told them about Sydney and my plan to visit a ranch in the country. I didn't mention Vietnam, and they never brought it up. My last words were. "Mom, Dad, I gotta go. It's almost ten dollars per minute!" I walked down to the hotel front desk and paid for the phone call.

I returned to our bar in Kings Cross and slipped back into the conversation with my crew. It seemed as if I had never left. Only a day and a half in Sydney and these GIs had a corner spot at the bar and they didn't move.

While at the bar, we met many of the locals, and they all thanked us for our service. They knew where the Americans hung out in Sydney, and many made it a point to say hello and buy us a pint. There were no TVs in the bar, so we were left to our wits and good conversation. I told my friends about my pending trip to Goulburn. They said they were finished with sightseeing and were happy here in the bar.

Sunday morning arrived; it was a cloudy, cool day. I loved it. It was such a relief from the heat of Vietnam. I took a taxi to the train station and found a seat on the almost empty train. It would be a three-and-a-half-hour journey. The local train would make every stop along the 125-mile route.

As the train pulled out of Sydney, I had an odd feeling that something would go wrong. I dismissed that thought, but it kept gnawing at me. I watched as the city of Sidney disappeared and the train passed through lush green hills and valleys. I nodded in and out of sleep, and I began to daydream about my host family.

I imagined a middle-aged couple meeting me at the Goulburn train depot. They would be well dressed with broad smiles. On the ride back to their estate, they would tell me about their only child, a daughter, Penny. She had just turned nineteen and was away at the university. When she heard of the Yank coming to visit, she canceled all her plans and was rushing home to entertain the American GI, me! The ever-chatty mother told me more. Her daughter had been the high school prom queen and had just won first prize in the New South Wales beauty pageant. She went on, "Maybe the two of you can run out to our club tonight for an early meal."

My fantasy continued. "Our poor daughter," the parents said in unison. "She just broke up with her boyfriend, and we do hope you will be able to cheer her up a tad. Oh, one more thing," the mother leaned over the seat and whispered. "She is seeing a doctor for a rare hormone imbalance. This condition gives her an insatiable appetite for men."

"Oh, is she cured?" I asked. Just then, I felt a kick against my foot. I opened my eyes to a bulbous, red-faced man with a cigar sticking from two rows of yellow teeth. It was the conductor announcing my stop.

The train platform at the Goulburn station was deserted. I was the sole passenger who disembarked. I looked up and down the platform, the streets, and the tracks. I saw no one. I walked to the station door only to find it locked. I thought, *Maybe my host family is running late. Duffy, don't panic.*

I waited and waited and then looked at the three-by-five card with my contact's name and address printed in a legible hand. There was a pay phone at one end of the station platform. I pulled some coins from my pocket, deposited the correct amount, and dialed the number. It rang and rang, there was no answer. I thought, *You probably dialed a wrong number.*

This time I deposited the coins, then slowly and deliberately redialed the number. Again, there was no answer. I took a deep breath and tried to figure out plan B if plan A went south. I thought, *Okay, maybe they blew you off, but you can still get back to Sydney in time for a Sunday night out at the Kings Cross pubs.*

A train schedule was posted on the station window; I read it only to find that I had just missed the last train back to Sydney. I would have to wait until the next morning, Monday, and take the 7:00 a.m. train back. I thought, *Now what?*

I remembered I had the address of my contact in my pocket, and I could inquire around town to try to find the house. I began to walk the streets of Goulburn, feeling sorry for myself and worrying about my wasted day of precious R&R. A kind soul a few blocks from the station pointed me to the correct street. I walked a few blocks and found the address. It was not a house but a business, a travel agency, and it was closed. Then I did panic, thinking, *Why in the hell did you sign up for this nutty trip to the country?* Duffy, you are an idiot. I imagined all my friends back in Sydney drinking beer, laughing, and meeting good-looking women.

I continued to walk the Goulburn streets cursing myself. Every shop I passed was closed. It was three o'clock on a Sunday afternoon. Not a soul was on the street. I was distraught. As I passed one small shop, I heard laughter from within. A sign on the door read Goulburn Social Club, Members Only.

I walked back and forth in front of the shop, mustering enough courage to step inside and see what all the laughter was about. However, the members-only sign made me hesitate. I opened the door to find a large man seated on a stool. He looked me over and then asked, "Are you a member?"

From the doorway, I glanced into the room. The place was packed with smiling people sipping tall glasses of beer. The fellow at the door asked me again if I was a member. I told him no, then I turned to leave. He stopped me, and then in a deep Australian accent, he said, "Well, mate, want to join? It's only a dollar."

I nodded my approval and pulled a dollar bill from my wallet; I handed it to him. He welcomed me and pointed to the bar. As I ordered a pint from the bartender, my accent gave me up as an American. The bartender handed me the beer, then asked, "How did a Yank end up here in Goulburn?"

I told him my story. What got his attention was my status as an American GI on leave from Vietnam. During the course of the Vietnam War, over 60,000 Australians fought alongside the Americans: 521 died in the war and over 3,000 were wounded. They had a large stake in the Vietnam War and they were very proud of their fighting boys.

The bartender loudly announced to the customers that a Yank was in the house, just back from Vietnam. Soon people approached me, shook my hand, and thanked me for my service. They began to buy me pints and tell me about their lads fighting in Vietnam. People formed a line to greet me. I heard about a cousin or a brother serving in Vietnam. They told me of their laws in Goulburn shutting down all businesses on Sunday, except social clubs.

A young Catholic priest approached me and listened to my story. I pulled the crumpled three-by-five card from my pocket with the name of Mrs. Hall and an address and phone number neatly printed on the card. He looked it over and then began chatting with some patrons at the bar.

After we finished our pints and the social club was about to close, the priest told me to come with him to the rectory office and he would try to find the missing Mrs. Hall. We walked over to the rectory, and he got on the phone. After a series of calls, he located Mrs. Hall. Soon a very apologetic Mrs. Hall arrived. As it turned out, the women at the Sydney reception center were unaware that host families began their visits on Monday, never on Sunday. The staff at the reception center was all volunteer. It was a misunderstanding. I thanked the priest for his help then got into the car with Mrs. Hall. She told me that my host family had a ranch outside of town, but because of the mix-up, I would spend the night at her home.

The Halls had a modest, white stucco house on the edge of Goulburn. When I walked in, I thought I was back home in Chicago. There was a clean kitchen, a living room, and a dining room. The dining room had a beautiful oak table. The table was set for Sunday dinner. There were curtains on the windows and pictures on the walls. It all seemed so welcoming to me. I mentally compared this homey atmosphere with the filth of our lives in Vietnam. The Halls' home was wonderful.

Mrs. Hall had two grown children, Joan, an attractive nineteen-year-old, and her older brother, Robert. Mrs. Hall was a widow. We sat down to a pot roast dinner, something I had not had in close to a year. It was fantastic. There was conversation about the United States and my home in Chicago. Joan asked me what Vietnam was like. I put my knife and fork down and tried to collect my thoughts and answer with an accurate description, but I couldn't. The few words that formed in my mind were blocked by the death of the soldier and the cowards on the helicopter. I flashed to the assassination of the schoolteacher. In an awkward moment of silence, I shook my head and said nothing.

Mrs. Hall saved me from embarrassment and asked if I wanted dessert. "Yes, please," I said. I looked out the window to budding trees and thought of Chicago at this time of the year. Our trees were turning color and soon they would lose their leaves. It was springtime, 1968, in Australia, so very different from Vietnam and Chicago.

After dinner, there were still a few hours of daylight. Joan had her brother drive me around town for a sightseeing tour. He drove us in his new car, a Morris Mini. This twist of fate that brought me to the Halls' home turned my entire day around. In just a few hours, I had gone from a handwringing mess walking the deserted streets of Goulburn to a happy tourist.

Joan asked me if I needed anything. I told her I needed a coat. It was cool in the evening, and I hadn't brought one. It was settled. They would drive me to the dry-goods dealer in the morning. Mrs. Hall phoned my host family. I would be with them the following night.

The next day, Joan became my personal tour guide. Our first stop was the dry goods shop. This was a very old-fashioned store with the wares behind a long counter. The proprietor looked me over. Then, from a large stack of blue coats, he pulled out one and asked me to try it on. It was called a Norwellan Bluey Junior. The coat was made of fine Australian wool. The coat had large wooden dowel buttons hanging from navy blue cords. I tried it on. "Sold," I exclaimed.

The shop owner picked up a pencil and a receipt book. He wrote down a few figures, then looked at me and said, "That will be eight dollars and thirty cents."

I could not believe the value. Two nights before, I had paid twenty-nine dollars for a terrible phone connection talking with my parents. I counted out the money and thanked him.

Joan gave me a second tour of Goulburn and the surrounding area. We arrived back at the Hall home after a stop for lunch. Mrs. Hall told me my host family was now ready for me. Joan drove me out to my host family's farm. She and I got on well, and I was disappointed that we had to part.

The farm was located in a picturesque group of rolling hills. The owner and his wife welcomed me. They had two boys, Paul, ten years old, and Michael, eleven years old. The boys took to me quickly and began pummeling me with questions. I was shown their property, the barn, and the apple storage facility. They took me to watch a farm hand shear their sheep. The man was skilled at his trade. The wool was cut from the sheep still intact. The naked sheep looked puny compared with their woolly profiles before the shearing.

The boys dragged me outdoors to walk their property lines up one field and down the other. Their mother protested, but I waved her off and said it was fine with me—I was enjoying myself. The only problem I had was my rented oxford shoes. They weren't designed for a wet barnyard. The boys wore Wellington boots, or as they called them, "gumboots." They dragged me by the hand and pulled me all over the ranch. They even took me to their secret fort under a stand of bushes and branches. Then we climbed a small hill to view Mount Baw Baw. Just when I thought the tour was finished, they insisted I see the river. I asked them what river. They shot back, "Why, the Wollondilly River. You haven't heard of it?" I lied and told them that I had heard of it, and now I would see it. We stood on a hill, and from a distance; I saw a sliver of the river.

The boys reminded me of my brother Dan and me. He and I had had our escapades in the woods and built forts and secret hideouts. I told them that my brother and I had also lived near a river before our dad moved us to Chicago. They began to ask about my river. I told them it was named the Fox River, and its waters flowed all the way to the Mississippi River, then down to the Gulf of Mexico.

"Did you have a boat?" they asked.

I told them that my brother and I kind of had a boat. They became very inquisitive.

"How can you *kind of* have a boat? You either have a boat or you don't have a boat."

"I'll tell you both about our boat later," I said. "We better be getting back to your home."

That night after dinner, we settled ourselves into their den. There was no television. The boys told me of a boat that they and their father were going to build in the summer. The boat would be made of wood, and they were going to fish from it in the Wollondilly River. They told their dad that I "kind of had a boat." Then they both pressed me with questions about my boat. I told them that my brother and I had found it.

"How can you find a boat? Tell us about your boat." I said, "Okay, but only if you let me start from the beginning." They listened as I told them my boat story.

>Our small town of Cary, Illinois, held a fair each sum-
>mer. The fair was held on Main Street. Cars were not
>allowed on the street, only pedestrians. There were
>rides, food vendors, a dunk-the-fireman tank, and
>lots of people. My dad took my brother, Dan, and me
>to this fair on a Saturday night. I was ten years old
>and Dan was eight.

We walked around together and greeted friends and neighbors. Then I spied a treasure sitting next to the curb in front of Peter's Bakery. This was what I wanted and wished for since our move to Cary. Best of all, it was not for sale; it was to be raffled off to a lucky winner that night. It was a beautiful brand-new speedboat with a big outboard motor and leopard-skin seats, and it even had a trailer.

I ran to my dad and begged him to purchase some raffle tickets for the boat. He thought for a moment and then said okay. We walked over to the table where tickets were being sold. My dad asked for five tickets at fifty cents each. He handed the man a five-dollar bill, then he took his change. We sat at a card table with pencils in his hand. Dan and I helped him fill out each paper ticket. When we finished, I watched as the man unlocked and opened the door of a large drum. The drum was made of wood and stiff metal screen. It sat on an axle with a crank at one end. The man put our five tickets into the drum and gave the crank a turn. I looked in as our five paper receipts mixed with the others. I stood at the drum, peering into it and trying to find our tickets. They became lost with all the others. But now we had five chances to win the boat.

I had been pestering my dad about a boat since we had moved from Chicago to Cary. Most of the families that lived on the river had boats. I would see families jump into their boats and speed away for hours of fun. I tried everything I could think of to convince my dad a boat was truly a necessity if one lived on a river. I played the "What if?" game. "Dad, what if the river flooded, and everyone was able to leave their homes in a boat but us? We could die!" "Dad, what if a tornado blew down the bridge, and we needed to get to Fox River Grove for food?" "Dad, what if the Communists invade Cary? Like Senator Joe McCarthy says they will. We could float down the river to Algonquin and escape before they brainwash us." Nothing worked. I pestered him so much that he wouldn't even say no. He would just twist his head back and forth. One hot Saturday in our yard, he got angry with me and said, "I have had it with your boat talk, Mike. Stop it. My no is final!" But now things were different. If we won this boat at the Cary fair, my prayers would be answered.

I spent the entire night at the fair walking in circles around the boat. I pictured myself at the wheel speeding down the river as envious boys and girls watched from the shoreline. I would give them a wave as we roared past their houses. Maybe I would slow the boat to a crawl, then push the throttle to full speed and leave a white wake as I waved goodbye.

We left the fair before the raffle was held. On the drive, home I began to worry about not having a pier at our house.

"Dad," I asked, "if we win, where will we dock it?"

"Dock what?" he said.

"*Dad,* dock the boat?" I couldn't believe that he wasn't thinking about winning our new boat. He told me that we would worry about that when and *if* we won the boat.

Our neighbors, the Roth family, let us fish from their pier; I was sure they would let us dock our new boat until we arranged to build a pier. That night I had trouble sleeping. I kept thinking of boat problems. We didn't have a hitch on our car. How would we get the boat from downtown Cary to our house? The phone rang about 10:00 p.m. I ran to it, convincing myself that it was the call about the boat. It was not; it was one of my sister's high school boyfriends. The next morning, I asked my dad if the call had come in. He said, "What call?"

"*Dad,* the call about the boat."

In a flat voice, not raising his head from the Sunday paper, he said, "No."

About 10:00 a.m. we left for church. I saw a few friends on the steps of the church and asked them if they knew who had won the boat. They didn't. After church, I walked up to another friend and asked him about the boat. He didn't know who had won, but his dad did. His dad told me the name of the winner;

it was not the Duffys. I looked at my dad, he looked relieved. It was a long ride home from church.

When we got home, my brother and I walked into our yard and watched the Sunday boat traffic on the Fox River. It was a perfect boating day, hot and sunny. There were big boats, boats that had chrome Chris Craft logos on the bow, little speedboats, and fishing boats with small motors. They went back and forth all day. Soon evening came and the boat traffic slowed. By nightfall the boat traffic stopped. It began to rain, and then it began to storm. Lightning filled the sky.

The next day, my brother and I walked down to the river bank. The river was swollen from the night's storms. We began throwing rocks at the railroad trestle above the river, and then we picked up rocks and tried to skip them across the river. Our stones never got far from shore. We stood and watched as the river's current washed down tree limbs, wood planks, and other debris. The previous night's rain added a great volume of water to the river's flow. I could see the water level had come up under the Roth's pier, almost touching the bottom. I watched more junk float by. It was all heading down toward the dam in the town of Algonquin. I soon made out a familiar form floating downstream. It was submerged, but the form was unmistakable. It was a wooden rowboat, and it was headed straight for the Roth's pier. I screamed at Dan for help, and we quickly waded into

the river and grabbed the submerged boat as it floated near us. Dan and I struggled and pulled the boat
into our yard. It was heavy and waterlogged. At once
I could see why it was submerged. There was a floor
plank missing near the back. I looked over the boat
and thought, *We can fix this.*

The green paint on the boat was peeling away and the
row boat was half-filled with river water now spilling out the back. With great effort, Dan and I pushed
and shoved and then turned the boat over. There in
full view was a gaping hole. *Okay*, I thought, *now all
we need to do is replace the missing plank.* Dan and
I ran to our garage and found the things we needed. A board, window putty, black tarpaper, and some
rusty bent nails. I hammered the nails straight on
our walkway. Then we began to work on the missing
plank. After taking some measurements, I grabbed
my dad's rusty hand saw and began to saw a board to
fit the open space. I would saw the board, then check
to see if it fit. If needed, I would saw again. When I
was finished, the board measured about seven inches wide and the hole was about eight inches wide. I
thought, *Not to worry, we can fill in the space with
window putty and tarpaper.*

I hammered the board to the bottom of the boat, but
the wood was so rotten that only a few nails stuck. The
board also didn't quite fit the curvature of the boat. It
stuck out on both sides, but just a little. We filled the

space with putty, nailed the tarpaper to the bottom, and then pushed more window putty in and around the tarpaper. We were ready to launch. Dan and I turned the boat over and pushed it into the water, bow first. Remembering that we didn't have oars, I stopped. We ran back to the garage, where we found two long wood planks; I thought that the planks would work fine as paddles. We ran back to the boat. I had Dan sit in the front as I pushed off and jumped into the back. We drifted out into the river, and almost immediately, the boat began taking on water. Our repair job gave us about two minutes on the river, then we sank.

Dan and I pulled the boat back on shore. I had another idea. If we both sat in the front of the boat and placed large rocks next to us maybe the back of the boat would rise above the water line and we could stay afloat. We ran around our yard picking up the large painted rocks my father had set out to border the property line on his rented house. He painted them white and spaced them evenly near the end of our long picket fence. The rocks were heavy. We pushed and rolled the rocks to the boat then struggled to lift them, they slammed down on the boat floor. We put five rocks into the boat, I had Dan sit in the front, and I pushed off, but this time I didn't get into the boat until it was floating. This idea worked; the back of the boat was high and not taking on water. I gingerly climbed aboard and moved toward the front. We slowly paddled out into the current of the river, and the boat began to move quickly in the swift flowing water. Because the back was so high, our front was near the water line. Even a strong paddle movement brought water over the side.

We began our ride down river, passing the piers in our subdivision then crossing into the next subdivision. I thought this was great. We hardly had to paddle. The river current was strong and it was moving us without effort. As we floated toward the subdivision of Trout Valley, I began to hear a noise that spelled trouble. It was the sound of a motorboat. It soon came into view. Uh-oh, I thought, the motorboat was moving fast and had deep swells in its wake. We needed to get to shore quick or we would be swamped. Dan and I began paddling as fast as we could to get to the Trout Valley shoreline. We were near the middle of the river, and the faster we paddled, the more water came over the side of our boat. The motorboat roared past us, turning just at the right moment to create a large wave, which was now moving toward our craft.

Soon the motorboat's swells caught up to us. We weathered the first, but the second wave swamped our boat and we had to abandon ship. We both swam to the river's edge and left the boat to sink. As we climbed on shore I remembered my father's white painted rocks. *Oh, no,* I thought, *what can I tell my dad about the lost rocks?* It was late afternoon, very hot, and Dan and I began the long walk home from Trout Valley. We passed the opening in the chain-link fence and walked through Root Springs, over a small bridge, and through a path into Jandus subdivision. I worried about the lost rocks all the way home.

At dinner Dan and I told my father our story, and we included the missing rocks. He wasn't angry that they were gone, and he said he didn't think they looked very good anyway.

The boys loved the story and asked for more, but their father ushered them off to bed. When he came back, we had a glass of his Scotch whisky. As we sipped our drinks in front of his hearth, he asked me about Vietnam. I stumbled over my thoughts and ended with a pause, then said, "*It's just horrible.*" He asked me one more question about the war. He asked me if we were winning. I had no answer. I didn't know. I told him I didn't think even the commander of our troops knew the answer to that question. But I told him I did know one thing I could do here in Australia I could never do in Vietnam. I could relax.

The next day, my last day on the farm, was spent with the boys and more journeys around the hills. They showed me their livestock, including one large bull. This reminded me of my boyhood growing up in Cary, Illinois, and its absolute freedom from harm or responsibility. I promised the boys one more story about a huge bull.

At dinner I was told of the plan for the next day. Either Mrs. Hall or Joan would come to pick me up. I thought, *I hope its Joan.* I would spend my last day with the Halls. Through her travel agency, Mrs. Hall arranged an airplane trip back to Sydney. I wouldn't have to spend three and a half hours on the train. I watched the boys help clean up in the kitchen. When they finished, they grabbed my hands and pulled me into the den. They demanded another story. Their father was lighting a fire, and the boys had me join them on the floor to tell one more story, I began.

In the early 1950s, my Dad moved our family from a small apartment on Chicago's West Side into a rented house in Cary, Illinois. The house sat next to the Chicago and Northwestern Railroad tracks and fronted on the Fox River. My younger brother, Dan, was seven years old, and I was nine. We were ecstatic about the move. We now had a yard to play in and a river outside our front door. Although Dan and I were happy with this move, my mother hated her new home because it was so far from her brothers and sisters living in Chicago. She also despised driving, but now she was forced to drive our lumbering four-door Pontiac sedan, without power steering. What she hated most was a telephone party line with three neighbors listening in on her conversations. The long and harsh winters in Cary just added to her woes. In the summer she tossed us both out the door after breakfast and told us to stay out of the house and out of her hair.

The summers in Cary, Illinois, were heaven for a kid. Dan and I would ride our bikes from one end of town to the other. We would explore every corner of our new town, population 900. We even went over the bridge to explore the exotic village of Fox River Grove. When Dan and I heard about the giant bulls stabled at the Curtiss Farm we decided to ride our bikes over to see them. The Curtiss Farm was a 200-acre cattle-breeding operation, complete with an agricultural school. The farm had milk cows, breeding bulls, and a large, well-tended vegetable garden. The fruits of the garden went to the many employees and helped keep their grocery bills down. The fruits of the bull-breeding operation were sold and rushed to Chicago for transport to all corners of the United States. In some cases, the semen was sold for shipment to Europe.

One Monday morning, Dan and I jumped on our bikes and rode over to the large barn at the Curtiss Farm. The barn was cavernous with a high ceiling and huge wooden doors. We arrived midmorning and stood in the open doorway. Dan and I watched as the bull technician led one after another enormous bull to the back of a cow. The cow was chained to a post. After a moment of bull-and-cow foreplay, the bull would leap on the back of the cow. The first time we saw this, I thought, *Either the bull was angry or the workman was training the bull for the circus.* Dan and I watched in amazement as this theater unfolded. Dan and I couldn't figure out how the back legs of the cow could hold the weight of the huge bull. Dan asked me what was going on. I told him I didn't know, but I thought the guy standing near the cow had better watch out because I was sure the cow's legs would give way at any moment. If that happened, the bull would keel over on the workman, crushing him.

At times the workman would glance at us and yawn; he looked bored. Other times during this performance, we heard loud noises, mooing, grunting, and the occasional sidestepping of hooves smashing on the concrete floor. This whole process was very strange to me because the workman would try to get between the bull and cow and position a three-foot firehose type of thing he held in his hand. I had no idea what was going on.

Soon we became bored and rode our bikes over to the upper pasture along River Drive, where horses grazed. Dan and I pulled handfuls of grass from the earth and fed it to the horses. As we fed them, one trotted over to Dan. The horse began to scratch his side on the fence post. As the horse did this, Dan jumped on his back and began riding the horse around the field bareback. I was impressed. I watched in envy as my little brother rode around and around the fenced pasture. Soon the horse gently slowed and trotted back to the fence and Dan climbed off. This was a lot more fun than watching the indifferent workman and the acrobatic bulls. At the end of the day we rode our bikes back to our home in Jandus subdivision and watched the commuter trains pass by our house. The trains were pulled by black coal-fired steam engines. They belched plumes of smoke from their stacks, and shrill whistles screamed as the trains approached a nearby grade crossing. We waited in our yard for my father to return from his work. We talked to each other, still trying to figure out what was going on inside the Curtiss Farm barn with the cow and bulls.

The boys told me I was a good storyteller. I thanked them, and then I thanked the whole family for a wonderful visit.

The next morning Joan arrived in her brother's Morris Mini, and we drove back to Goulburn. We spent the day together, talking and driving around town. She took me to the heights above Goulburn for a bird's-eye view of the village. We met a few of her friends. She asked me about coming back to Goulburn. I told her it was unlikely; the army gave me only one R&R, but I would ask. There was a Christmas dance in town, and she wanted me to attend with her. This sounded like my civilian life back in Chicago. I missed it, and this small slice of normal life lifted the weight of Vietnam from me. This is what a young man should be doing, going to dances, socializing, and enjoying life.

I said my goodbyes to the Halls, boarded a twin-engine Cessna airplane, and sat in the copilot's seat as we flew back to Sydney. The moon was bright and the pilot skimmed over the clouds until the lights of Sydney came into view. The flight was thrilling. As I left the plane, I tried to pay the fare. Again I was thanked for my service in Vietnam. The pilot shook my hand and said, "No charge, mate."

I took a taxi back to the hotel, threw my bags on the bed, and walked back to the Kings Cross bar. My friends were still in their favorite corner. Someone put a pint in my hand, and we toasted to our last night in Australia. They asked me about my trip; I told them it was good. I paused then said, "No, it was perfect."

Chapter 8

HANK

Shortly after I returned from Australia, my friend Jack Smith left our unit. He climbed into the mail truck one afternoon, shook my hand, and drove away. The artillery battery was now mine. I was the new executive officer. Once again, I was green and untested in this new position. As I watched Lieutenant Smith's jeep drive over our muddy canal and speed toward Saigon, I felt a knot grip my stomach. Jack's presence had made my job easy; now my job would become hard.

The major problem facing me, or so I thought, was gaining the respect of the men as the new XO. I soon found out there was a larger dilemma—Lieutenant Owen. He despised the fact that I was his superior and dedicated himself to making things difficult for me.

Lieutenant Owen's quick wit and sharp tongue took aim immediately. He was always fast with a joke or a glib remark, often at my expense. I, on the other hand, would stumble over my words. Owen was confident, secure, and pompous; he would talk over me as I tried to explain a fact, a rule, or a boring guideline about the guns. I was awkward at this game of language brinkmanship. However, I was still Owen's boss and this raised tension between us.

Lieutenant Owen had one perilous flaw, unnoticed by most, unnoticed by me at first. Lieutenant Owen was cavalier about the workings of the artillery battery. Later in the year, Owen's overconfidence would prove deadly. He believed that the enlisted men on the guns and in our FDC bunker knew their jobs well and did not need supervision, especially from a young, untested officer like me. Maybe an occasional walk-by was enough, but as he often said, "No one likes working when someone is looking over his shoulder."

During our meals, I watched Lieutenant Owen tilt back in his chair, laugh, and mock me after I stated some arcane artillery safety rule. Then, making sure that all the officers at our table heard him, he would say, "Duffy, the men on the guns have years of experience, much more experience than a green XO like you.

He would smirk, shake his head, and then continue: "Your walking around the gun pits during fire missions will not only get in their way but will also piss off the enlisted men. Your presence will cause discontent in the gun pits. Is that what you want?"

I watched Owen push his chair away from our mess table and then walk away with Lieutenant Hart in tow. The two of them began their talk about California. That's all I heard at our officers' mess table. Day after day, California, speedboats, a sunny climate, and what Hart and he were going to do when they got back to their beloved L.A.

Owen would discuss in fine detail the brands and models of speedboats, outboard motors, and even the type of boat trailer he was going to purchase. Then on the weekends, he told us, he was going to drive his new boat over to Lake Havasu in Arizona. I watched as Hart and he would lock eye to eye, then review and refine their fantasies. I had little interest in their daydreams. I wanted to do my job, get out of the army, and go to college.

I began to hate the California myth of milk and honey. I listened as it was served up each day. Then I watched as Lieutenant Hart put Owen on a pedestal as the Grand PooBah, Lord of California Knowledge. Hart was Owen's most treasured audience.

I felt alone and isolated. Captain Tom was seldom seen; he spent most of his days and nights in his small bunker. I spent my free hours reading periodicals, rereading my letters, and trying to teach myself to play the guitar. Mail call became my most coveted moment. When I received a letter, I would find a secluded spot in our camp and carefully open the envelope. I would read and reread the letter, deliberately examining the paper, the envelope, and the handwriting of the author. My sister, Irene, five years my senior, always sent the news from our family. She wrote about our annual Labor Day picnic—who attended and what food was brought. Those were details I had always overlooked, but in Vietnam they became important to me.

In my sister's letters, there was usually a photo of some family event. I would focus on those pictures and try to imagine myself in the small backyard behind our apartment building. When our family hosted the Labor Day party, that was the spot we gathered. In late August and September, our apartment was hot and uncomfortable. Although we did have one window air conditioner, it worked only when most of the lights were turned off; otherwise a fuse would blow. In the summertime, our back steps became the place for conversation. While in Vietnam, the conversations I had taken for granted at home became precious. I missed them so. During those family parties, Dan and I would pepper our cousin Burt with questions about the Vietnam War. He had just returned, and we thought he was an expert on the topic. Although we fired nonstop questions at Burt, he rarely spoke about his tour in Vietnam.

After my letter reading and daydreaming respite, I would walk circle after circle around the guns. In the afternoon, when the guns were cleaned and the ammunition was restocked, the men would lie on their cots and wait for the nightly fire missions. I waited for the sun to set and the night air to cool our compound. As the day ended, I crossed off another day on my short-timer calendar. It was now fall 1968. I was scheduled to leave Vietnam in late January. After my walk, I would sit on my cot, write letters, and go to the mental comfort zone of home. I planned my life after Vietnam—college, friendships, and peace. My daydreaming was usually short-lived. A fire mission would arrive or a problem would find its way to my boxlike room; relaxation was impossible. Then there was Owen—he had a way of creating problems for me with his constant challenges to my authority.

Lieutenant Owen was correct about one thing. The men on the guns did know their jobs. They were well trained, and they fired every night, honing their skills. I'm sure that my presence around the gun pits did bother some of the men. But, regardless, each night as I walked the gun pits, I noticed mistakes. I found small errors late at night, when the men were sleepy or hungover from warm beer. These were men who wished only one thing in life—to finish their tours in Vietnam and return home. They hated the heat and filth we lived with each day.

The mistakes I found were minor errors in deflection or elevation. Most of the errors were harmless. An errant artillery round would fall in a muddy field, and no one would know, no one would care. But even an error of only a few millimeters at the gun pit had the potential to be lethal. An artillery tube that was raised to a point of 300 degrees when it should be raised to 305 degrees put us all at risk. It sounds like an error of little consequence, but like an immense triangle, a small error at the apex becomes a large error at the triangle's end. If the end is seven miles out from the apex, the small error at the gun position turns into a large error as the artillery round explodes in a fireball. If the error puts the impact near a unit of troops, then death and destruction from friendly fire occurs.

Directly under my command and being groomed for the executive officer position after my tour ended was Lieutenant Hart. Over the months, I watched as Lieutenant Hart and Lieutenant Owen became inseparable; they were always together. Being the stronger personality, Owen would sway Lieutenant Hart into his sphere of influence and away from me.

One day while standing in the FDC bunker, I heard Owen talk of leaving Vietnam and returning home to Los Angles via Europe. This conversation intrigued me, and I wondered to myself if the army would let him do that. Owen talked of flying to Rome and then traveling through Germany, France, and Great Britain. He loudly exclaimed that Lieutenant Hart and he would take their time getting home and see a bit of Europe.

As Owen took a breath and momentarily stopped talking, I jumped in with what I thought was a good idea, "Hey," I said, "why don't you guys visit Ireland on the way home?" Ireland was my ancestral home; to me it was sacred.

"Ireland!" Owen screamed. "Who wants to go to that shithole?"

He said those words with such conviction and hate that I was taken aback. Perhaps Owen's ancestors were Orangemen from Ulster, and they had given him a thorough dousing of papist hatred. I knew one thing—whoever taught him to despise Ireland did their job well. After Owen's "shithole" comment in front of the enlisted men, I felt embarrassed and hurt. I thought, *Duffy, keep your fucking mouth shut.*

I walked out of the FDC bunker and back to my isolation. I reread the *Stars and Stripes* newspaper, old letters, and my acceptance letter from Colorado College. I turned on my radio and tuned in Hanoi Hannah. Her soothing voice was a pleasant respite from Owen's rants. I fed one of the many stray dogs and scratched its head as it rested in the dust.

I thought back to my life in Chicago and the time I spent with my brother Dan playing sixteen-inch softball in the alley. I thought of the vendors driving colorful panel trucks, honking their horns and shouting the word "vegetables." Using a small scale, the seller weighed and sold produce to my mother and our neighbors. I vividly remembered the junk dealer who drove through every week looking for bed springs, old pipes, and any type of metal he could find; sometimes he would pay cash for large pieces. He always would smile and wave to Dan and me as his ancient Ford pickup truck passed us. I longed to be back there playing catch with my brother. We hit the softball with a wooden bat that had its knob at the end worn off from years of use. In the fall we threw a ragged football with the leather stitching torn at each end from hitting our concrete alleyway.

We attended Mass on Sunday at St. Ignatius Church on Glenwood Avenue. After Mass my mother cooked and served us Sunday dinner. Her menu rarely changed—pot roast with potatoes and carrots. On Monday we went back to work or school, and we were never late. Loafing was considered a sin. I felt guilty even if my mom caught me lying on our sofa. Our grandparents had Irish brogues, and they saved their money for a "rainy day." They rarely if ever made a purchase on credit. Debt was considered evil.

I missed those days so much. I thought nothing of them while growing up, but now, here in Vietnam, they seemed precious. Sadly, when I returned home from Vietnam, this rich culture seemed to have vanished. Our alley fell victim to air conditioning. Almost everyone on our block shut the doors to the peddlers, content to hear the hum of a window unit cooling their apartments.

As I reread a letter from my boyhood friend Joe Kiefer, I thought back to my first delivery job in our neighborhood. I was fifteen years old when I began working for the R&N Food Market on Devon Avenue. Every day after school and all day on Saturday, I rode a delivery bike with a large wire basket full of groceries. The basket sat over an undersized front wheel and was bolted to a plywood frame. My job was to ride throughout the neighborhood delivering kosher groceries to the store's many Jewish customers. I learned a hard lesson one winter afternoon. It was Friday, and I was late getting to my job. Chicago daylight fades fast in December, and there were more than the typical number of orders to deliver. As I started my rounds, it began to snow, further slowing my pace. By the time I arrived at my last customer in a large apartment building, the sun had set and the Jewish Sabbath had begun.

I made my way into the building through two heavy oak doors then up a long flight of stairs. The hallway was dark and narrow and it held the aroma of boiling cabbage. In my hands was a large cardboard box filled with canned goods, milk, ice cream, and lox wrapped in white butcher paper. I knocked on the door and waited. Soon a very angry man thrust the door open and began raving at me about the time. "You're late! I told Ira to get the groceries delivered before the Sabbath. Don't you people listen?"

I apologized and offered to walk into his apartment and put the ice cream and milk in his refrigerator. He was shouting at me in either German or Yiddish. He spoke so fast that I couldn't tell the difference. He had me put the box of groceries outside his door in the hallway. Then he gave me a cross look and slammed the door. I didn't get a tip.

Our squawk box screeched and brought my daydreaming to an end and back to the reality of Vietnam. It was a false alarm—no fire missions, just a reminder that all the targets were plotted and I needed to lay the battery for the evening's fire missions. With trepidation, I walked into the FDC bunker just as Owen was finishing another story. He ignored me. I got the azimuth (direction) for the night's fire missions from the enlisted chart man and walked out.

Captain Tom gave me a lecture one night about the job of training Hart. Then he asked me, "How is it going? Is he learning?" I answered him with an affirmative nod. I told him every night I had Hart walk the guns with me. We would go over the night's fire missions together and then decide what guns would fire. What I didn't tell him was the difficulty I had with Owen and getting Hart out of the FDC bunker to do our job.

My squawk box crackled and I heard another fire mission come into FDC. I walked back over to the FDC bunker to get the azimuth just as Owen was holding court. He was serving up another sermon about boats, big boats, little boats, what saltwater did to boats. He went on and on, disregarding my presence. I waited patiently for a pause. When Owen took a breath, I looked directly at Lieutenant Hart, then I said, "We need to walk the guns. Let's go."

Owen stared at me with hateful eyes, then he exploded with a mocking mantra. "Duffy, you don't have to go near the fucking guns; the men know their job, let them do it."

I ignored Owen and looked at Hart eye to eye, then I said again, but this time forcefully, "Let's *go.*"

Owen was furious that I was taking his audience. I could see the glances from the enlisted men as tension built in the room. I made the mistake of arguing with Owen. I said to him, "Look, I'm the XO;

it's my job to walk the guns and soon it will be Hart's job." I turned to Hart and said, "Lets go."

Owen loathingly peered at me. I felt his hatred. He screamed, "Duffy, they have more experience than all of us put together—give it a fucking rest and let them do their job." It was all he could do to contain his rage. After this outburst, a dead silence filled the room. I walked out of the FDC bunker with Peter in tow.

Although Peter cherished his time with Owen, he knew full well that Captain Tom had given me the task to ready him for the day of my departure. That day couldn't come quickly enough.

As Peter and I began walking the guns, we approached a group of GIs talking. When they saw us, they tossed their lit cigarettes into a drainage ditch. Peter said to me, "Did you see that?"

"See what?" I said. I was confused.

"The roaches," Peter said.

"Roaches?"

"Yeah, roaches. Don't you know what roaches are?"

"What do you mean roaches—bugs?" I asked.

I was still puzzled. Peter spoke easily with me and told me about the marijuana roll-ups smoked in Vietnam and in California. He told me the ends were called roaches. Thank God it was Peter telling me this and not Owen. He would have lampooned me for a week, making sure that all his enlisted buddies knew how stupid I was.

***

In the fall of 1968, I had a GI take my picture as I sat in the portal of my ammo-crate home. I made sure that I looked grim and menacing as I held a captured Chinese AK-47 rifle. I imagined the photo being published in the *Chicago Tribune* with the caption "Our Men in Vietnam." The *Chicago Tribune* published pictures of local boys in the paper with a short blurb about them and what neighborhood in Chicago they came from. My brother, Dan, was featured in one of those short articles in 1967. The *Tribune* stopped publishing the photos and short bios in 1968, after the Tet Offensive and after Walter Cronkite's famous negative comments about the war on the nightly news. My picture was developed, and I foolishly thought it made me look like a tough GI, albeit a skinny one.

My days and nights in Nhá Bé seemed endless, walking the gun pits and making sure that maintenance was performed and logged into the record books. After a few hours of sleep, I would rise at 8:00 a.m. Our guns fired until 4:00 or 4:30 every morning. By 8:00 or 9:00 a.m., in the lowlands of Vietnam, it was too hot to sleep. I would get up still wearing my clothes and boots. Putting on one's boots in the middle of the night was a slow process. I needed to be ready to supervise the fire missions quickly; there was no time for the luxury of looking for boots.

Behind my hooch was our generator; it was constantly humming. Beyond the generator was a path leading to an outlook position on the edge of the Sông Nhá Bé River. Two of our men were on duty there day and night. The guns were a short walk from my quarters. I was ever present, ever vigilant. This was a twenty-four-hour, seven-day-a-week job; there was no escape.

Standing behind the guns, I could hear the elevation and deflection numbers coming over the squawk box in the gun pit, and before the gunners turned the gun tube, I would mentally compute where the tube should be pointed. When the gunner finished his job, I sometimes would ask him to recheck his figures. I would do this if I thought the gun tube was pointed incorrectly. Often a tired, grumpy gunner would recheck the numbers on his gun site, then say to me, "Sorry, sir, my numbers were off." The guns had metal sights with metal dials and numbers engraved within each dial; when it was dark, the men used flashlights to view the hash marks and numbers. They were hard to read in the daylight hours and even harder during the evening hours.

Another part of my responsibility was the FDC bunker, Lieutenant Owen's turf. Jack told me every day my responsibility did not end at the guns. Mistakes also occurred in the FDC bunker. If the gun pits were the blue-collar point in our unit, the FDC bunker was the middle-management point. I was now part of the upper-management team.

During the dusty dry season, the guns became a problem. We cleaned out the dust with oily rags, wiping out the breech and the firing mechanism. We made sure that the moving parts were oiled and operating with as little friction as possible. An hour after cleaning the guns, they would be covered with dust again; it was an impossible job.

It wasn't all work at Nhá Bé; we did have our small club, a small building with a corrugated tin roof. It had a few tables and chairs and a homemade plywood bar. Warm Pabst Blue Ribbon beer was always available. On Sunday afternoons, most of the officers and noncommissioned officers (corporals and sergeants) drifted in, except Captain Tom.

One Sunday afternoon I was sitting at a table with Peter Hart when our first sergeant walked into the club. With him was his Saigon drinking buddy, Hank. Both he and Top (Top was short for first sergeant) shared the same stateside politics, and they both hated "gooks." Hank lived in the upscale quarter of Saigon near the officers club. He had a wife and children back in California. Here in Vietnam he was making big money as a civilian contractor. Our first sergeant walked him around the guns, the ammo bunker, and our FDC bunker, then they headed for our club. Following the first sergeant and Hank into our club was Hank's "girlfriend"; she was the most stunning Vietnamese girl I had ever seen.

I sat quietly with Peter and watched as Hank and Top tossed down beer after beer in a faux display of masculine bravado. They would laugh at their stupid jokes then tell each other about their lives back home in the States. Hank began talking about his wife, "Yeaaaah, my wife is married … but I'm not." After that declaration, they both broke into a toothy laugh, coughing out phlegm and the smoke they had just inhaled, and showing their yellowing teeth.

Peter Hart and I sat listing to Hank and Top's blather, but we were both watching Hank's girlfriend. She was hanging on his arm. When she entered our club, Peter and I watched as this stunning figure glided past our table. She stopped at an empty chair, put her foot on its edge, and, with a damp bar towel, wiped the red dust off her high-heeled shoes. She did this slowly then glanced at Peter and me. We watched as she threw the towel back on the table. She had long, straight black hair that fell far below her shoulders, and her lips were brilliant red. Her American blue jeans were tight, and her shoes were scarlet. Peter and I were speechless. Everyone in the club watched her as if she were onstage. She was the only woman in our club, and she was striking. After cleaning her shoes, she walked over to our pinball machine, turned to Hank and, in almost flawless English, said, "Hank, you got a quarter?"

Hank reached into his pocket and handed her a fistful of change, then he turned to the first sergeant and began a nonstop barroom speech about his gambling adventures. He stopped only to guzzle his warm beer.

Hank was an overweight bragger. His fat stomach hung well over his belt line. We guessed he was in his mid-fifties. He had a puffy, red face and greasy gray hair. He wore a short-sleeved Hawaiian shirt that was tight on his large frame. His dusty shoes were made of blue canvas with white rubber soles; they were slip-ons.

In a loud semi-drunk voice designed for all of us in the club to hear, our first sergeant began the business of impressing his buddy Hank. He started with a story about a recent poker game. At full volume he barked, "Yeah, I kicked ass. I took those stupid shits for over five hundred bucks." Then he stopped, took a drink of his beer, and slammed the can on the bar. He squeezed the sides of the can until they bent.

Not to be outdone, Hank opened his mouth and in an earsplitting and obnoxious voice began his rant: "Yeah, me too. I kicked butt in Saigon, playing against those stupid-shit dockworkers. I took them for over eight hundred skins."

Hank raised his cigarette to his mouth and took a long, deep drag, then he looked around the room to see who was watching him. Although we all heard Hank, no one was watching him. We were, to a man, motionless and gazing at his Asian beauty. She was springing a small steel ball up a narrow channel on the pinball machine. Then she watched it roll down the incline, bouncing off small rubber posts and ringing a bell inside the machine. She had both her hands on the flippers, one on each side of the machine. Her lithe body moved to and fro as she pushed the flippers back and forth. She was as stunning from behind as she was from the front.

When Hank realized that no one was paying him any attention, he turned to his trophy girlfriend. He put his fat, tobacco-stained hand on his girl's ass. He pulled his open fingers through his oily gray hair. She turned to him, stretched, then gave him a long, slow kiss.

Peter looked at me, and we rolled our eyes. "Bought and paid for, Duffy," he said.

Satisfied that we all saw his kiss, Hank went back eyeball to eyeball, talking trash to the first sergeant.

I turned to look at Hank's girl. I wanted to get her attention. I had read somewhere about mental telepathy. I thought if I stared at the back of her head, I could make her turn to me. I imagined she would walk to our table and sit down with us. Then she would tell us that she wanted to dump her lard-ass contractor friend and join us. As hard as I stared at the back of her head, it didn't work. She never turned around, and she never seemed to notice us.

"Did you see that?" I asked Peter. "That fat ass is in our space pulling that shit. I can't watch this. I'm leaving." I got up to go, but Peter grabbed my arm and said, "Wait a minute, how can you leave this show?" He was right. I sat down again as the voyeur in me kept my eyes glued to this Asian beauty.

"Hey, Sarge," Hank belted out. "What you need in this joint is an air conditioner. You wanna air conditioner?"

Peter and I nodded at each other. We both thought if that could be pulled off it would make the club comfortable. Hank continued.

"Shit, I can get most anything I want off the docks—air conditioners, refrigerators, all new stuff from the States," he said. "They bring it in for the big-shot brass in Bien Hoa. But me and the dockworkers—see, I take care of them and they take care of me. They can't buy booze—you know the hard stuff—'cuz they're too young. I take care of them. Then, when I ask, they look the other way. Five-finger discounts."

Hank began to laugh again, showing his yellow teeth. They were pointy with gaps between them. He took a long drag off his Marlboro. Hank looked around the room to a quiet audience and then belched. He seemed a little annoyed that no one was paying him much attention. He put his hand back on his girlfriend's ass and said, "Hey, baby, maybe you and me shoullld"—Hank was beginning to slur his speech—"shoullld go back to my pad."

Hank began to laugh a slow drunk laugh. Tobacco smoke wafted out of his open mouth as he chuckled. He looked back at us and then took another deep pull off his fag. He turned to his girl and said loudly, "My bachelor pad, baby. You know what I mean?"

I looked at Peter and said, "What is he? Some kind of jag-off fucking beatnik? Bachelor pad," I exclaimed, "what the hell is that?" Peter and I thought Hank had probably started drinking that morning. At his quick rate of pounding down our beer, it would not be long before he passed out.

I told Peter I needed to take a walk. I got up and walked out of the club, past our mess hall, and over to one of the guns. I began making small talk with the men, trying to get my mind off that girl.

"Ready for tonight; I think you're firing."

"Yes, sir, we're ready."

I walked past the humming generator and into the swampy field toward our outpost on the river.

"Everything okay, guys?"

"Yes, sir, not much going on today, not even a boat to watch."

We often saw tanker and cargo ships glide past our position headed for the tank farm or the docks of Saigon.

I began walking back across the field and fantasized that maybe Hank would be passed out when I got back to the club. I would ask his companion if I could be of some assistance, perhaps I could drive this Asian beauty and Hank home, because Hank was in no condition to drive. Peter would want to drive or at least to come with us, but I outranked Peter. "Not this time, Peter, you're needed here." I imagined myself driving into Saigon with Hank passed out in the back seat. I would help his beauty shove his fat contractor ass through the door of his bachelor pad and then ask her if she would like a drink, perhaps a cup of tea. She would quickly answer yes. We would slam the door on Hank then drive to a club, a French club, and then have an early dinner. She would tell me how horrible it was being with Hank, but she needed to support her family. I would tell her that I understood and perhaps we could meet again, perhaps I could be of some assistance to her.

I walked past the generators onto the dirt path that led to the main road and Saigon. I saw the first sergeant waving at Hank; his girlfriend was kissing him as they drove away. I passed Peter. "Remember, Duffy," he said. "She is bought and paid for."

✳ ✳ ✳

On another Sunday afternoon while reading a book, I heard loud shouts from our compound. I walked out of my shady cubbyhole and saw a Sunday afternoon volleyball game. The Americans, with Owen as their leader, were playing a few South Vietnamese Army troops. These games were always one-sided. Owen put together a California volleyball squad, and all the players towered over the Vietnamese. Week after week it was no contest, the score was always lopsided and the Americans would crush the Vietnamese. It took me a few moments to figure out what was going on, but when I did, I could hardly believe my eyes. This time the Vietnamese were about to beat Owen's California beach boys.

The game was almost over, and the Vietnamese were excited and had a crowd of their friends cheering them on. The serve was with the Vietnamese, and Owen shouted orders to his teammates. I watched the ball fly back and forth, secretly hoping that the Vietnamese would win. A hard spike into the American side finished the game, and the Vietnamese cheered and began celebrating. Owen was visibly angry and stormed off the dusty road.

The next day Captain Tom called me to his hooch. He ducked under the small portal into the sunlight to talk with me. I never did see the inside of Captain's Tom's hooch. He thanked me for my service, then he handed me a letter. He told me that he had written me a letter of appreciation, and it was going into my permanent military file. He went on to say that he would be leaving for the States soon, and perhaps this letter would help me if I decided to make the army a career. I took the letter, read it, then thanked him and walked back to my bunker. The letter was flattering, but I couldn't understand Captain Tom's motivation in writing it. I just did my job like everyone else in the battery. I couldn't explain my feelings about the letter or the Vietnam War. After being there close to ten months, I was numb. I stuffed the letter into my cardboard folder and waited for the next fire mission.

As I walked back to my bunker, all I could think about was home. Although the letter was flattering, I would have gladly exchanged it for one less day in this war.

Chapter 9

THE BRONZE STAR

Every GI serving in Vietnam received two medals. The first was the Vietnam Service Medal. It was awarded by the U.S. government. The ribbon holding the medal was bright yellow with three red stripes running down the center and it has bright green edges. The second medal was awarded by the Republic of Vietnam. The ribbon holding this medal was green and white; it honored the GIs service helping the Republic of Vietnam during their war years. Before I arrived in Vietnam, I would look for these medals on officers or enlisted men during military functions or while passing through airports. I was interested in the soldiers that had been to Vietnam and I wanted to engage them and ask them about the war and what their job was.

Medals and insignia were and still are a very important part of the military's dress uniform, we nick named the medals fruit salad. The medals show everyone who is familiar with the decorations where a GI has been and what he or she has accomplished in military service. When I found myself at one of the large military bases in Vietnam or in the United States, I would always look over the colorful posters of these awards. The posters were usually pinned to an office wall or in the day rooms on military bases. The medals shown on the posters dated from World War II, Korea, and now Vietnam, I always enjoyed looking at them. That said, while serving in the bush of Vietnam, no one wore medals or for that matter thought much about them. Medals were a stateside luxury with little use in the jungles of Vietnam or in the grime of Nhá Bé.

I was looking over a reprint of one of the medal posters in our *Stars and Stripes* newspaper one morning; I was finishing my last cup of coffee. The mess hall women were in the kitchen talking and laughing and, I was alone at a table. I had a perfect view of Captain Tom's bunker; it seemed to me that it kept getting larger. This was no ordinary bunker. Captain Tom made some remodeling "improvements." The walls were now four sandbags thick, and he added an extra layer of sandbags to the roof. This was a lot of weight, so the men had to find more wooden beams and add them to keep the roof from sagging. The bunker was finished off with two additional sandbagged walls facing our muddy road; it now looked like the entrance to an igloo. Captain Tom spent a large part of the day and night in his bunker. I think it made him feel safe.

After Lieutenant Smith's departure, I took over the everyday operations of the unit. I performed my duties with a deep respect for our deadly artillery. I constantly checked our guns. I checked on the men, the ammunition, and the nightly fire missions worked up in our FDC bunker. The worrywart in me emerged, and I checked everything once again. I was scared to death about making a mistake.

My frequent visits to the FDC bunker were upsetting to Lieutenant Owen. I knew this, and it made us both uncomfortable, but I did it anyway; it was my job. What was most important to me was preventing an error. A mistake on the guns could mean huge problems for everyone. It could put a huge, black spot on our records, and it could keep Captain Tom from getting his next promotion. An errant artillery round landing in the wrong place was sure to bring a reprimand. But my worst fear was a case of friendly fire— killing our own troops. It certainly would have lasting consequences for a career army officer like Captain Tom and bring punishment to all involved, not to mention the guilt I would feel about wounding or killing our own men.

Our position at Nhá Bé, adjacent to the giant fuel storage tanks, put our unit in the line of VC fire. If they decided to send off a volley of rockets and blow up the tank farm, our unit would surely be in their path. A constant stream of ships from the Middle East steamed up the Nhá Bé River and kept the tanks full of gasoline and jet and diesel fuel, and a hit would be a huge prize for Charlie. The tank farm was on the VC target list, and we all knew it.

My evenings at Nhá Bé were spent preparing for our late-night fire missions. This was a routine job I had down pat. After checking ammunition stores and the guns, I made my nightly stop in the FDC bunker. If Owen was on duty, I would get a blank stare. If Owen was not on duty, I could relax a bit. Each night, I scanned the targets for the evening's fire missions. The targets were designated by a series of pushpins stuck in our velum charts. The charts had red hash marks here and there representing villages and military bases. I reviewed the targets then decided what direction to point the guns. The night's targets were radioed to us earlier in the day from headquarters. Once we computed the distance and the direction to the target, we then figured the elevation and deflection using our slide rules. I always studied the topographical maps pinned to the FDC wall to ensure the targets were not near an overlooked fishing village or a cluster of huts. When

I became familiar with the targets, I walked out to lay the battery or point the guns in the right direction.

Our cannons had limits to their left and right movements. We needed to make sure that all the targets were within the traverse range of the guns. The 105-milimeter artillery tube could turn only so far then the tube stopped.

With the azimuth for the guns written on my ever-present clipboard, I walked to our aiming circle, an optical device designed to position the gun tubes in the direction of the target. This instrument stood on a wooden platform elevated above the guns. Each gunner needed a line of vision from the howitzer to the aiming circle to fix his gun sight and aim the cannon in the correct direction.

The path I walked from the FDC bunker to the aiming circle took me past Captain Tom's hooch. I usually peeked through the small opening to see if I could see a light or hear the typewriter. After checking the maps and charts, I walked over to the aiming circle platform, climbed up a small set of steps, then instructed the gunners to move the tube of the gun in line with the light on my aiming instrument. I used a flashlight so the gunners could get a gross fix through their sights. After that, we fine-tuned our instruments until the guns were pointed in the exact direction shown on our velum charts.

Late one fall night, I glanced up from the aiming circle to see a pitch-black sky—there was no moon. As I stood on the platform looking through the aiming instrument, I heard an enormous roar over my head. It was the sound of Chinese or Russian 122-millimeter rockets screaming into our camp. I jumped from the platform and ran to a gun pit. We all listened as the rockets landed in a muddy field just beyond our position. The rockets didn't explode. The muddy field did not offer enough resistance to ram the plunger and ignite the fuse. The rockets would stay buried until some unlucky farmer hit them with his plow. We all looked at one another. We knew we had just dodged a very large bullet; it was only with luck that it didn't land on us.

I quickly figured we had some time before the next volley arrived. The Viet Cong used bamboo supports to prop up the rockets. When the rockets were launched, the back blast from the rockets scattered these rickety platforms. Before the VC could launch another volley, they needed to reassemble the flimsy bamboo launch pad. That done, they carried the large, six-foot rockets, one at a time, and then pointed them toward our position. I figured we had about ten minutes before the next volley, if there *was* a next volley.

I told the men to turn the guns in the direction of the rocket fire. I had a good sense of direction, and I was sure they were coming from the south. I stuck a pole into the ground and told them to point the tube in the direction of the pole. I would be back with an elevation after I looked over the charts in the FDC room. I ran to Captain Tom's bunker and called to him through his small doorway. "Sir, we're getting hit," I shouted.

There was dead silence from his bunker. I stood in front of his small doorway and waited, but still there was no answer. I thought, *He may have already gone to our FDC room to help with operations.* I was about to leave when I heard a soft voice from within, "Lieutenant Duffy."

I answered with a question in my voice, "Yes, sir?"

"Lieutenant Duffy, can you handle the situation?"

I paused then asked, "Sir, you're not coming out?"

He answered with a firm no.

I answered him back, "Yes, sir, I'll handle the situation."

As I sprinted to the FDC bunker, I thought, *Why is this guy here?* A career army soldier—this is what all those guys were trained for. Why do they go into the army if they don't want the risk?

This was the second time in Vietnam I had this experience with a career soldier. I didn't get it. I was the draftee, the citizen soldier, just doing my duty for God and country.

I forgot about Captain Tom and ran into the FDC bunker. I picked up a pushpin and stood over the velum chart. Owen saw the determination on my face. He began a modest protest, but I waved him off. I don't think the men in the bunker heard the rockets because a large fan was humming in the room. I said, "We're getting hit, and the rocket fire is coming from …" I paused, then I placed the pushpin high on the chart, "here."

I motioned to the chart man, and he carefully moved a metal straight edge toward the pin I had just placed on the chart. I took a pencil and drew a long straight line running down the metal edge, from the top of the chart all the way to a second pin representing our position. I looked up, the room was quiet. I made eye contact with Owen and said, "The rocket fire is coming from somewhere along this line. I need a deflection number."

Then, as if by providence, our radio crackled. An officer at the small navy base to the south of us announced that he had seen the rocket fire and had a fix on the launch site. He slowly read the azimuth numbers.

With the azimuth from the navy, I placed a second straight edge on the chart representing the navy's position. Then I positioned the long, metal ruler in the direction the navy gave us. I followed it out until it crossed my pencil line. We now had a target. I had the chart man push another pin at the intersection of my pencil line and the navy's line. That was where the fire was coming from. I quickly glanced at the wall map and saw the launch area was a mangrove swamp with no nearby villages. I looked directly at Owen and told him to work up numbers for the guns. "We're gonna blast away," I said. He quickly worked up the numbers on his slide rules then wrote them on a piece of paper. I grabbed the paper and ran out to the guns.

Once at the guns, I had the gunner begin turning the tube toward our target. But as he spun the small wheel that moved the tube, it stopped short. The tube had reached its traverse limit. We were close, only a foot or two. I shouted at the men to bump the trails. If the tube on the gun carriage would not move, we could move the entire carriage by lifting the trails. Those were the long iron gun supports dug into the ground. This was an unrefined measurement, but I had done it before and I was confident it would work. There was no time to re-lay the guns with the aiming circle.

The men on the gun began lifting the trails then pushing and shoving the artillery piece. It was hard work in the cramped and crowded gun position. I jumped into the pit and began helping. As I pulled the trails in pitch darkness, my left heel caught the edge of an unseen ammunition crate. I fell back into a stack of 105-millimeter ammunition. My upper back muscles wrenched in pain. I used my right hand to break my fall, only to fill it with slivers from a wooden crate. I got back on my feet just as more rockets screamed over our heads. We all jumped deep into the gun pit and waited. This second volley exploded in a flash of white light and ear-piercing sound just beyond our position. A moment passed, and then I motioned everyone to get back to work. We elevated the tube to the correct elevation, the charge was set and shells were chambered, then the breech was closed. The crew chief yelled, "Ready, *fire.*"

The gunner pulled the lanyard, and in a deafening roar, the shell exploded out of the gun. Then we fired again. After the barrage from our gun, I quickly glanced at my watch. It was just a few minutes since the last volley from Charlie. I had everyone jump back into the gun pit. I was watching the timing between volleys of incoming rocket fire. I figured the time between volleys was the time the VC needed to reload. My estimation was correct because another volley flew over our heads. This time the rockets smashed into the fuel tanks, starting a ferocious fire. The flames and smoke began filling the air. We were lucky—a soft breeze from the southeast kept us out of the path of the dense black smoke.

We continued to fire, and the VC continued to fire back at us. Time seemed abstract. Our adrenaline was up, and we all were focused on firing our guns and stopping the rockets. Some of the men in our unit were called to help fight the fires now raging at the tank farm. The flames and smoke were towering high above our compound. The fire was raging out of control and threating a tanker ship docked close to the flaming storage facility.

Our FDC bunker called down another fire mission. An infantry unit was engaged with the VC and needed artillery fire. I ran to guns four and five as the men quickly set the new azimuth then spun their tubes in the direction of the target. They began firing nonstop. There were explosions from the incoming rockets and our guns firing back, blasting round after round. The noise was thunderous.

After a time, the rocket fire stopped. Maybe we stopped it or maybe the VC ran out of rockets. Dawn broke, but the fires at the tank farm were still burning. I laid eyes on a massive cloud of smoke as it billowed into the morning sky hundreds of feet above us. The metal tanks were melting from the heat and they were collapsing in on themselves. The tanker ship was cut loose from the dock and now sat idle in the middle of the Nhá Bé river. We were exhausted. I told the few men left on the gun to take a break. I walked to my small hooch and lay down. This time I took off my boots and socks. My eyes closed, and I fell into a deep sleep.

At about 8:00 a.m., I was summoned to Captain Tom's bunker. Groggy and exhausted, I pulled on my wet socks and boots, then I walked over to the opening in his bunker. I announced my arrival with a "sir?" He emerged into the morning light and looked at me with a curious expression. He told me that headquarters had called him early that morning and requested a full written report detailing last night's rocket attack and the actions our unit took to destroy the enemy fire. He paused then said, "You will have to write the report. When you are done, bring it to me for a signature." He turned and disappeared into his bunker.

As I walked back to my hooch, I thought, *Of course I have to write the fucking report since he had never left his rocket-proof box during the attack.* I grabbed my clipboard with the previous night's azimuth and deflection numbers scribbled on it and walked over to our headquarters bunker to borrow the typewriter. I sat at an olive-drab table, over an olive-drab typewriter, and pecked out my report line by line. At one point, I tried to use my typing skills from high school. I put my fingers on the home keys and looked at my handwritten notes. Then I began to type. I looked up only to find that my fingers had shifted one key away from the home keys and I had typed gibberish. I started again. The first rockets had hit our position at about 11:30 p.m. I guessed at the time of the next volley, then went on to explain how we got a fix on the VC launch site and fired back. I mentioned the navy's help and the computations made in our FDC bunker. I added that we had moved the gun carriage by bumping the trails when the tube reached its traverse limit. I tried to be as thorough as possible. The one thing I did not mention was Captain Tom's complete absence from the hellish night's attack. I wanted to, but I didn't.

When I completed the report, I walked back to Captain Tom's bunker and handed him the papers. He ducked back inside to read it. I walked to the mess hall and got a cup of coffee; this morning it had a metallic flavor with a hint of soapsuds. Then I walked outside to watch the fuel tanks as they continued to burn. I noticed that the women in the mess hall had not made it to work; maybe that's why the coffee was so bad. I also noticed that our barber was missing from his small Hot Toc barbershop. Jack Smith was right when he said that we would never get rocketed with either the women or the barber on base. After a short time, Captain Tom called me back to his bunker. He had a small problem. A change in plans had been radioed to our unit by the brass at headquarters. He explained to me, with some concern in his voice, that headquarters called and requested a face-to-face oral report from him. He told me he had replied back to headquarters that I would be traveling to Bien Hoa to give the face to face. Then Captain Tom handed me the signed papers, nodded his approval, and ordered me to drive to Bien Hoa and meet with the colonel. I was to leave at once. I found a driver, got in a jeep, and nodded off as we headed to Bien Hoa. I was drained from our night of firing, and I had no interest in changing clothes or polishing my boots. I looked and felt like a worn-out slob. That morning I had even spilled grits on my pants. They made a stubborn stain, but it blended in with the dirt on my jungle fatigues.

We drove out of Nhá Bé, north into and through Saigon, then northwest to Bien Hoa, our headquarters post. As we pulled up to the building, I turned to see an enormous cloud of smoke from last night's attack hanging in the sky. I walked into the HQ building and I was surprised to find it air conditioned; it was comfortable. Two tidy office clerks stopped their typing and gave me the once-over. I'm sure they expected a well-groomed officer. "Sir," one of them said, "if you would like, we have a can of shoe polish here. You can brush up your boots before you go in to see the colonel?" I shook my head as I walked past him and said, "No, thanks." The poor man looked upset. I was a little nervous about meeting with the colonel, but I had all the facts typed in my report and I felt I had an answer for any question he might throw at me.

I was escorted into the colonel's office. I saluted, handed him my report, then stood as he read it. He never offered me a seat. When he finished reading, he looked up at me. I thought he was about to give me a lecture on my filthy fatigues, but he didn't. He began asking questions. He asked me how we got a fix on the enemy rocket launch site. I could see he was impressed with our quick response. After fifteen minutes of questions and answers, I was dismissed and began the trip back to our unit. The colonel never mentioned Captain Tom, and I never brought his name up.

When I arrived back at camp, Captain Tom called me to his bunker and asked for yet another oral report, this time about my meeting with the colonel. I guessed he was worried about his absence. I told him the meeting was quick and it had gone well. Then I asked to be excused; I was exhausted and I needed some sleep.

Weeks after the rocket attack, I was told of a small assembly near our helipad. A few citations were to be awarded by the battalion commander, and I was ordered to attend. I walked to the helipad just as a Huey was landing. A colonel and his aide jumped out of the helicopter as a few of us stood waiting. They walked over to us, and we were called to attention. I watched as the colonel's aide handed him a few papers. The aide wore a bright metal yellow bar on his shirt collar. He had clean, polished boots and neatly pressed and starched fatigues and he looked nervous. His tidy image was a stark contrast to our filth and our weary eyes. This disparity bothered me. I wanted to grab this fucking butter bar and have him spend a few sleepless nights here with us. I wanted to see his clean-shaven face covered with dust and mud, then watch fear build in him as night approached. We owned the daylight hours, but the VC owned the night. The aid looked out of place.

After a few words, the colonel walked over to me, nodded, and then pinned a Bronze Star on my chest. I was flattered. I thought, *What did I do to deserve a medal?* I looked around at our small formation; there were just a few people in attendance. Soon we were dismissed, and the colonel and his aide quickly walked back to the helicopter and flew off. There was no congratulatory gathering or a toast to the three of us who had received medals. There was no joy. I jotted a note to my parents and mentioned my medal.

Although Lieutenants Owen and Hart were invited, they did not attend our small ceremony, and my award was never mentioned. I stuffed the small, black case holding my Bronze Star into my duffle bag. In the evening hours before our guns began firing, I would take the medal out of its case and look it over. The black case also held a small lapel pin. The pin was made of cloisonné in the same colors as the Bronze Star. It was designed for the lapel of a civilian suit coat. The medal hung from a red silk ribbon and it had a blue line in the middle. I liked holding it and looking it over. However, I would have gladly traded it for a ticket home.

DEPARTMENT OF THE ARMY
HEADQUARTERS, UNITED STATES ARMY VIETNAM
APO SAN FRANCISCO 96375

IN REPLY REFER TO

AVHAG-PD

2 6 NOV 1968

SUBJECT: Transmittal of Award

Commanding Officer
54th Artillery Group
APO 96491

1. /‾X‾/ The attached Medal, Certificate, Citation and General Orders,
pertaining to the award of the___ Bronze Star Medal_____ to
_1LT Michael J. Duffy_____,_____ _____ are forwarded for
appropriate presentation.

2. /‾X‾/ Copies of the Citation and General Orders for the individual's
Military Personnel Records are included.

3. /‾X‾/ If the individual has departed your command, request this
correspondence be forwarded to his present commander.

4. /‾‾/

FOR THE COMMANDER:

4Incl
as

JAMES E. LOVE
Major, AGC
Asst Adjutant General

USARV FL 158a Revised 15 Mar 68 PREVIOUS EDITIONS OF THIS FL MAY BE USED.

Chapter 10

THE MISTAKE

I was exhausted, and it was beginning to show. One night I found myself shouting at my radio operator, "Get me the deflection and elevation!" I couldn't understand why he was not responding. Finally, I heard his voice. He kept repeating himself, "Sir, there is no fire mission." I was sleepwalking and had awakened standing in front of him. Only then did I realize my mistake.

Most every night when I walked over to the FDC bunker, I would find Lieutenant Hart talking with Owen. In my awkward way, I would inform Hart it was time to walk the guns. This ritual was like tooth extraction. Even though Hart always joined me, Owen always made it unpleasant. Owen had successfully convinced Hart that an officer's presence on the guns was unnecessary. I felt that Owen was intentionally trying to impede my every decision, and he never let up.

Captain Tom was now gone; he had rotated back to the States. Captain Tom's replacement was also a career military captain. We gave him a bit of distance because he was new, and we were still getting to know him.

I lingered in the mess hall after our meals and talked with the Vietnamese women—Baby-san, Mama-san Mop, and the others. They told me of their all-day shopping trips to Saigon, trips that would have been impossible without the wages we paid them. Life for those women was filled with poverty, but it was better than the subsistence farms that most came from. Their small farms required nonstop manual labor, and there was never money for a Saigon shopping trip. I enjoyed those short conversations in the mess hall; they took my mind off my work, if only for a short fifteen minutes.

One night the gunnery sergeant and I tried to contact the two men on duty in our guard tower. The guard tower sat on the edge of the Sông Nhá Bé River about 500 feet from our main camp. We were using our squawk-box system of communication, but it wasn't working. After repeated attempts to establish contact, the gunnery sergeant and I walked out to the tower. We found both young privates in a deep sleep. The gunnery sergeant woke them and gave them a thorough tongue-lashing. As punishment, I decided to give each man two weeks of latrine duty. The men in the unit hated latrine duty, or the shit detail as they called it. Every few days, the men on this duty pulled out metal drums from beneath our wooden outhouses; the drums were filled with feces and urine. Fifty-five-gallon metal drums were cut in half, then positioned under our outhouses, they collected this fecal cocktail every day. The men on the shit detail poured diesel fuel into each half barrel and set them on fire. A foul-smelling smoke filled the air. It was a cursed job. Either the gunnery sergeant didn't hear me or I was misunderstood, because the next morning, I was informed that both men were turned into the captain for Article 15s.[17] The gunnery sergeant upgraded the punishment without consulting me first.

The pending Article 15s put me in a difficult spot. Just a few weeks earlier, I had used the two-week latrine punishment for a sim-

---

17. An Article 15 is a formal military punishment placed on a soldier's permanent record.

ilar offense. I did it quietly and without notifying our first sergeant. My latrine duty punishment kept any formal written penalty off the soldiers' records. Soon word got out that the two new offenders were facing Article 15s. I was now seen as an officer who worked with a double standard. It made no difference that our gunnery sergeant had turned the men in without my knowledge; I took the heat.

One night less than a week after the Article 15s were issued, I was confronted by one of the punished men. He was visibly intoxicated. A crowd gathered around us, and in slurred speech, he began his rant. He called me an officer who played favorites. I stood my ground and listened as the crowd of enlisted men grew. I let him finish, then I told his fellow crew members to put him to bed. I thought about handing him more punishment, but I didn't. I did manage to tell him that his biggest mistake was getting caught sleeping on duty by our go-by-the-book sergeant. The crowd dispersed, and I went to my hooch and waited for the squawk box to call out the next fire mission.

I was in a constant state of sleep deprivation. Every few hours, I jumped from my cot to the piercing words from the squawk box, "Fire mission." I rolled from my narrow bed and listened, then scribbled the powder charge, elevation, and the deflections numbers on my clipboard. That done, I walked to the guns that were about to fire; the guns were rarely fired without my presence.

The constant night and day firing, along with my executive officer responsibilities, drained me. Amoebic dysentery found its way back into my system, and I began to lose weight again. I started each new day with a mantra murmured to myself, "One day down and one day closer to home." Sometimes I counted half-days.

Late one afternoon, Lieutenant Hart walked over to my hooch. After some small talk, he suggested that I take the night off and get some rest. He had been working with me for more than a month in preparation for my departure and his appointment as the next XO. He knew our procedures and he knew his duties well. But although I was beat-tired that night, I was uneasy about handing him the responsibility of the battery. I held a sense in my gut he didn't take our job seriously, or as seriously as I did. Each day and night we worked together, this doubt surfaced and it troubled me. I believed there was a risk in handing my XO duties to him, but I didn't know why. I stalled Hart and said I would think about his offer and get back to him. I went on to tell him that I was not that tired. My body didn't believe that lie, and as hard as I tried, I could not fight off the fatigue.

That afternoon while reading a copy of *Stars and Stripes*, our local paper published in Saigon, I was approached by one of the enlisted men. "Sir?"

It was Burgess, one of the men from our gun crew.

"Burgess, what do you need?" I asked.

"Sir, I was won'er-in' if you could sign my allotment papers."

The army's allotment papers were documents designed to send a portion of a GI's pay into a savings account or back to the United States to a spouse or a family member. I looked at Burgess and said, "Well, I guess I could Burgess, but that task is usually handled by the first sergeant. Have you talked to him?"

"Yes, sir, he told me to come to you."

That was odd since our first sergeant barely gave me the time of day. He thought of me as an inexperienced twenty-two-year-old lieutenant. He was a forty-five-year-old decorated veteran of the Korean War. I looked at Burgess then asked, "How do you want to change your allotment?"

I watched him nervously twist the allotment papers in his hand, then Burgess began a dialogue. "Well, sir, right now I am sending ninety percent of my pay back home to my folks. They are saving it for me, you know, for when I get back to the States." He continued, "Well, sir, now I wanna send it to my fiancée."

I thought this seemed like a reasonable request. I looked at Burgess then asked, "Okay, so now you want to send ninety percent of your pay to your fiancée. Burgess, is your fiancée the same girl you have a picture of in the gun pit?"

"Oh, no, sir, this is a new girl."

I was puzzled. Burgess had a small black-and-white photo of a girl pinned above his bunk. It looked like a high school yearbook picture. The girl had her hair combed in a sixties bouffant style and wore glasses that flared to a point at the edges. Her mouth almost revealed a smile, but some hidden self-control or a case of nerves kept it off her face. If I was asked to rate her looks, I would probably call her plain, and even that description might be a stretch. I looked at Burgess and then asked, "Burgess, if your fiancée is not the girl pictured in the gun pit, then who is your fiancée?"

"Well, sir, it's a new girl."

I congratulated Burgess.

"Great, best to you and the bride to be. Tell me about her."

"Well, sir, we are in love. We are going to get married just as soon as I get home and bring her over."

The words "bring her over" puzzled me. Once again I stopped Burgess from talking and asked, "Bring her over—what do you mean by bring her over? Bring her over from where?"

"Well, sir, Taipei."

"Burgess when were you in Taipei?"

Burgess looked at me, paused, and said, "Sir, don't you remember I was off on R&R last week?"

I lied. "Oh, yes, now I remember. Did you meet this new girl in Taipei?"

"Yes, sir, I did."

Taipei is the capital city of Taiwan, the Republic of China. It's a favorite of the GIs—lots of bars and lots of girls. I continued to ask Burgess questions. "Burgess, how did you meet this girl?"

As Burgess continued twisting the allotment papers, he looked at me and began his story. "Sir, I met her in the hotel. She was down in the lobby, and I was walkin' around looking things over, and we just met right there in the hotel lobby. She was real nice to me. She was nicer than any girl I ever met in the States. She said she could show me around town, 'cuz she was off work and had some free time. I thought, sure, why not. So we took a walk, and then she says, 'Let's take a boat ride.' So we did, and we went up and down the harbor on this tour boat. She tried to pay, but I said no way 'cuz my folks had just sent me $400 for R&R. She told me about her life and how she works in a club as a dancer. She hates it and wants to quit, but she can't. You see, sir, her boss is real mean, and he tells her if she quits he will sell her contract to the Chinese mob."

I was puzzled. I looked at Burgess and then asked, "The Chinese mob?"

"Yes, sir, the Chinese mob. Well, sir, we spent the whole day together, and she asked if we could see each other the next day. I couldn't believe it, sir. No girl has ever asked me that."

I stopped him and said, "Burgess, tell me about the picture of the girl you have in the gun pit. Who is she?"

"Well, sir, she's a girl I knew from high school. I had my friend back home send me her picture. She really isn't my girlfriend. I just told everyone she was 'cuz they all had pictures of girlfriends and I didn't. You know, sir, all the guys were teasing me about not being able to get a girlfriend."

I took a good look at Burgess. He was short and pudgy. He had a face full of ripe pimples, and his hair was greasy and pushed to one side of his head. Burgess looked about eighteen years old, but he may have been younger. Often a kid from the States would drop out of high school and get his parents to sign a release letting a seventeen-year-old join the army. I guessed Burgess was probably a high school dropout. I was sure the girl in Taipei was the first girl who had ever taken notice of him. I was also sure that she had taken him to bed, and now she was wanted to take him to the cleaners. It was a twist on the old confidence game. Only this time, it was not money and greed that seduced the victim but lust and loneliness. Here in Vietnam there was plenty of each.

The girls working the Taipei hotels needed elementary English to hunt their prey. If they were good and the American GI fell for their story, a Taipei working girl could get more cash out of her mark after he returned to Vietnam. And if the girl was very good, she could convince the mark to continue sending checks, even after the GI was discharged and back home in the States.

Some girls used professional letter writers to compose sweet love sonnets doused in cheap perfume. The stories were endless and always ended with the words, "I love you and send money." The letters should have read: send money, then I'll love you. Some of the real professional girls might get five or six sucker GIs to keep mailing them checks.

A jaded and savvy GI on R&R would hook up with a girl for a week, slip her a tidy tip, then head back to Vietnam with a smile on his face. The innocent and love-struck Burgess swallowed the bait.

I looked at Burgess as he continued to twist the allotment papers in his hands. "Okay, hand me the papers." I said. I pulled a black ballpoint pen from my clipboard and signed his papers. I handed them back to Burgess and wished him luck. A smile crossed his face—he was happy. Burgess thanked me and walked away.

I headed straight to our headquarters bunker and to our first sergeant. As I walked into the office, I saw the first sergeant pecking away on our battery typewriter. He looked annoyed. "Good afternoon, Top."

He turned from his typewriter irritated, looked at me, and said, "Sir?"

"Sergeant, it's about Burgess."

"Yes, sir, the captain left for Long Binh this morning. I was busy, so I sent Burgess to you."

"Well, Top," I said, "I just signed Burgess' allotment papers."

He heard my words, and his face contorted. He rose from his desk and faced me, then with a controlled anger he blurted, "Shit, sir, you don't believe that story about him getting married, do you?"

"No, Top, I don't believe the story, but Burgess does."

Top was furious as he ranted on. "Sir, Burgess is one of my men, and I don't want any of my men fleeced by some Chink whore."

His words stung. They were filled with hate. Top despised and mistrusted all Asians. It didn't matter what country they were from— he put them all in his not-to-be-trusted file.

I looked at him then said, "Sergeant, it's his money. If he wants to send it to the Queen of England, he has that right. It's not your money or my money; it's his. I signed the papers." I turned and left his small office. I made another enemy that day trying to accommodate an enlisted man. I also was sure that Top would wait until our new captain returned from Bien Hoa and then talk him into tearing up Burgess's allotment papers. But Burgess was happy, if only for a little while. As I walked back to my bunker, I saw Hart, and I was reminded of *his* request.

Hart's request to take over command of the guns that night was rattling around my head all afternoon. I thought, *I could use the sleep*. But would he check the guns the way I check them? Would he watch the guns as they fired, looking for mistakes from men who were equally tired? I was torn and I couldn't make up my mind.

As afternoon turned to evening, my doubt of Hart's ability gave way to fatigue. I approached him in his hooch and told him to take over the night's duties. I looked him in the eye and said, "You are now in charge of the guns. Make sure they don't fire without your supervision." He nodded.

Then I walked to my bunk along with the grime of the day. Not caring to wash, I fell into a deep sleep because, for one evening, I had shifted my responsibilities to Lieutenant Hart.

I awoke the next morning to a horrific situation. During the night, our guns had dropped two rounds of friendly fire into Saigon. We sat about eight miles south of Saigon and just a small sliver of it was within our artillery range. But this sliver was a heavily populated area of rundown huts that housed the civilian work force of Saigon.

During the previous night, while I was sleeping, Owen and Hart had performed a series of frantic investigations rechecking targets, deflection numbers, powder charge numbers, and elevation numbers. Their hope was to shift the blame of this error to our ARVN neighbors, who had also fired during the night. It was concluded, however, that two rounds of "friendly fire" had come from our battery. During one

of the early-morning fire missions, a gun in our unit ran out of artillery shells. The gun was shooting a number-four charge that would
drop the shell a few miles short of Saigon in a suspected enemy area.

The crew chief radioed the FDC bunker reporting they had run
out of ammunition. After discussing the situation in the FDC bunker,
the officers in charge, Hart and Owen, decided to pull two rounds of
ammunition from an adjacent gun and finish the mission. They made
this decision without leaving the FDC bunker.

It was easy to borrow two shells from a nearby gun crew. The
normal supply procedure of pulling artillery shells from our ammunition dump would take time and effort, albeit just a little effort. The
men on the gun were lazy, they didn't want to walk out to our ammo
dump and check out more ammunition. The crew in the adjacent gun
pit quickly placed the high-explosive bullets into the brass canisters
and passed the two shells over. The mistake was there. The gunners
receiving the two shells failed to check the powder charge inside the
canister. The powder charge was now incorrectly set at a charge of
seven. A charge seven sent the round another three miles north into
a squalid section of Saigon.

When I found out what had happened, I ran to the gun and
demanded to know who caused this monumental fuck up. Where
was Lieutenant Hart last night? I soon found out. He had spent the
entire night in the FDC bunker with his buddy Owen in a feckless
orgy of jokes, laughs, and coffee. Meanwhile, an exhausted gun crew
had made a sequence of errors that, under proper supervision, could
have been avoided.

Hart was seduced by Owen to forget his responsibility and forget
my nightly mantra to him as we walked the guns, "Don't let the guns
fire without supervision!" I knew I would have caught this error, and the

mistake would not have happened. I audibly cursed myself for taking the night off, "You stupid fucking shit, Duffy!" I said to myself.

I also felt betrayed. With his arrogant attitude toward me, Owen dismissed all our training from Officer Candidate School back in Fort Sill. Lieutenant Hart fell for Owen's picture of me as an overcautious micromanager. The guns fired without supervision; there was no officer at the guns as our SOP (standard operating procedure) required.

For the first time since he had arrived in our unit, Owen looked worried. His haughty attitude vanished. I stood in the FDC bunker demanding an explanation. He and Hart told me that they were aware of the error shortly after it happened. The gunners informed FDC that an error had probably occurred. Soon after this horrible news, an emergency radio message came from our command ordering all the artillery batteries to check their fire (cease firing) and review their missions. A military post in Saigon had reported seeing incoming rounds.

Hart and Owen did not wake me because they believed nothing could be done until morning anyway. That was the only wise decision they had made. I was furious.

I left the FDC bunker distraught and seething with anger. I walked to the headquarters bunker and waited as our new captain finished a discussion with the first sergeant; they both looked terrible. When he finished, he turned to me and in a somber voice told me that our guns were responsible for three civilian deaths. He asked me if I would travel to Saigon to survey the damage and talk to the family of the dead. I hesitated, thinking to myself that this visit to Saigon should be a job for Lieutenants Hart and Owen. He looked at me with near panic in his face, then he said, "Duffy, I need to debrief Hart and Owen. Battalion headquarters is flying a major to our unit this afternoon; he wants to review all of last night's fire missions." He hesitated then said, "The major wants to review this fuckup himself." I said okay. That was the first and the last time I heard him say the word "fuckup." Lieutenant Nguyen, our ARVN neighbor, would accompany me as an interpreter because I could not speak or understand the Vietnamese language. I found a driver and a jeep, and we were off to Saigon.

We drove out of camp and headed north. The normally pleasant drive through the lush rice paddies was blurred with my anger. The road from Nhá Bé to Saigon received light military traffic. Beyond our camp, there was only the small navy base.

As we neared Saigon, I watched the rice paddies give way to lots filled with trash. The garbage the Americans left behind became the treasure of the Vietnamese scavengers. They would spend whole days looking for beer cans, lumber, nails, or anything on the junk pile that could be sold on the streets of Saigon. Lieutenant Nguyen leaned forward and in broken English explained the area in Saigon we were traveling into was very dangerous. He told me he would handle things, and we must not stay long. He took a deep drag off his cigarette and nodded to me. He looked worried as he repeated the words, "We must not stay long, very dangerous."

We wound our way through the narrow streets of Saigon, kicking up dust from the unpaved streets. Women and children and old men stood in the portals of tin-roofed shacks made of weathered boards and held together with rusty nails. They quietly watched us pass. I felt good about having Lieutenant Nguyen with me. He could speak the language, and these people could see that I had one of them as a friend. But the people did not look friendly; they stared at me with blank eyes. My heart began to thump as fear rose in me.

From my quick glance at the charts this morning, I knew that we were coming close to the point of impact. I didn't know what to expect. God, how I wished I had Owen and Hart with me so they could feel the despair here and experience this awful mission. We passed a Saigon cowboy. He flicked the butt of his cigarette at us as he yelled, "Fuck you, GI."

Lieutenant Nguyen guided the driver through a series of narrow dirt streets. To me, this was nothing but a maze of confusing lanes, where, if left alone, I would never find my way out. There were no street signs, no curbs or sidewalks. Everything seemed to be built without thought or planning.

Lieutenant Nguyen had our driver stop near a narrow canal filled with a fetid liquid the color of used motor oil. Barges and sampans were lined up against each bank of this narrow waterway. I saw people living on the vessels, their laundry hanging from ropes stretched from the craft to a post on the dock. The stench from the canal made me breathe through my mouth. I watched a young boy urinate off the side of a sampan into the water.

This channel was a dead-end slip built by French businessmen at the turn of the nineteenth century. At one time, the canal provided a transfer point from land to sea for the bountiful Southeast Asian rubber product. The commercial vessels that had docked here fifty years earlier were long gone, replaced by paint-chipped wooden sampans. Poverty, filth, and hopelessness had a new home here.

Lieutenant Nguyen looked at a piece of paper he held in his hand and motioned the driver toward a lane leading away from the canal. I secretly thanked him. As we passed a group of children, they yelled in unison, "Numba one GI." That was a common signal to the GIs to toss a candy bar or gum. I was in no mood to toss candy today. Our driver slowed at

Lieutenant Nguyen's request and then stopped in front of a rusty wood and tin structure. It had an open portal with a long, narrow hall leading into living quarters. There was a second story to this house; with a low ceiling, it was also made of corrugated tin and gray wood planking. A rope ladder provided access to the second floor. This was poverty in pure form: no running water, no electricity, and no sanitation.

At first glance, the house looked unharmed, but after a closer look, I realized there was no roof. Our shells had fallen toward the rear of this shelter and scored a direct hit on this family's sleeping quarters. We were told that a young woman and her two children, a twelve-year-old girl and a nine-year-old boy, had occupied the space. A small crowd gathered around us, and they wore looks of sorrow. I began looking over the damage as Lieutenant Nguyen talked to an old man with a wispy white beard.

The old man, who I assumed to be a grandfather or some important family elder, was grateful we were here, and he accepted our words of sympathy from Lieutenant Nguyen. Now he wanted us to view the bodies. We followed him as he walked us down a passage. My breathing became heavy, and all I wanted to do was leave. I did not want to follow this old man, and I did not want to see the corpses. I had seen dead VC on the roads during the Tet Offensive; that didn't bother me because they were armed combatants, but the thought of seeing a dead woman and her children made me feel wretched.

We entered a dimly lit room. An old woman in the corner was sobbing, and a few other people were standing near her. All eyes met mine as I entered, except those of the old woman. She continued sobbing quietly. I greeted the people with a nod, and I lowered my head in an awkward sign of respect. The old man introduced us to the others and explained why we were there. My eyes fell on the woman in the corner again. She barely responded to our presence. The old man gestured toward a table in the room. It took me a moment before I realized why.

There on the kitchen table was a white sheet with three forms beneath it, one larger than the others. The sheet was covered with flies, and they were buzzing around our heads. As I began to comprehend what I was viewing, my composure changed; fear and panic replaced my ignorance. My throat dried, and it was hard to swallow. The old man reached for the top of the sheet. Something inside of me pleaded with him to leave the bodies covered. God, how I wished Owen and Hart were there to smell the death and feel this grief. These innocent children had every right to live, and this woman who was in the prime of her life was now gone. Our guns had taken their lives because Hart and our crew had not done their jobs.

The old man didn't hear my silent request, and he pulled back the sheet, revealing a horrific sight. I stared at the lifeless remains of a mother and her children. Their bodies were charred beyond recognition. They looked like grotesque clay figures fired in a kiln with a matte black glaze. Their arms and legs were contorted, as if even in death they were telling me how horrific the night before had been. I felt an overwhelming sense of guilt for taking last night off.

I turned to the faces in the room. All eyes were now on me. Even the woman in the corner had stopped sobbing and she too was watching me. I felt for a moment I had been betrayed by Lieutenant Nguyen. He lead me into this room of despair to punish me for the death our guns delivered to this family and to his countrymen. I glanced his way and quickly realized he was as uncomfortable as I was.

I turned to leave the room. As I walked down the narrow passage, my head swelled, and my anger was overwhelming. I staggered onto the street and into a brilliant sunlight. It took all my effort to keep from vomiting. The dusty heat on the dirt road was now a relief. I tumbled into the jeep. My driver, half asleep, started the engine. Lieutenant Nguyen followed close behind me, nodding his head to the somber crowd as they walked out into the daylight. I could tell he, too, wanted out of this hellish place.

We silently drove back to the battery. I was sick with anger, not only at Owen and Hart, but also at myself for taking the night off. This would not have happened had I been on duty. I kept thinking to myself, when I was on duty I watched every move the gun crew made. I was aware of their fatigue. I knew where mistakes could and did occur. I now felt an enormous sense of responsibility. I also had a stinging anger at the gun crew; they knew better than to cause a stupid mistake like this. The NCOs on duty should have checked the powder charge. The men fired the gun in a sloppy, unthinking, and careless manner. They killed three innocent people, and then they went to bed.

After we arrived back at our compound, I passed Owen and I stopped him. I told him of the scene I had witnessed in Saigon. Owen all but shrugged, and then he turned and walked away. I was left alone with this horrible image. I wanted to share this picture with someone and pass along my sorrow and my rage.

I called the gun crew into our empty club for a meeting. They slowly filed in one by one. They knew I had just returned from Saigon. They were quiet and reserved. They sat and gave me their full attention. I started by asking each one of them if they had children at home. Each man looked at me and spoke. Some had small infants, some had toddlers, one man had a six-year-old girl. The others shook their heads. I persisted, "What about a niece or a nephew?"

They nodded their heads; they all knew someone at home of a young age. By this time they looked puzzled. They thought I was going to give them an "ass-chewing" and a punishment, maybe even a letter of reprimand. I continued.

I asked the men gathered in front of me to picture these children they loved and cared for back at home. I waited a moment and then I asked, "Now, do you all have a picture of a child in your mind?"

They nodded, and I went on: "Now I want you to picture that child burned and twisted in some horrible state of death, because that's what I saw this morning. This was the result of your carelessness and disregard for procedure." They looked away from me, my voice cracked and I stopped talking. I regained my composure, then with a wave of my arm, I dismissed the group. They quietly filed out. I hoped my words gave them some feeling of the gravity of their error. There wasn't a punishment I could think of that would match the consequences of this horrendous mistake.

Later that night, I found myself behind one of our buildings near our generator. It hummed away as tears filled my eyes. Physically, I was spent, and emotionally, I was exhausted. I felt I was drowning in a sea of responsibility that I never could have imagined, and it was crushing me. I was staggering under the weight of decisions I did not want to make.

I longed for the comfort of Chicago. For a moment, I thought of the familiarity of my old neighborhood, of my friend Joe Kiefer and our political talks in Cindy Sue's Coffee Shop. I thought of Chris, my old girlfriend, and our good times riding around in her father's Buick. Vietnam was overwhelming, and now I carried one more horrifying image; God, how I wanted to go home.

As the generator continued to hum, I heard a voice call out. "Lieutenant Duffy, sir?"

I was surprised anyone would find me here. "Yes?" I turned and answered.

"Sir, it's Corporal Link. He's hurt."

"What happened?" I barked, annoyed that my grieving was interrupted.

"Well, sir, he was drinking again, and he fell against a gun site and cut himself just above his eye. Sir, it's all bloody; should we drive him to the navy base?"

I didn't want to deal with another problem. "Have you told the first sergeant?" I asked.

"No, sir. Remember, he's in Saigon on a three-day pass."

I was twenty-two years old. Corporal Link was twice my age and he had a chronic drinking problem. Time after time, the first sergeant covered for him. I walked to the gun pit and gave Corporal Link a long look. He was half asleep, and he had a gash over his eye that our medic had just bandaged. I told the gun crew chief to put Corporal Link on the mail truck in the morning and send him back to our base camp. "As of now, he is off this gun," I said.

One of the men protested. "But, sir, the first sergeant would give him another chance."

I viewed the scene and it was all I could do to hold my anger. Then I said, "I want him off this gun and on the mail truck when it leaves in the morning."

After the day I had just experienced, I was through with mistakes and excuses. I was through with incompetence.

Our squawk box began barking out another fire mission. I jotted the powder charge, the elevation, and the deflection on my clipboard and then sprinted to the guns. Out of some mechanical mindset, I began to function again, and I pushed myself through the night.

Chapter 11

PRIVATE CONNOR

Weeks after our deadly mistake, I could still feel the stress between Owen and me. I despised his cavalier attitude, and he despised me. After that horrific day, I took back complete responsibility for the guns. I did this at a dear cost of sleep. But I knew when I was on duty there would not be another error; I left nothing to chance. Soon, I would hand the battery to a new executive officer. Lieutenant Hart was out of the picture. Our command in Bien Hoa had handed him a letter of reprimand, and it was placed in his permanent file. That letter and some punitive words from battalion headquarters put his future in doubt.

I noticed a greater respect from the enlisted men. They were all aware that the mistake had placed a huge black mark on our unit, and now they realized just how easy it was to screw up. More value was put on my presence during our nightly fire missions. When I noticed an error, no matter how small, I was given a quick, "Oh, sorry, sir." I was also sure that the lecture I gave the gun crew just after returning from the point of impact in Saigon was passed along to the men in every gun pit. There would not be another incident in our battery.

Our new commanding officer was now comfortable in his job, and he fit in well with the junior officers. One hot, muggy morning in December, following a long night of firing, I was called to his bunker. I was exhausted and I was now working on three or four hours of sleep a night. All the officers and NCOs in our unit were assembled just outside his doorway. He was standing and waiting impatiently with a sheet of paper in his hand; I was the last to arrive, and I got a quick, scornful glance from him. He began to speak. He informed us that we were moving from Nhá Bé. This move, he said, would be quick. He paused as we looked at one another, puzzled. We were all thinking the same thing: *How quick was quick?* He explained that our new base would be on a hill in the massive military compound at Bien Hoa. Then came the punch line—we were told to get ready that morning; we were moving that afternoon. "HQ ordered us out of Nhá Bé, and our six guns must be in place at Bien Hoa ready to fire by nightfall," he said. "Now get to work; you are all dismissed."

In a frantic display of effort, everyone began loading trucks and breaking down tents and chart tables. We rolled up our maps and stuffed them into tubes. We packed up ammunition, poncho liners, cots, duffle bags, and boxes of C-rations, then we hooked the howitzers to the trucks and waited. In the early afternoon, our convoy was assembled and we were ready to leave. This time, as the executive officer, my jeep was at the head of the long line of trucks and howitzers. I waved my arm, and we began to snake our way out of Nhá Bé. A few Vietnamese army troops and their families watched as we left. I saluted Lieutenants Bo and Nguyen. I glanced toward Mama-san and Baby-san's ammo-crate home and winced as I thought of the towel I had never given Baby-san, then I turned my head toward the dusty access road. Our journey took us through Saigon then northeast to Bien Hoa. We arrived about 4:00 p.m.

The trip, thank God, went without incident. Our trucks pulled through the Bien Hoa gate; we passed two sentinels surrounded by a sandbag wall. They were both hunched over M-60 machine guns, and they gave us a wave. We drove deep into the compound, arriving at a series of empty bunkers. The howitzers were backed into the pits, and the sandbagged walls were quickly rebuilt. I set up the aiming circle and laid the battery. We were ready to fire just as the sun was setting.

The FDC bunker was located down a long flight of stairs and was almost completely underground. I kept up my routine and checked every operation in the battery. By this time, Lieutenant Owen was avoiding me, and it was clear to me he despised my authority and my presence in the FDC bunker, even if it was just a quick stop by. I was a constant reminder that his laissez-faire attitude toward the workings of the guns was a disaster. We all had an operational handbook, but the officers on duty needed the brains to follow it. Although Lieutenant Owen bristled when I entered his bunker, the enlisted men working with him gave me a measure of respect and cooperation that had been absent in the past.

This was the middle of the dry season, and our constant companion, the red dust of Vietnam, was everywhere. Because we were now on one of the army's largest bases in Vietnam, the enlisted men found it easy to visit the PX and spend their meager monthly earnings, about a hundred dollars a month. One evening before our fire missions began, I walked into a gun pit. I looked over the howitzer and walked around the bunker where the men lived. The quarters for the men consisted of small bunkers with sandbagged roofs held up with a series of wooden beams. The bunkers looked like small caves. The men had cots arranged in nooks and corners with photos of their families and girlfriends pasted around their spaces. I stuck my head into one of those caves. As I viewed the clutter, I saw a new stereo record player propped up on two boards sticking out of the sandbagged wall. It was cantilevered inches above a young private's head.

The stereo, just a few days old, was covered with red dust. The one lone record sitting on the turntable was also covered with dust. There was no way the private could play the machine because there was not an electrical outlet in the bunker. I inquired about the logic of the purchase. The private told me that it reminded him of home, and it didn't matter if he couldn't play his Patsy Cline record. He looked at me and said, "Sir, when I get up in the morning, it's the first thing I look at. It's just like my room back in Little Rock."

On another occasion, I was walking the guns and waiting for a fire mission when I was told there was an accident. "What is it?" I asked. "Where?"

"Out by the trucks. Sir, you can follow me. I'll show you."

We ran to our small motor pool. It was dark and a thick fog had rolled in from the South China Sea. "Sir, over here."

I heard a man screaming. As we approached the truck park, I saw a group of men crouched over a GI. He had his hands over his eyes. "What happened?" I asked.

I was told that the young private was working under a truck when a battery tipped and then fell over spilling acid onto his face. He was screaming for a medic. The men were pouring water over his face and eyes, but we needed to get him to the hospital. "Keep him here," I said. "I'll get a Medevac right away."

I ran to the FDC bunker and radioed for help. In a moment, a helicopter was on its way. We monitored the pilots as they made the short trip to our position. We soon heard the helicopter blades and then the bad news: "We can't land; there's too much fog. We are unsure of the landing area."

I remembered what we did earlier in the year when I was flying as an artillery spotter over Saigon. I had two jeeps pull up and turn on their headlights. The jeeps were facing each other, and there was enough space for the helicopter to land between them. I turned to the crowd that had gathered around me and told them to pull the red flares from our trucks and jeeps and make a large circle around the landing area and then light them.

The helicopter pilots and I began conversing over a portable radio. "Listen," I said, "we're going to light the landing area with red flares. Watch for them." It took a few moments, and soon the flares were lighted. "Can you see them?" I asked.

There was a pause and then a positive reply, "Yes, we see the red outline. We're coming in."

The ship landed, and we heaved the wounded man onto the helicopter. It flew off to the hospital, and I had one more calamity under control. It sometimes seemed to me that my days went from one problem to the next. There was no room to breathe, just decisions, problems, and stress.

✳ ✳ ✳

Most of the GIs serving in Vietnam were marking time waiting to get out and resume their lives in the States. It was a mistake to think that the soldiers in Vietnam were the lowlife dropouts and problem kids of America; this often-held opinion of the GI in Vietnam as an undereducated dropout was a common misconception. The logic went like this: if a kid was smart enough to attend college, he could avoid military service. If the same kid had poor high school grades and couldn't get into college, he quickly received a draft notice into the army and a tour in Vietnam, just as I did. We had a mix of people serving in our unit, including a few college graduates, unlucky enough to graduate from college and then quickly get drafted. We also had a few troublesome kids in our unit, kids who were offered enlistment in the army versus a prison term, but those were the exception. If a soldier was conscripted into the army and then successfully passed the rigorous training of both basic and advanced artillery school, he probably was not a deadbeat.

The army didn't want losers operating artillery. The guns were dangerous weapons, and the army needed levelheaded men with the skill to maneuver them and shoot them straight. Our men needed a working knowledge of math and good reading skills. They needed to be able to set the gun sites, turn the wheels, and point the tube in the right direction. Then the correct powder charge needed to be cut and, if required, a fuse setting was necessary. There were many different shells and fuse options, so the GI in the artillery needed the skill to read the manuals and follow written directions.

Not everyone who entered the army went to Vietnam. Many of the men I met while serving at Fort Sill, Oklahoma, ended up in Germany, Korea, or the South Pacific. The deadbeats in the army, either in Vietnam or in the U.S., usually ended up in jail or they went AWOL, and when the AWOL GI was caught, and they always were caught, they went to LBJ (Long Binh Jail). Some were such losers that we didn't want them in our unit and we got rid of them.

Most of the men who served in Battery C, 7th Battalion, 9th Artillery were homesick and tired, but they were dedicated to their jobs and would help one another accomplish our mission. It seemed to me that most of the men in our battery got along. We had a mix of people in the army reflecting the demographic make up of the United States. About eighty percent of the unit was white, fifteen percent was black, and five percent was Hispanic.

I often wondered about racial undertones in our unit. I'm sure they were there, but perhaps not on the surface. That said, during my tour in Vietnam, I never experienced or witnessed a racial issue—but I did experience plenty of conflict between the men. The last issue I had to deal with was between two GIs in Bien Hoa, my last post before rotating back to the States. The conflict was the result of two strong personalities clashing.

The problem occurred one night about 8:00 p.m. I was dreaming of home, of buying a car and then driving from Chicago to Colorado College. My dream continued and took me to dating good-looking college women, but it was interrupted, as I was about to pick up the best-looking girl on campus for a night out. The squawk box hissed, then a voice came over the speaker. "Lieutenant Duffy, sir, this is Sergeant Massey. Can I see you, sir, now?"

"Okay, come up to my bunker." I said.

Sergeant Massey had arrived from the states just a few days earlier. I had met him only once, and I remembered him as a short, stocky man with short blond hair; his fair skin was sunburned red from the Vietnam sun. He was still wearing his green army-issue fatigues from the States. His shirt had a gold embroidered nametag and gold embroidered chevrons on both of its sleeves. In Vietnam we all wore black embroidery to designate our rank; gold embroidery could make you a target. Sergeant Massey told me the army had lost his duffle bag with his new jungle clothes and boots. I told him I understood. I thought back to my arrival at Cam Ranh Bay when the army had lost my bag.

Sergeant Massey quickly arrived at my small bunker, and he was visibly upset. "Sir, I need to talk to you," he said.

"Okay, sergeant, what is it?" My stomach tightened as my beautiful dream vanished.

"Well, sir, it's Private Connor."

It took me a moment to figure out who Private Connor was, but I soon remembered him arriving in our unit a week before Massey. Private Connor came to our battery labeled as a problem soldier. He had been to every unit in the battalion. Ours was the last. He was angry about his lowly position here in Vietnam. Also, during an afternoon meeting, the captain told us that Private Connor did not take well to authority.

There was little privacy in my small bunker, and I didn't want the rumor mill to crank up. I walked Sergeant Massey to a spot behind my hooch and away from curious ears. I sat down on an empty ammo crate, and Sergeant Massey stood, his chest was heaving with anger, his fists clenched. What he didn't know was that I was angry at him for interrupting my daydream. I glanced up at him and in a flat, annoyed voice I snapped, "What is it, sergeant?"

He began talking rapidly. He told me that Connor had refused to perform a task. His face was filled with rage. He paused and then blurted, "Sir, Connor mouthed off to me." I waited a moment before I spoke. I thought, *I'm going home in six days, and this guy just fucked up my beautiful dream. I don't need this shit.* Then I took a deep breath and I asked Sergeant Massey this question: "What was the task Connor refused to perform?"

"It was the shit detail, sir."

This unwelcome detail was reserved for those who committed minor infractions or for whomever the sergeant in charge of the detail had a grudge against. When Private Connor heard that he was placed on the shit detail, he decided that no green-from-the-States sergeant was going to order him to do this shit job. He refused.

After this breach of authority in front of the other men, Massey was furious. He was ready to file formal charges against Private Connor. I continued asking Massey questions. "Did he threaten you in any way?"

"No," Sergeant Massey replied. "But, sir, he was insubordinate, and at the minimum, I want an Article 15 written up. No enlisted man I outrank talks to me that way."

I nodded to him in a false gesture of sympathy. I thought, *This guy is in for a long year.* Trying to act concerned, I told Sergeant Massey what he wanted to hear. I said that I would file the papers for the Article 15 as soon as I had a chance to talk to Private Connor. I dismissed Sergeant Massey and asked the RTO (radio telephone operator) to summon Private Connor to my bunker.

Private Connor arrived. This was our first meeting. He was tall and broad-shouldered, maybe six-foot two. He was black, and like Sergeant Massey, he was upset. I had him take a seat on an ammo crate. Again, I made sure that we were out of the hearing range of my small office.

I asked Connor what had happened between Sergeant Massey and him.

Private Connor began a nonstop rant. "Sir, I don't take any stateside bullshit from no one. I'm not pulling shit detail. I've done my time here in Vietnam, and I am ready to go back to the world, sir." He paused, shook his head, and then said, "I'm not pullin' shit detail for no one. Massey comes in here with his stateside bullshit attitude." His lips pursed as he continued to twist his head back and forth.

As I listened to his rant in the evening light, I keep wondering when he would stop; it went on and on. This was probably the first time an officer had taken the time to hear him out. He continued to vent, talking in circles and repeating himself, all the while shaking his head back and forth.

Connor was a private in the army—not a private first class but a lowly private. He had been busted (lowered in rank) probably more than once. My guess was this: he didn't have a lot to lose, and an Article 15 served to him would accomplish little. At this point in his army "career," he didn't give a shit.

As he talked, I thought back to my time at Fort Polk, Louisiana, and my basic training. I was a private just like Connor. A private in the army has zero leverage. It is the lowest rank for a GI. As a private at Fort Polk, I spent each day getting screamed at or double-timing around the post because some sergeant felt like exerting power.

Most of the men in our barracks at Fort Polk were draftees from Chicago. We arrived together from Chicago's Polk Street induction center. About half of the men were white and half were black. During our eight weeks of training, we got on well together. If there was any racial tension, I was unaware of it. I certainly never saw it in our barracks. We were all in the same boat, and we made the best of our situation.

After six weeks of training at Fort Polk, we were all given a Saturday afternoon pass outside the fort. There was only one town close enough to Fort Polk to visit—Leesville, Louisiana, a small Southern town next to a large military post. The town survived because the GIs spent their money in Leesville. One would think the barkeeps in Leesville would love to see the GIs arrive on a Saturday afternoon with pockets full of cash. They didn't. In every establishment we entered, we were treated with contempt.

After our Saturday lunch on base, we formed ranks outside our barracks. We were given a stern lecture about behaving in town. Then we were ordered to be back on the post by 10:00 p.m. Our sergeant brought us to attention and then he dismissed us for a night out in Leesville.

We ran to the bus stop, our pockets full of payday cash. By the time the bus left the post, it was overflowing with GIs. Soon we arrived at our final stop, downtown Leesville.

Our group, Company D, 3rd Battalion, 5th Infantry Division stayed together. We had formed friendships in the barracks. We talked and worried about Vietnam daily. But today we were going to drink cold beer. Louisiana's drinking laws let you drink beer at the age of eighteen.

Our small crowd soon found a bar not far from the bus stop. We walked inside and sat at a large, round table. We were the first group off the bus and the first group into this bar. It seemed to me an excessive time passed before the waitress made her way to our table, but when she did, it was not to take our beer order. She pointed at us and said, "I can serve you." Her finger pointed at the white troops. "But I can't serve you." Her finger was now waving back and forth at the black troops.

With a scowl on her face, she turned her back on all of us and walked away. I watched her standing at the far end of the bar puffing on a cigarette. She watched our table with visible contempt.

We all looked at one another and then said, "Let's go." We got up from the table and quietly walked out into the Louisiana sun. One of the black soldiers, a fellow from Chicago named Dyer said, "Sorry, fellows, looks like we can't have that beer together, but I am going to have a cold beer somewhere." We separated, and the black troops walked down a street to "their" part of town.

Like Dyer, we all wanted a cold beer, but we didn't go back into the bar that had refused us service. We found a bar a block away. We walked into a dark, unfriendly atmosphere where no one smiled or greeted us. They just wanted our money. I handed our waitress a five-dollar bill for a fifty-cent beer. After waiting for my change for what seemed like a very long time, I stood up from the table and tracked her down. I looked at her and asked for my change. She began to argue with me. She took a deep drag off her cigarette, then she blew the smoke back in my face, and snapped, "I already gave it to ya." I persisted and stood my ground. I told her I wanted to talk with the manager. Only then did she reluctantly reach into her apron and pull out my change. It was obvious to me that GIs—white or black—were despised by the bar owners and their staff.

I had my cold beer in an unfriendly barroom while surly waitresses scowled at us. I boarded an early bus back to Fort Polk, happy to be traveling out of this foul town. With all its faults and military ugliness, the fort was far friendlier than Leesville, Louisiana. I never returned to Leesville. From that day on, I would always think of Leesville, Louisiana, as America's pigsty.

I looked up at Private Connor as he momentarily paused from his never ending story, and then I asked him where he was from. I needed to get him off the shit detail topic.

"St. Louis, sir," he said.

"Okay." Then I asked him, "Connor, how short are you?"

A smile crossed his face. He closed his eyes, and then said, "Thirty-two days and a wake up sir."

"Connor," I said, "that's nothing. It's four lousy weeks. You're almost home."

"Yes, sir," he smiled and replied.

"Listen to me. You have to live with Massey for thirty-two days. That's all. Not one day more. So put up with his stateside bullshit and play the game. After thirty-two days, you're home free, no Article 15, no court-martial, nothing but St. Louis. Can you do that for thirty-two days?" I asked.

"But, sir," he said, his eyes now open wide, "what about the court-martial and the Article 15?"

"Forget it—that won't happen. Just set your mind to make it thirty-two days, and you're home free, okay? Remember, an Article 15 or a court-martial could mean a less-than-honorable discharge, and you don't want that."

He thought for a moment and then said, "Okay, but, sir, Sergeant Massey promised me an Article 15."

I looked at Connor and said, "I promise you that as long as you get through your thirty-two days without trouble, there will be no Article 15." He nodded, got up from the ammo crate, and walked back to the gun pit.

Now I needed to get Sergeant Massey to back off on his promise of issuing Connor an Article 15. I threw the dice in a risky psychological maneuver. I had to win Massey over to my way of thinking to keep the peace in the gun pit. I asked my radio man to call Massey. He arrived still upset. "Sir, did you talk to Connor?"

"Yes, I talked to him."

"Then, sir, I wish to follow through on the Article 15."

"Okay, I will do that, but I want you to understand what that means for you." I paused to make sure he was listening, then I continued. "Sergeant Massey, I am leaving Vietnam in six days. You just got here. You have one long year ahead of you. You have to live with all these troops, including Connor, in a cramped gun pit. Unlike in the States, you can't go home at

the end of the day; you are stuck in that small bunker for one long year."
I held out the word "long" to emphasize his yearlong predicament with
Connor and the others on his gun.

"So, before you punish Connor with an Article 15, I want you to
think about that year ahead of you. I will file the papers for you. But
remember that you are the one who will be around to take the shit
from the troops on your gun."

His tone softened, and then he said, "Maybe we should wait until
the morning, sir."

"Okay, see me tomorrow morning, and I will file the papers."

Massey saluted me, turned, and walked away. He never came
back to my bunker, and I never heard a word from Connor. I gam-
bled, and I won.

Chapter 12

HOME

In the fall of 1968, I submitted paperwork to our command at Bearcat to leave the army thirty days early. I wanted to enter Colorado College at the beginning of its spring semester, starting in early January 1969, but my discharge date from the army was in late January. After a flurry of paperwork from battalion headquarters and then letters to and from Colorado College, my request was granted. Colorado College moved my start date to January 1969, and the army granted me a thirty-day early release.

But I had one administrative job facing me, and I was putting it off. Our new commanding officer, Captain Hawthorne, reminded me daily of this task.

There were five officers under my supervision, all first and second lieutenants. Before I could board a plane for home, I needed to fill out five efficiency reports. I dreaded this job. The reports were typed on a one-page Department of Defense document that had a series of preprinted questions, and there was a blank space on the form for my written comments on each officer. The army didn't want a thesis on people, so the report was limited to one page, front and back.

After completing each form, I would hand the finished reports to Captain Hawthorne. He would review each one, reading my comments and my answers to the preprinted questions. If he thought I was

THE COLORADO COLLEGE

COLORADO SPRINGS, COLORADO 80903

November 20, 1968

1Lt. Michael J. Duffy
"C: Btry 7th Bn 9th Arty
APO San Francisco, California 96530

Dear Lt. Duffy:

Thank you for your letter informing us that your early separation
has been approved and that you plan to join us in January, 1969.

I have enclosed a room application form which you should complete
and return together with your $100 deposit. Concerning the resi-
dential requirements at Colorado College, as you will have reached
the age of twenty-one prior to your registration for the spring
semester, it would not be necessary for you to reside on campus.
If you prefer to live on campus, however, I can assure you that we
will be able to accommodate you and our residence halls will open
on the morning of January 12, 1969.

We look forward to your safe arrival from Viet Nam and welcoming
you as a member of the Colorado College community.

Cordially yours,

William A. Ferguson
Associate Director of Admission

WAF/bg

Enc.

cc: Mr. Jack Goodnow

THE COLORADO COLLEGE

Colorado Springs, Colorado 80903

December, 1968

TO: Students Entering Spring Semester 1969 and Their Parents

FROM: Robert W. Broughton, Vice President and Business Manager

SUBJECT: Some Special Payment Plans Offered by Colorado College for
           Meeting College Expenses.

     We thought it might be helpful to you if I summarize the
arrangements that can be made, with respect to paying tuition and other
fees for the coming academic year. You have already been notified that
the basic costs for the Spring Semester are:

Tuition and Fees	$ 850.00
Room and Board	475.00
Health Insurance	16.00
Total -	$1,341.00

The College has two payment plans:

1. All semester charges are payable on or before registration.

2. All semester charges are payable in four equal monthly
   payments. The schedule for payments for Spring 1968-69
   follows:

   Spring Semester

   First payment due on or before registration
   Second payment due February 1
   Third payment due March 1
   Final payment due April 1

     When the deferred payment plan is used a $10 per semester
carrying charge is added.

     We also cooperate with the Insured Tuition Payment Plan and
the Education Funds, Inc. so that those of you who wish to pay your edu-
cational costs over a longer period of time may do so. In these instances

To Students entering Spring Semester 1969   -2-

your contract is with the Company you select which, in turn, pays the College.
Descriptive literature of each plan is enclosed for your information and
appropriate action if such arrangements appeal to you.

       Many parents find it convenient to pay fees in advance of
registration. You may do this if you wish, by mailing your check to Colorado
College, Colorado Springs, Colorado 80903 - Attention: The Business Office.

       Perhaps I should remind you that the $100 room deposit required
of all students living on campus is refunded, less any outstanding charges,
at the end of residence in the halls or fraternity houses.

       We look forward to having you on campus and if now or during the
next four years you have problems I can help resolve, please write or come in
and see me.

PJB /vs

Enclosures

overly harsh or too easy on an officer, he might ask me to do a rewrite. After his read, the captain would call each officer into his small bunker and have them read their reports in his presence. After their reading, they would sign the report acknowledging that they had read and accepted it. There was only one copy of the efficiency report, and that document was placed in each junior officer's permanent file. It was now time to collect my thoughts and put them on paper.

The most vexing issue for me was the task of ranking each officer on a scale of one to five—one the best, five the worst. There was a box on the form that needed to be marked with each officer's standing. The report was incomplete without those boxes filled.

I got on well with most of the lieutenants and rarely had an issue or problem with their performances. The exception was Lieutenant Owen. He continued to harbor resentment toward me and challenged almost every move I made.

Until the day I left our unit, Owen bristled when I entered the FDC bunker. I became good at ignoring him. One night when I had only a few days left in my tour, I heard a fire mission come in over our squawk box. It was called into us just after dark by an infantry unit under attack. I ran to the FDC bunker to get a deflection for the guns. I engaged one of the corporals standing over his chart table. As he worked up a deflection and elevation for me, Owen entered the room. In a final act of childish petulance, he demanded to know why I was in *his* FDC bunker. This time, the young corporal turned from the chart table toward Owen and said, "Sir, there's a fire mission. Lieutenant Duffy needs a deflection for the guns."

That surprised me, and the comment from the corporal quickly put Owen in his place. I was pleased that even the enlisted men under Owen were aware of his unprofessional behavior.

As I thought about writing Owen's efficiency report, I reasoned that I could easily slam him with a few disparaging words about his performance and then label him number five of five. I probably would never see any of the officers again, so I had no reason to worry that they might confront me in a state of rage.

Captain Hawthorne stopped me one morning, looked me in the eye, and said, "Duffy, get the efficiency reports done, understand?"

I answered him with an affirmative nod.

That afternoon, I pulled out a small, olive-green table from our headquarters bunker. I moved it to a shady spot away from the gun pits and any nosy GIs who might wander by. I took the typewriter, placed it on the table, and began one of my last tasks as the executive officer.

I already knew whom I would label number one of five and whom I would label five of five. My problem was the middle. I was wrestling with the labels four of five and three of five.

Three new lieutenants had arrived in the fall of 1968, and they all worked shifts in the FDC bunker with Lieutenant Owen as their superior. Every time I began to discuss the new lieutenants' performances with Owen, he would brush me off and provide no real substance. So it was up to my personal observation to figure out who would get the lower rank and who the higher. I used my knowledge of the officers' skills and deportment around our unit. Did they offer help with a task or volunteer for a duty when the captain asked for assistance? This was easy to observe because we were together every night for a short meeting. During those meetings, Captain Hawthorne might ask for a volunteer to oversee a small project or duty. I was usually exempt from those tasks because of my full day of duties as executive officer. I would watch as hands were raised or not raised. From that, I could tell who put forward the extra effort that helped our unit and Captain Hawthorne.

Two days before I was to leave the unit, I was summoned to our headquarters bunker for a private meeting with Captain Hawthorne. He sat at a small wooden army-issue desk; it was painted olive-green. I remember his face and his words. His first question was, "How are the efficiency reports coming?" He gave me a look and then he said, "Well?"

I told him they were written, but I wanted to reread them one more time. I asked if I could turn them in the next morning, my last day as XO. He nodded and said okay. I, too, had an efficiency report written about my performance; the author of this report was Captain Hawthorne. This document would be placed in my permanent military file. Captain Hawthorne looked at me and said, "Okay, have them on my desk in the morning. Now, have a seat and read your report." He handed me the one-page document. He sat back in his chair as I read the report. I was flattered. The captain had given me high marks in every category, including a glowing one-page short essay. I signed the report and thanked him.

Then he handed me a second piece of paper to read and sign, a one-page document offering me the rank of captain. My signature on this document would confirm the offer of captain's bars had been made and I had declined the promotion. I was pleased. I had been commissioned a second lieutenant less than two years before, and now I was offered captain's bars. I signed the document, and the captain handed me a carbon copy, which I still have in my file of documents from Vietnam.

Although the offer of captain was tempting, the promotion would keep me in Vietnam another six months and derail my plans to attend the 1969 spring semester at Colorado College. Declining that promotion may also have saved my life. In the spring of 1969,

DISPOSITION FORM
(AR 340-15)

REFERENCE OR OFFICE SYMBOL	SUBJECT
AVGA-P	Declination of Extension of Service for Promotion

TO	FROM	DATE	CMT 1
Commanding Officer ATTN: AVGA-P APO 96376	1LT Michael J. Duffy Btry C 7th Bn 9th Arty APO 96930	27 Nov 68	

I have this date been informed of my eligibility for promotion to Captain-AUS and of the requirement to extend my obligated service for this purpose, as provided in DA messages 837567, 24 Oct 67, 851760, 15 Feb 68, and 860986, 23 Apr 68, and do not desire to do so.

Michael J. Duffy
MICHAEL J. DUFFY
1LT ARTY

DA FORM 2496-1 REPLACES DD FORM 96 (STENCIL), EXISTING SUPPLIES OF WHICH WILL
1 FEB. 62 BE ISSUED AND USED UNTIL 1 FEB. 63 UNLESS SOONER EXHAUSTED.

the Viet Cong attacked Battery C in the village of Xuân Lộc and we suffered many casualties, both dead and wounded.

The next day, I pulled out the completed efficiency reports from my attaché. I slowly reread each one. I signed the reports, walked to the captain's bunker, and handed him the completed paperwork. He took his time reading the reports. When he finished, he looked at me surprised and said, "I thought you and Owen didn't get on well?"

"We had our differences," I said.

The captain continued, "Okay, they make sense to me—good job."

I had given Owen the top ranking one of five. During his time in the unit, we had had our differences, but I was able to separate my personal feelings from my professional duty. Although I despised him and his behavior, he did his job well. I thought back to the night of the mistake and reasoned that it was Hart's acceptance of an invitation from Owen that had kept him in the FDC bunker and not at his duty station as ordered. I gave Hart the five of five, the lowest ranking because of his total disregard of his duty the night of the mistake. I still believed that if he had been on duty, at his assigned position, he would have caught that careless error. I also believed that if I had been on duty that night, the error would never have occurred. Just the thought of that night and the following day was agonizing for me.

I shook the captain's hand, said goodbye, and walked out of his bunker. I grabbed my few belongings and left quietly for the out-processing building a short jeep ride away. I would be on a plane for home the next day.

I was reading a copy of *Stars and Stripes* newspaper at the processing center when I saw a jeep pull up with Captain Hawthorne and Lieutenant Owen. I thought, *Did I forget to do something back in the unit?* I walked onto a small porch and greeted them. Owen had a rare smile on his face. He said, "You didn't stop to say goodbye."

Then he thanked me for the one of five on the efficiency report. Since it was unlikely that I would never see him again, I'm sure he expected the poorest of the rankings, five of five, and a typed tongue-lashing in the comment section. I told him I used my judgment as an officer and did not let my personal feelings interfere with my efficiency reports. I went on to say that I was sure he would have done the same thing if the tables had been turned. I said this even though I didn't believe my words. Lieutenant Owen and Captain Hawthorne shook my hand and drove off.

The next day I boarded a dark green bus with wire grating and bars on the windows. We left Bien Hoa for Saigon's Tan Son Nhut Airbase. When the bus arrived at the airport, we were issued travel vouchers to board a Trans World Airlines plane back to the United States. I watched from the waiting room window as a red-and-white TWA plane landed on the tarmac. A shipment of new GIs walked off the plane, fresh from the States. They looked terrified.

The plane was cleaned, the doors were opened, and we walked across the tarmac and up a flight of stairs and into the cabin. I took a window seat near the back of the plane. My new orders, sending me to the army terminal in Oakland, California, were on my lap, safely tucked into my attaché. After arriving at the Oakland Army Terminal, I would be honorably discharged from the military and resume my life as a civilian.

As I sat looking out the window, I couldn't help but think of my past year in Vietnam. My thoughts were cluttered with painful events and emotions. For the few Vietnamese people I had encountered, I could think only of their wretched poverty and the ever-present risk of living in a war zone. There were no safe towns in Vietnam. Injury and death were everywhere. This country had been ravaged by different wars for almost thirty years. But now this would be behind me, and I could forget Vietnam, or so I thought.

It was close to Christmas Day, and as the plane lifted off, a roar of excitement filled the cabin. I sat quietly, peering out the window at the

Mekong Delta. Our first stop would be Hawaii. Most of us slept on the flight. We were awakened only once, when the pilot informed us that we had just passed the International Date Line, and it was now the previous day. I was confused and had to figure in my head just what day it was, December 23rd or December 24th. When we arrived at the Honolulu Airport, we were told to disembark and prepare for a six-hour wait. There was a mechanical problem with the plane.

It was early in the morning and still dark. I walked outside the terminal, away from the crowd of sleepy GIs and into the open air to watch the sun rise over Diamond Head. It was beautiful, and I promised myself that I would return someday. The plane was repaired, and we boarded for Oakland, California.

A line of olive-green buses greeted us at the Oakland airport. These buses did not have bars and wire mesh on their windows. The buses shuttled us from the airport to the army terminal. I walked off the bus and into a large hall, where a madhouse of GIs were milling about. In the hall, the size of three large gymnasiums, queues of men were anxiously waiting in front of long tables. They held papers in their hands, ready to complete the discharge process. The Oakland Army Terminal was a major point of discharge on the West Coast. Our planeload of men was added to those from Cam Ranh Bay in Vietnam and from other Asian bases. Step by step, each GI went through a series of stations. We were examined by doctors in white lab coats and asked about our health. I told the doctor about my dysentery, still not cured, and my back injury in the gun pit. He was busy and seemed preoccupied. He listened and scribbled notes on a clipboard. He glanced at me and then said, "Lieutenant, I want you to listen for an announcement about filing a claim to use the veterans' hospital; you can get treatment for both problems there." He handed me a signed piece of paper and sent me off to another line.

The discharge process was painfully slow, and no one could leave the hall until every GI completed the procedure. By late afternoon, we waited impatiently as a form labeled DD214 was typed and handed to us for our review. The officer that handed it to me said, "Lieutenant, now listen to me, this is important. If there is a mistake on your form, this is the time to correct it—there will be no other chance." I nodded at him and slowly read each line on the form. The Department of Defense form number 214 documented a GIs active duty service, citations and medals earned, and most importantly, whether the GI was discharged honorably or less than honorably. After carefully reading each line of my DD214, I looked up at the young lieutenant and told him the date on the form was wrong. It was dated December 25th, but today was December 23rd. He looked at me, shrugged, and said, "The army wants it that way. If everything else on the form is okay, sign it."

Shortly after signing the form DD214, I watched an officer dressed in tidy khakis mount a set of risers. He raised his hand to hush the crowd of impatient GIs then he put a microphone to his mouth and loudly shouted, "Attention." He waited a moment until the hall was quiet. "At ease, you all have been processed out of the army, and you are now free to go."

A howl of approval rose from the crowd. Then the lieutenant raised his hand again and hushed the assembly, he continued. "Wait, there is one last thing. If any of you wish to file a claim for a medical problem, you will have to spend the night, and I will deal with the paperwork in the morning. If you do not wish to file a claim, you will now be dismissed." In a command voice, he shouted, "*Attention.*" Everyone in the hall stood silently at attention. Then he shouted, "Dismissed."

The hall carried the sound of a stampede as hundreds of men ran out the doors and out of the army. I waited until the hall had emptied and then I approached the lieutenant. I didn't want to spend the night in the Oakland Army Terminal, but my back was killing me and I was not sure if I was completely cured of dysentery. He told me to move to the side, have a seat, and he would deal with me when he was done with his paperwork.

An hour passed, and the hall was now almost deserted except for a few of us waiting on the Lieutenant. The discharging officer glanced over and realized that only three of us were willing to spend the night to file a medical claim. "Well, if there are just three of you," he said, "I'll fill out the paperwork now and you can leave."

The paperwork was quickly issued and signed. We were told that a letter would arrive at the addresses we had listed on our discharge papers. This letter would direct us to a veterans' hospital for an examination. He dismissed us.

I walked out of the Oakland Army Terminal and into a darkening winter sky. It started raining as I hailed a taxi. Then I tossed my green duffle bag into the trunk. Before the driver had a chance to close the trunk, another cabbie drove up and jumped out of his car. He ignored me but went straight for my bag, which was now sitting in the open trunk of the first cab. He shouted at the driver, "That's my fare."

The two argued as I watched, confused about the taxicab etiquette I had breached. The tug of war with my duffle bag went on for a moment until I grabbed it back. I gave both drivers a look of disapproval, then I tossed the bag into the first cab. I looked at the driver, and in my Vietnam officer's command voice, I said, "Take me to the San Francisco airport." I climbed into the car while the driver vented about what had just happened, his eyes darting back and forth from the rearview mirror to me. I ignored him.

The image of the San Francisco airport that evening is vivid in my mind. It was late evening, and I thought I might have to spend the night in the terminal. I had enough money to buy a one-way ticket home and a little extra for a cheap motel. I wore my khaki dress uniform, now very wrinkled. As I exited the taxi, I noticed a man walking aimlessly across my path. He was a bearded hulk of a man, and he gave me an unfriendly glance. He wore a faded, blue denim jacket, blue jeans, and black motorcycle boots adorned with brass buckles. Printed on the back of his jacket in appliquéd letters was Hells Angels, Oakland. His nonchalant manner and his uniform seemed foreign to me.

I had read about this California motorcycle club in Vietnam. The article said the members of the Hells Angels dressed up in a pseudo-threatening fashion and enjoyed nothing better than beating people up, always making sure the odds were in their favor. The article also said they dealt in drugs and other nefarious trades.

I watched this man pass me. Patches of his fabricated bravery adorned his denim jacket—chevrons and other senseless symbols. His uniform was topped off with a red bandanna pulled tight across his head. To me, he was all show. He reminded me of the medal riders back in Vietnam. My mind flashed back to the Hells Angels article that I had read in *Stars and Stripes*. I had an overwhelming impulse to shout an obscenity at this fucking punk. I wanted to engage him and intentionally piss him off, but I kept my cool.

After my year in Vietnam, his cheap patches meant nothing to me. I had no fear of him. What I did have was a rage within me. As I entered the airport, this feeling passed, but it alarmed me, and it would come up again and again my first year home from Vietnam.

I walked up to the airline counter and purchased a one-way ticket on the last plane to Chicago's O'Hare International Airport. Then I found a payphone and called home. As I talked with my mother and father, I could hear the relief in their voices. I told them I would take a taxi home from the airport because it would be late when I arrived. The plane was half-full of sleepy people. I dozed off, but I was too anxious for any restful sleep.

The plane landed at a deserted O'Hare Airport. I jumped into a cab for my trip home to our apartment on Bosworth Avenue. I had to give the driver directions. When he pulled up to our building, it was after 10:00 p.m. It was cold and I had no coat. I rang the doorbell and waited to be buzzed in through the vestibule and into the staircase that led up to our first-floor apartment.

My mother hugged me in her nightgown with tears in her eyes, my father shook my hand, and they both welcomed me home. There was a little conversation, and then they quickly went back to bed. I walked into the bedroom I shared with my brother, Dan. It hadn't changed since we left for the army. Our two roll away beds were made up; on the wall there was a black and white picture of our grade school football team. A few shirts were hanging in our tiny closet. On top of the dresser my brother and I shared was a beer mug I had won at Riverview, a now-shuttered Chicago amusement park. Beside the beer mug, there were a few pens and pencils and two letters. One letter was from a high school acquaintance, now working for an insurance company. It was a form letter welcoming me home from the army and wishing to sell me $10,000 worth of whole life insurance. In the letter was a graph showing me what the policy would be worth in thirty years. The letter stated that I would be a millionaire if I followed its advice and purchased the insurance policy. The other letter was from my boyhood friend Mike

Brady. He was serving in the Air Force and wanted to know how I was getting on. He was unaware that I had been sent to Vietnam.

Dan was still in the army, stationed in North Carolina. He would not be discharged until later the following year, 1969. I took off my uniform and pulled on civilian clothes from my closet; they were now large on me. I walked into our kitchen and listened to the wall clock. It made a buzzing sound. There was a metal coffee pot on the stove with a small blue flame under it. I turned it off. Next to the kitchen was a third bedroom, the smallest of three in our apartment. My mother had turned it into a TV room. She would never allow a TV in the living room. She told us the living room was for socializing and conversation. She convinced me of this, and to this day, I feel the same.

I switched on the TV. It sat on a wire table with wheels and it was a color TV. When I had left for the army three years earlier, it was a black-and-white TV. I turned through the channels—there were only four—and found a movie. It was a John Wayne shoot-'em-up cowboy movie in black and white.

I sat in my father's recliner and looked around the room. On the wall was a color photograph of John F. Kennedy, cut from a *Life* magazine, and a crucifix with dried-out palm reeds from Palm Sunday; the reeds were probably a few years old. Next to the crucifix in a silver frame was the word "Duffy" spelled out in Kennedy fifty-cent pieces. It was a gift to my dad from his close business friends when he retired from the New York Central Railroad. Sadly, later in the year, thieves broke into our apartment. They ransacked it and took the framed Kennedy fifty-cent retirement gift, but they left the crucifix.

Next to the recliner, in a woven wicker basket, was a cloth clown puppet used to amuse my now two-year-old nephew, Matthew. Each wall in this small room was covered with beige wallpaper. The single window in the room faced the brick wall of the apartment building just five feet to the north of us. I turned off the TV, pulled on a winter coat, and walked through the kitchen. I opened the back door to our first-floor landing and descended the back steps to a patch of concrete. The Nichols family lived on the third floor of our three-story apartment building; on the second floor was a new tenant. My parents had moved into our first-floor apartment ten years earlier, when our landlady, Mrs. O'Toole, lived on the second floor. She sold the building and was replaced by an absentee landlord—a cross, middle-aged man from Northern Ireland named Mr. William Ball. He chastised my father one summer day in 1968. He was upset that my father had had a few friends over for a barbecue in our tiny common yard. He placed a small unwelcome sign in the yard that read Keep Off The Grass. After that encounter, my father wrote a strongly worded letter to Mr. Ball. Since that day, they had not spoken. My brother and I thought Mr. Ball was probably an Orangeman from Belfast who hated all Catholics and lived for the Twelfth of July parades, the day in 1690 when England's King William of Orange's army had conquered Ireland.

I walked down our narrow gangway and then north up the alley. I turned east on Arthur Avenue and walked toward Sheridan Road. I was hoping that Cindy Sue's Coffee Shop would be open. Maybe I would run into a friend. The coffee shop was closed, but a tavern down the street called Bruno's was open. I walked into a smoky bar with middle-aged men hunched over their drinks; the TV was blaring the latest news from Vietnam. They all glanced at me and then they turned back to their drinks. I recognized the bartender, Tom Kelly. Tom smiled at me shook my hand and said, "Welcome home, Mike." Almost everyone in the neighborhood knew my brother Dan and I were in Vietnam. I ordered a beer, paid for it, and left it on the bar, not even taking a sip. I felt uncomfortable and I didn't want to engage anyone at the bar, especially about the war in Vietnam.

The news clip on TV upset me. I almost felt that I should be back with my unit; I felt a strange kind of separation. I tried, but I couldn't explain that feeling to myself. It was an odd mix of emotions—a little anger, a little remorse, and a strange feeling about arriving home. Home didn't seem like home anymore. On the plane ride from Vietnam, I imagined a group of friends gathered at the airport smiling and patting me on the back. My arrival at O'Hare, my walk around the neighborhood, and the next few days would be marked by indifference. Most people, including my parents, felt awkward asking me about Vietnam. And I, in turn, was not ready to open up and discuss the war and my feelings. This would change, but the change would be slow in coming.

I walked up Loyola Avenue past my old school and our church, St. Ignatius. Then I walked back home and tried to fall asleep. Early in the morning, I dozed off.

The next day was Christmas Eve, and our apartment was full of relatives. It felt strange eating from clean plates with silverware. My mother's food seemed foreign to me. It tasted wonderful, but it was shocking to see so much food and so much left over after dinner. The conversation in the house was about football, national politics, and Chicago politics. I was never asked about Vietnam, and I was thankful for that.

Christmas Day came and went in a blur. My body was still fatigued from the long flight home and my year in Vietnam. I turned my attention to the trip ahead of me, my drive to Colorado Springs. First, I needed a car.

On Thursday the 26th of December, I took the 'L' train down to the Art Institute of Chicago. I walked the halls and found some of my favorite paintings by Turner and Constable. And I sought out one of my favorite American painters, Edward Hopper, and his painting *Nighthawks*. I walked up and down the Art Institute's grand staircase marveling at its massive form. My visit ended in the basement coffee shop, where wall-sized 1960s-designed black-and-white graphic posters filled the south wall.

When I arrived back at our apartment that afternoon, there was a letter from the U.S. Government sitting on my dresser. It contained the fruits of my frugality while serving in Vietnam—a check for more than $5,000, my needed funds for college.

After depositing the check in the Northern Trust Bank, I took the 'L' train to Evanston and purchased a used 1963 Volkswagen at a dealership on Chicago Avenue, just north of Main Street. The car was pale green. Now I was set for college. I watched the calendar as my few days at home came to an end. Just before New Year's Eve, on Saturday, December 28, 1968, I decided to drive down to Rush Street and experience the social life of Chicago once again.

I got into my Volkswagen Bug on a raw, just-above-freezing night. The weather had warmed, and an intermittent cold rain had been falling all day. I pulled my new Volkswagen from its parking space onto our wet street and started the drive to Rush Street. As I turned west onto Schreiber Avenue, I watched a woman slip and fall in front of my car. I slammed on the breaks. I pulled the car to the curb, got out, and ran to her, asking if she was okay. She held a toddler by one hand and a half-empty bottle of Smirnoff vodka in her other hand. I took the child and walked her to the sidewalk. Then I began the business of moving the woman, whom I assumed to be the child's mother. Before I helped her from the street, I threw the vodka bottle down the alley; it smashed against a brick wall. Then I started pushing the woman.

She was headed to a doorway in a yellow-brick apartment building, but she was so drunk that she couldn't stand, much less find her keys.

For years, this apartment building had been filling up with our new Southern Appalachian neighbors. My father watched year after year as this once tidy corner building changed from polite family people to hardcore drinkers with glue-sniffing kids threatening any kid who dared cross "their turf." Junk cars began to litter Schreiber Avenue and the small grassy strip in front of the building became muddy and littered with cigarette butts and beer cans. My dad hated this change, but there was nothing he could do short of moving.

After digging through the woman's purse, I found a set of keys and tried each key until one opened the front door. I was then able to shove her into the vestibule, and the little girl followed us. At least we were out of the rain. I looked the woman over in the dim light of the vestibule. She was heavyset with messy brown hair. She wore no hat or gloves and she looked to be about thirty years old. Her hands were red from the cold, and her toddler was hardly dressed for winter. I asked the woman what floor she lived on, and in a slurred voice she muttered, "Three." That was the last word I got out of her.

To get into the stairwell, I had to open a second door. That was difficult because the woman couldn't stand. I pushed, shoved, and twisted against her dead weight; the young girl followed behind us. With great difficulty, I got both of them to the first floor landing. Once there, I began knocking on her neighbors' doors, hoping that someone would help. No one answered my repeated knocks.

I continued to wrestle the woman up the stairs on to the next landing and then the next floor. It was a slow process, but by pulling and pushing, I got her and the child to the third floor. Then I needed another key to open her apartment door. I looked through the woman's purse searching for her apartment door key. Just as I found a second set of keys, I turned to watch as she fell backward down the flight of stairs, her limp body smashing on the landing below. Her head hit the radiator with a thump. The little girl and I viewed this scene in amazement. I walked down to the landing, picked up this poor drunk soul and did a fireman's carry back up the stairs. This is when I realized how heavy she was. I propped her against the door, then I tried each key until I found the one that fit the lock. As I turned the key, the door opened and she fell forward onto the floor, but this time it was inside her apartment. I looked around at a sparse household. There was a playpen in the center of the room, but I saw no other furniture. The small kitchen had a single light burning; the second bulb in the fixture was out. There was a stack of dirty dishes in the sink. I saw a small kitchen table with a jar of jelly tipped over; it was open, its lid sitting on a vinyl tablecloth. A wooden captain's chair was pushed to the table, and there was a baby's highchair in the corner. I picked up the young girl, took off her sweater, and then placed her in the playpen. Her hand was in her mouth, and she looked at me with bright blue eyes. I switched on the living room overhead light, walked over to her mother, and pulled her away from the door so I could leave the apartment.

I wished them both a happy New Year. The little girl watched me as I closed the door, and she mumbled. I felt she was safe in her playpen, and in the morning, the woman, probably with a splitting headache, would figure things out. I drove down to Rush Street.

Along with the local crowd, the street was filled with revelers back from college. I walked into a bar. People were dancing, and waiters in white shirts kept asking me if I wanted a drink. To stop the pesky waiters, I ordered a beer. The waiter quickly turned to the bartender and shouted, "Draw one." The beer was too cold. I was used to drinking warm beer in Vietnam, and I found that warm beer had more flavor. I looked around the room to see if I could ask someone to dance, but I realized I would then have to make small talk, and I was not ready for that. I left the bar and walked south on Rush Street all the way to Chicago Avenue, then I headed home.

The next day, Sunday, December 29, 1968, turned cold. I filled my VW Bug with a few belongings, among them my attaché with my army records and my college letter of acceptance. I said my good-byes and began my trip to Colorado Springs. I spent the first night in Omaha and arrived in Colorado Springs the next evening.

My self-imposed budget allowed for a few nights stay at a cheap Colorado Springs motel, then I needed to find permanent housing. I didn't want to live in the dormitories, mistakenly thinking I would be out of place with the younger students. I didn't realize that it was in the dormitories where friendships were made. I ended up living alone in a motel on South Nevada Avenue called The Western Hills. I was able to work a deal with the owner for a room and an evening meal in exchange for work in the kitchen. This arrangement seemed perfect, but I soon found I was isolated from the college campus.

As school opened for the spring semester, I walked into the college gymnasium; it was filled with students and professors seated at tables. The professors were registering students for their respective classes. Each professor had paperwork and books stacked in front of them. They were answering questions and greeting students.

It was here in the school's gym that I first met a fellow Vietnam veteran, Jim Perlmutter. He was one of the first returning veterans to enter Colorado College. Jim had served in Vietnam as an army medic. In 1967 he was awarded the army's Silver Star for valor. While in Vietnam Jim had applied for admission to Colorado College, but he quickly received a letter of rejection. Jim was not deterred. He drafted a second letter and reminded the admission staff that he was serving his and their country. He went on to say that he soon would return from this war and wanted to attend a college in his hometown of Colorado Springs. If Colorado College was not interested in him, perhaps the committee could recommend a suitable school. This was a good move, and it made the admissions people stop and think. Jim soon received a second letter, a letter of acceptance. He led the way for other Vietnam veterans and me. Jim greeted me in the gym and introduced me to a few other students back from the war; there was just a handful of us. Those few veterans I met in the gymnasium were the beginning of my social life at Colorado College.

I put every effort into my classes that spring; I spent long hours at the library working on my rusty writing skills. In my free time, I joined the track team. The track coach, Frank Flood, was twenty years my senior and fascinated by the war in Vietnam. He asked a lot of questions, and I enjoyed answering them. He was the exception. Most of the people on campus avoided the topic of Vietnam; even other veterans avoided talking about the war.

On cold, snowy days, when we couldn't run outside, Coach Flood wrapped our hands with tape and then fitted us with sixteen-ounce boxing gloves for an aerobic workout. We entered a makeshift boxing ring in the basement of the gymnasium. Coach Flood had been a professional fighter in the 1950s; he fought in New York and Chicago. He loved boxing and made a great effort to promote it to the students. I soon found I enjoyed the boxing ring more than running. One day, Coach put the gloves on me and told me that a hockey player would be over soon to spar. The hockey player, an excellent athlete, was broad-shouldered, tall, and heavier than I was. There was a point in our sparring match when I threw a left hook and quickly followed it with a right. My glove smashed into his nose. He dropped to his knees, then he fell to the mat face down. The scene frightened me, but Coach Flood assured me he was okay and ended the match.

Late in the school year, Coach put together a team to fight in an amateur boxing competition held each year in Pueblo, Colorado; it was called The Pueblo Smoker. The match was organized by a local civic organization and drew more than a thousand fans. It was the highlight sporting event of this gritty steel mill town. One snowy afternoon, Coach Flood pulled me out of the ring, and as he began unlacing my gloves, he said, "Duffy, you have a lot of natural ability as a fighter. I want you to fight in the upcoming Pueblo match."

I knew this question was coming because some of the other students were already on board. I told the coach I didn't know. I asked for some time to think about it. As I thought about getting into a ring with a thousand people watching me, I hesitated. It was like being onstage, and it didn't appeal to me. I decided to decline the invitation, but I would wait until the last minute, because I didn't want to be pressured to join the fight. There was to be a weigh-in at the venue in Pueblo. At the weigh-in, each fighter would be matched with another fighter near his size and ability. As the day came closer, I pulled the coach aside and told him of my decision. I saw his disappointment, but my no was final. It wasn't the fear of boxing that kept me away but the fear of boxing in front of an audience. The coach understood, and he didn't push.

By mid-semester, I had had it with motel life, and I began to look for another living arrangement. I found a room on Weber Avenue near campus and made the move. Now I was faced with paying rent and losing my evening meal at the motel restaurant. I applied for a job with the college food service, and I was hired on the spot. I was sent to the Kappa Sigma fraternity house, where I served food at their evening meals and helped clean the kitchen. I was paid an hourly wage and my dinner was provided during each shift I worked. This was the perfect job for me. As weeks passed, the fraternity men adopted me, and my social life blossomed. I was included in every social event and developed lifelong friendships. The Kappa Sigma house became a social anchor for me and saved me from the isolation of the motel.

My days at college were filled with classes and my nights with long hours studying at the library. I also spent time painting and printmaking at the Colorado Springs Fine Arts Center. During this busy time, I thought little of Vietnam. I mistakenly believed that I had moved on from the war, and I assumed that it was now in my past. But I soon discovered my war memories were just below the surface of my student life.

The nightly news readers on TV discussed potential peace talks as the fighting in Vietnam raged. Then the news readers turned to the anti-war protests in the United States. I watched those broadcasts in our student union. Some students cursed at the image of President Nixon. They also cursed the war and hurled obscenities at the television set. I quietly watched those outbursts of anger, never letting on that I had fought in Vietnam. I knew there was no joy in Vietnam, but I soon learned there was no joy or celebration for the Vietnam veteran. Instead, we often were met with distain and judgment.

On only one occasion at Colorado College was I put under the microscope about my Vietnam experience. One of the college's well-respected history professors and an antiwar leader on campus found out I had served a tour of duty in Vietnam. While I was sitting in his class toward the end of one of his morning lectures, he began comparing the soldiers serving in Vietnam with the Nazi storm troopers in World War II. His intention was to get my goat. Of course, he did get my goat, and I called him on this foolish comparison. As we exchanged words he looked down at me then said, "Okay, you were in Vietnam, tell us about it."

His demand surprised and silenced me. What followed was a long pause as I tried to collect my thoughts about my year in Vietnam. I thought, *How could this guy compare me, an American draftee, to Hitler's Nazi war machine?* The classroom was silent, and I felt every eye focused on me. As I thought back to my year in Vietnam, I realized that nothing I said could come close to a description of that horrible time in my life, and for a moment, I wanted to run from the room. The silence continued as I soon grasped that I was being set up for an argument, an argument that I was sure to lose against a skilled, well-spoken professor. As I sat at my desk, I looked up at the professor, and slowly shook my head.

"So you don't want to tell us about Vietnam?" he said. I continued to shake my head. I stood to leave the classroom, feeling thoroughly insulted and empty of words. As I walked out, the professor dismissed the class. I was the first to leave, and I was upset and hurt.

Outside the classroom, I stopped and turned. I watched as the other students quietly filed out. I felt a measurable affront inside the room, but even now I couldn't talk. The students surrounded me. They each looked at me; some nodded and some smiled. Barb Wilson, my friend from California, gave me a smile and said, "It's okay, Mike." Many of these kids had friends or relatives who were serving in the military, and I was sure they realized the gravity of the professor's needless insult. What was even more disturbing to me was that he had served in the military during World War II.

Although I felt insulted by his comparison in an odd way, I now knew that someone in this college besides my track coach recognized my service, albeit in a negative light. For the most part, the other professors and most of the students ignored the topic of Vietnam. There was one exception when it was acceptable to bring the war to the surface—the campus war protests.

I moved on from that day. I did my work for the class, but from that point on, I kept my mouth shut, and each morning I couldn't wait for the class to end. In a strange twist; as time went on, I became friends with that professor. There was a curious bond because of our military service. He would greet me on campus and ask how I was getting on. He also attended the fine art functions held on campus, and we would discuss painting and drawing, but the Vietnam War was never brought up again, either inside or outside the classroom.

What I did not understand that semester was the indelible mark that my year in Vietnam had given me. I was so busy catching up academically with the other students, reading books, and closing the library each night that I had no time to think about the war. I did receive one letter from a young private in my old unit. He liked me and he wanted to know how things were going for me at home. I answered his letter with a few lines. After that, I never wrote to anyone in my old unit. I ended my first semester with solid marks in my classes and an excitement about returning to school in the fall. One afternoon in late May 1969, after my last class of the semester, I packed my Volkswagen and started for home.

Chapter 13

SUMMER 1969

I arrived home from Colorado College on a warm Sunday afternoon and quickly emptied my car. My goal now was to find a summer job. On Monday morning, my father and I walked down to the office of Chicago's 49th Ward Regular Democratic Committee on Devon Avenue. My father, a lifelong Democrat, knew the ward office handed out patronage jobs to loyal neighborhood Democrats. He had phoned the office earlier in the week and mentioned that I had just returned from Vietnam and I was in need of summer employment. The word "Vietnam" was cause for an instant argument on most college campuses. However, in Chicago's working class neighborhoods, a GI returning from Vietnam garnered respect and, in my case, a summer job driving a truck for the Cook County forest preserve district.

As we waited in the ward office, I watched a clerk type up a letter of introduction. She walked through a side door to have our ward committeeman, Neil Hartigan, sign it. I had hoped to meet Mr. Hartigan, but he never came out of his office, or he was never in the office and his secretary signed his name for him.

The letter of introduction was the necessary document needed for summer employment, either with the City of Chicago or with Cook County. My letter of introduction from Mr. Hartigan was a job ticket. Every ward in Chicago had patronage jobs. For the most part, those jobs went to the people living within the ward boundaries. Sometimes, a sympathetic ward boss might give a relative living outside his or her ward a job. But he did that at the risk of losing votes.

The patronage jobs were voting magnets. My dad would tell our neighbors his son had just returned from Vietnam. Then he would continue and mention that the ward committeeman helped his son get a job. The story of this job would circulate over dinner tables, in barrooms, and at churches and synagogues. People would nod their heads in appreciation, and that appreciation would find its way to the ballot box.

The efficient 49th Ward secretary told me to take my letter to the offices of Cook County in downtown Chicago. There, she said, I would fill out more paperwork and be assigned a job with the Cook County Forest Preserve. After a long day of waiting, filling out paperwork, joining the Teamsters Union, and paying my first month's dues, I was given a position. My summer job was in the Bunker Hill Forest Preserve just off Caldwell Avenue on Chicago's Far Northwest Side.

Early the following Monday morning, I arrived at the forest preserve office ready for work. My new boss, Joe, was late. When Joe finally arrived, he handed me the keys to a large, yellow dump truck. Two college kids who also got patronage jobs were assigned to me as my work crew; I was in charge. The two boys were close to incompetent. One day they set a lawn mower on fire by carelessly flipping a lit cigarette on it's gas tank. The two of them watched as the mower went up in flames. They stood watching it burn in a state of helpless stupidity. I extinguished the fire by throwing damp grass on top of the mower. Both of them talked incessantly about themselves and their sorry lives at college. They told me how bad the food was, how terrible their dorm rooms were, and how hard it was to get good tickets to rock concerts. I quietly listened and thought about how lucky they were to have the opportunity to attend college and not get drafted. They, of course, did not even think of the war in Vietnam. When they found out I had served a year in Vietnam, their only question was this: "Did you get laid?"

The job at the Bunker Hill Forest Preserve was easy, but it left me with too much time on my hands. After work I would head home, eat dinner, watch a little TV, and then walk to Lake Michigan. Vietnam was beginning to seep into my every task and every endeavor, and I couldn't get it off my mind. I longed for the busy schedule at college and my nights studying in the library, painting at the Fine Arts Center, or boxing with Coach Flood.

I decided to get a second job. A new bar on Division Street called Mother's was hiring waiters. The bar was down a long flight of stairs that led into a set of cavernous rooms. I drove to Mother's late one afternoon and spoke with the manager. When I mentioned that I was just back from Vietnam, he shook my hand and hired me. He told me that he had missed the draft because of a bad leg. Soon I was pumping customers for drink orders on the crowded dance floor. On weekday nights, work at Mother's ended at 12:30 a.m. I would head home, sleep a few hours, and then drive to the forest preserve for an eight-hour day. On weekend nights, I didn't get home from Mother's until 2:00 or 3:00 a.m.

Things seemed to be going well, and I pushed away my Vietnam thoughts. But I had this latent anger circling inside me. I think part of that anger had to do with the young men I met that summer who had successfully avoided the draft. Some men would get a letter from a sympathetic doctor listing a myriad of physicals problems, or some had the money to stay in college and continue getting draft defer-ments. Others I met told me they quickly married their girlfriends and by doing that they could apply for a marriage deferment.

One night at Mother's, I was assigned to help a bartender at a small triangular bar situated like an island near the dance floor. As I washed the dirty glasses stacked beneath the bar, the bartender, a wisecracking blunder-head, began loudly mocking me. He made sure his customers heard his insulting remarks. There was a silly pecking order between the bartenders and the waiters. The bartenders were on top of the hierarchy; the waiters were at the bottom. I cared little about the pecking order. I only wanted to make money and then head for home. I socialized with none of the staff.

As I continued to wash glass after glass, the bartender kept showering insults on me. He would look at me while I was washing the glasses and make a crack about how slow I was, then he would laugh out loud and shake his head. This juvenile behavior began as soon as I entered his small bar and continued for twenty or thirty minutes. I was close to walking away from his bar when I heard him tell a customer how he had avoided the draft. After I heard that, he made the mistake of bending down near the stainless steel basin. I stopped washing glasses and grabbed him by his tie near the neckline and I held him tight over the sink. I looked him in the eye and in an angry cutting tone I told him if he continued with his fucking insults he wouldn't make it to work tomorrow. I held him below the bar so the customers could not see. I had an urge to pummel him, but I gained my control and let him go. Then I watched a visibly shaken man try to compose himself. I felt the same anger I had in San Francisco toward the Hells Angel fellow, but this time I acted on it. I turned and ducked beneath the bar and onto the dance floor. The bartender never said a word to management, and he never came near me again. I told the boss I was finished washing glasses, and I went back to selling beer.

In the summer of 1969, I tried to put my life back together as I had known it before Vietnam, but it was impossible. The war I had left six months earlier was like a moving picture in front of my eyes. I couldn't rid myself of its presence.

I had one short week off that summer and took a road trip with two friends from my neighborhood, Don Suerth and Gene Diggins. Don had just purchased a new Volkswagen and wanted to drive to New York City. I quickly accepted his offer. We stayed in Queens, New York, with friends and made day trips into Manhattan.

One night, we found ourselves at a bar near Throggs Neck in the Bronx. We stayed much too late, and near the end of that long night, some of the locals in the bar began questioning our presence in "their" bar. I was still skinny; I hadn't regained the weight I had lost in Vietnam, but I carried myself with confidence. After my year

Pictured left to right: Mike Duffy, Don Suerth, Gene Diggins
(rear with cigar), New York City, summer 1969

in Vietnam, no one could insult me without some type of pushback. I approached the ringleader of this small group and told him that if he had a fucking problem with our presence, he and I could step outside. I was sure we could clear things up in the parking lot. I spoke with wrath and conviction, and I watched his face change. Cooler heads prevailed, and we wisely left the bar. He was lucky, but I was luckier. I didn't do anything stupid. I would not be so cool-headed later in the summer. The anger I carried continued to rear its ugly head.

We returned to Chicago on a Sunday night, and on Monday morning, I went back to work at the Forest Preserve. My boss, Joe, welcomed me back and began telling me how much money he had made over the weekend. He pulled out a fistful of twenty-dollar bills, and then he smiled at me and said I could make some extra money next week if I was willing to work on a Sunday morning. I told him sure, I was interested, Joe told me he would fill me in about the job later in the day.

That week we cut the grass and pulled picnic tables out of the North Branch of the Chicago River. Throwing picnic tables and beer cans into the river was a favorite late night teenage pastime. We cleaned up the trash from the small, sheltered picnic groves. On Monday mornings they were always filled with paper plates, candy wrappers, and lots of beer bottles and beer cans. Friday morning came, and Joe cornered me. He told me we had a big job to do. We drove over to one of the picnic groves and began moving tables from one location to another. After a few hours of work, one grove was almost empty of tables, but the other was now overflowing with them. I asked Joe if a big crowd was expected for the weekend. He smiled and said, "Yeah." At the end of the day, Joe turned to me and said, "Duffy, meet me here Sunday at 9:00 a.m. sharp." I told him I would be there.

Early Sunday morning I drove to the forest preserve. When I arrived and looked over the scene, I was puzzled. Joe was talking with a group of men in the picnic grove that was empty of picnic tables. He was speaking to the forward contingent of the Knights of Columbus planning committee. Joe walked over to me and said he had just a few more negotiations and then we could go to work. I stood next to my yellow Park District truck, still confused about our task.

Joe lit a cigarette and walked back to the group of men. He was in the middle of the crowd as arms waved and fingers pointed back and forth. Then I saw all of them take a belt of whisky from shot glasses. They shook hands, and Joe walked back to the truck. He said that he and I were going to pick up and move all the picnic tables we had moved Friday back to their original location. The original location is where the Knights of Columbus picnic was about to begin.

What Joe did was this: He knew the Sunday picnic was in grove A. So on Friday, while on the clock, he had us remove the tables from grove A and put them in grove B. On Sunday morning, when the Knights of Columbus group arrived to set up their picnic, they were surprised to see that they had only a handful of tables. This is where Joe made his move. They quickly cornered Joe, the Sunday morning forest preserve "official," and asked him why there were so few tables. Acting surprised, Joe said he thought the picnic was in grove B. He said he was sorry but nothing could be done now because he had only a skeleton crew. That's when voices were raised and arms began flailing. The men of the Knights of Columbus planning committee were beside themselves. In just one hour, hundreds of people would descend on their picnic grove, and they would have nowhere to sit. They pressed Joe about what could be done.

Joe had the answer. With the help of a little cash, he could have his small crew—the two of us—move all the tables back to grove A. After all the discussions, things were settled with a handshake, a shot of whisky, and a fistful of ten-dollar bills. Joe and I went to work. When we completed the job, Joe handed me twenty dollars. I think he kept fifty.

As the summer passed, I began to watch the calendar in anticipation of returning to Colorado College. My social life was all but dead because past girlfriends were either married or had moved on to other interests, and many of my old buddies were busy with their new wives. In the midsummer of 1969, a new bar opened in our neighborhood. It was located on Devon Avenue within walking distance of our apartment; it was called the Joker Pub. Gene Diggins told me about the grand opening, and we walked over one Sunday afternoon to a tavern full of people. There I began to patch together a second social circle. I had my friends in Colorado, but here at the Joker Pub, I made new friends and began to run into other Vietnam veterans. What was strange to me was that out of so many young men I talked with that summer, we—the Vietnam veterans—were in the minority. I often wondered, *How did so many guys get out of the draft?*

One Saturday afternoon on the sidewalk just outside the Joker Pub, I began a discussion with a fellow Vietnam veteran. He lived on the south side of Devon Avenue. When I was a kid, Devon Avenue was our dividing line. We had our social life north of Devon. Our beach was Albion Beach, our haunt was Loyola Avenue, and our hangout joint was Cindy Sue's coffee shop on Sheridan Road. All those places were north of Devon Avenue.

The fellow I began talking with, Donnie Conklyn, had just returned from Vietnam. He and I began to compare notes—where we were stationed, what our jobs were, et cetera. Donnie began to tell me a story not about the war but about an encounter with a local band of thugs called the TJO gang. TJO stood for Thorndale Jag Offs.

Donnie was five-foot six and weighed about 140 pounds. He wore round, rimless glasses, and they made his eyes look like big brown marbles. Donnie told me that just one day after he had returned from Vietnam, his mother sent him to Laurie's pizzeria for a takeout order. Laurie's was on the corner of Foster Avenue and Broadway in Chicago's Uptown neighborhood. After Donnie picked up his pizza and began his walk home, the TJO gang stopped him on Broadway. Five or six members of the TJO gang began hassling Donnie.

The TJO's modus operandi was to rob people, snatch purses from women, and generally make life risky for anyone who lived in or near Uptown.

The TJOs started this lopsided fight by punching Donnie in the face, knocking off his glasses, and throwing him to the sidewalk. The pizza flew onto Broadway, and the punks began kicking Donnie while he was curled up on the sidewalk. Still very much in the fight, Donnie got a hold of one of his attackers by his leg and then dragged him to the sidewalk. As he was getting kicked he found his face buried in the belly of one punk. Donnie opened his mouth wide and dug his teeth into the flesh of this combatant, ripping off a two-inch strip of skin and muscle tissue. As Donnie paused from telling me his story, he smiled and took a drag off his cigarette. Then he said, "Duff, I never heard a guy scream as loud as that fucker did after I ripped the flesh from his stomach."

Donnie went on. He told me that after his attacker's scream, the other gang members stopped kicking him, and they backed off. Donnie stood up with the flesh still in his mouth, blood dripping from his chin. He spat the flesh onto the sidewalk and stood his ground.

The TJO boys backed off in disbelief and fear, and they moved on down Broadway. Donnie walked back to Laurie's, he cleaned up, and then ordered another pizza.

Donnie told me this story with such nonchalance and confidence that I was sure he would be feared by this Uptown mob and never bothered again. A smile crossed his face as he puffed away on his cigarette. "Duff, I couldn't fucken believe it," he said. "I just got home from the war all pissed off and tired, then this TJO shit happens a block from our apartment."

He went on to tell me that he was even wearing his Vietnam jungle hat that night. He slowly shook his head from side to side and said, "My only regret about that night was the fucking punks backed off. I was ready to rip the flesh off any and all takers."

I walked away from Donnie knowing what he meant about being pissed off and angry. I couldn't understand why I was so angry. I wished I had been with him when he was jumped, I would have loved to have taken on the TJO boys with him.

I drifted down to Rush Street early one Sunday evening. I needed to report for work at Mother's at about eight o'clock. It was midsummer and Rush Street was crowded with tourists and revelers. I walked out of the hot, late-afternoon sun and into a bar. I ordered a beer and began looking around the room. Soon, from out of nowhere, a fellow walked up to me and asked what I was looking at? I didn't understand his question. "What do you mean?" I asked.

He continued staring at me and said, "What are you looking at?"

The fellow was short and thin; he had greasy hair combed straight back on his head. He was upset with me for what I felt was no reason. Puzzled, I answered him, "I'm looking around the bar. Why do you ask?"

"You're looking at my girl," he bellowed.

That was a surprise to me—I hadn't noticed him or his girl. They were seated in a booth across from the bar. I said, "I'm not looking at your girl."

He went on. "You fucker—you're looking at my girl."

As he stood near me, I couldn't believe what I was hearing. I didn't care about his girl or him. I thought, *Why am I in this situation?* I gave him a good long look and then I glanced at the entrance. There were two doors I needed to pass through to get outside. I eyed him and then I considered grabbing him by his collar and dragging him out to the sidewalk; once there I would pull him down the alley and thrash this piece of shit. God, how I wanted to do that, but I reasoned it might be too hard to get him through both doors. Also, what if a customer walked in just as I was pulling him out? That could be a problem. My good judgment prevailed. I turned back to the bar, finished my beer, and left. As I walked along Rush Street that evening, I felt a sense of relief that I didn't bow to my anger.

I walked up Rush Street toward Mother's and noticed that most of the bars had their TV sets tuned to the moon landing by Neil Armstrong. It was Sunday, July 20, 1969. People were glued to the TV sets, smiling and cheering. I was numb and could care less about Neil Armstrong, the moon landing, or my Sunday night of work ahead of me. For a short moment, I wished I was back in the military with its discipline and structure. I seemed out of place here and I could not unwind from the stress of Vietnam.

✳ ✳ ✳

August arrived, and I received an invitation from my cousin to visit her family's summer home in far northern Wisconsin. I was invited for a three-day weekend, and I quickly accepted. The drive north for me was new. I had never been past the city of Milwaukee; it's just ninety miles north of Chicago. Northern Wisconsin is home to a vast collection of large and small glacier lakes. Some of those lakes are linked together by small channels. In-between the glacier lakes are vast stands of hardwoods and coniferous trees it is truly a magnificent part of the Midwest.

My drive north was well over eight hours on narrow, two-lane roads. I arrived late that afternoon in the town of Three Lakes, Wisconsin. The beauty of the countryside was striking; there were tall white pines, maple trees, and blue inviting lakes. The sky was crystal clear with a brilliant sun. It was here at Three Lakes, Wisconsin, that I first began to relax and feel a sense of relief from my war experience.

The mood in northern Wisconsin was then, and still is today, laid back. I spent the better part of each day on a wooden pier, swimming and lying in the sun. One evening, as night fell and my tense muscles began to unwind, a group of family members and I took a long walk. On the way back to the house, I saw the aurora borealis for the first time. It was spectacular and a perfect end to my visit. I was ready to leave for Chicago and then return to Colorado College.

My brother, Dan, returned home from the army just a few days before my departure to Colorado. We talked over dinner one night and made plans to celebrate his return. On a Saturday evening, we both walked down our block to a small neighborhood pub called Connolly's. A few neighborhood friends joined us as we sat at this modest bar on Devon Avenue. Dan and I talked about Vietnam, and soon our conversation went back to the convoy from Xuân Lộc when our truck broke down. I told Dan of my concern as I sent my little brother to the back of the convoy with his loaded and cocked

M-16 rifle. I told him what I should have done that day was hook a chain to the broken truck and tow it back to Bearcat. As we talked in Connolly's, other neighborhood friends drifted in and greeted us. It was an innocent start to a Saturday night.

When Connolly's was about to close, we decided to drive up Clark Street to another bar with a 4:00 a.m. license. The other bar was across the street from a movie theater called the Adelphi. As we entered the bar, I heard a band playing country and western music and a tough-looking crowd eyed us. I turned to Dan and mentioned that it looked as if we had just entered a local hillbilly bar. The glue sniffers from our neighborhood were now of drinking age, and they had staked out a bar of their own.

There was a pool table in the center of the room and booths with tables along each wall. The bar had a good-sized crowd for 2:00 a.m. The first thing Dan did after entering the bar was to put a quarter on the side of the pool table. Dan was a good pool player. He had learned the game in the army. He told me that he could play all night and beat most challengers.

Pool table etiquette in a barroom was well defined. A new player had to place a quarter on the side of the table, often next to other challengers' quarters. The queue of quarters represented a challenge to the winner of the game or games, if multiple games were agreed on. The winner of the game or set of games had the right to stay at the table and continue taking on other challengers, sometimes all night. A loss meant that the loser had to leave the table, preferably in an agreeable manner.

All of us took seats in a booth near the pool table and ordered beer. I watched a tall man with bad teeth win game after game as Dan's quarter inched closer to marking his turn. The king of the pool table was cocky. After he won a game, he would cackle and mutter disparaging remarks about the poor skill of the loser. Soon Dan's quarter came up, and he walked to the table and racked the balls. As the challenger, Dan suggested that they play three games, and the winner of two out of three games would stay at the table. As this discussion went on, more challengers began placing their quarters on the side of the table.

The tall, lanky "pool champ" walked over to his booth and began a conversation with his crew. They laughed together, and I watched as they all downed a shot of liquor. The pool champion lit a cigarette and then sipped on his beer as Dan stood waiting at the pool table. Dan yelled across the room and asked if he was ready to play. In an impatient voice, the guy shot back at Dan, "Take your time, shorty." His "shorty" remark bothered me.

The champion pool player sauntered away from his crew and over to the table. He had a cigarette hanging from his mouth; he took his pool cue and then blasted the balls across the table. Both Dan and his opponent looked dead serious as they took their turns at the table. I lost interest in the game and turned to the conversation in our booth.

A loud yelp drew my attention back to the pool table as the "champ" strutted away in a victory walk back to his buddies. I watched him put a glass of beer to his mouth, take a drink, and then with a broad smile on his face shout to his friends, "I beat him real good." He continued to smile as he peered back at Dan.

Dan stood patiently at the table and then he reminded the winner that there was at least one more game to play before he had to give up the table. Reluctantly, Dan's opponent walked back. He took his cue and once again blasted the triangle of balls. They scattered across the table hitting the green felt bumpers and clacking into one another.

During the second game, Dan's skills improved. I watched from the booth as his opponent became frustrated and then angry when he lost game number two. This time he didn't walk back to his buddies. He yelled at Dan, "Rack 'em." He lit another cigarette as a bitter look crossed his face. Dan calmly stated, "The loser racks the balls," then he slid the plastic racking triangle down the table. His opponent racked the balls.

The last game was quick. Dan soundly beat his opponent, but his win was not without hazard. The guy was visibly upset. In a flash of anger, he began cursing Dan. His outburst got my full attention. Dan stood at the other side of the table, quietly listening to an obscenity-laced outburst. The only thing Dan wanted was the guy gone from the table so he could play the next challenger. In a seething rage, he threw his pool que at Dan. The flying cue bounced off the green felt of the table, and as I watched in shock, the thick end of the flying cue slammed into Dan's face. He was stunned and grabbed the table for support, his knees buckled and blood gushed from his nose. I watched as his opponent smiled and then began laughing. My anger at seeing my younger brother assaulted was overwhelming, and this time I didn't hold back.

I flew across the room and leveled two punches at Dan's assailant—a quick left hook, followed by a smashing right. Dan's attacker dropped to his knees. Now I had his crew to contend with as they began a vengeful charge toward me. I wasted no time. I took on the first one with a left jab, then a right cross, and his knees buckled and he withered to the floor. By this time, the barroom was in chaos. People were punching, pushing, and wrestling with one another. The band stopped playing, and the bartender called the police.

By the grace of God, I didn't get touched or hurt. That was not the case for Dan, who suffered a bloody nose and a nasty bruise with a lump on his forehead. The fight stopped when the Chicago police arrived and filtered through the front door. The police lined up everyone as the clock above the door struck 3:00 a.m. We were marched out to Clark Street to a waiting paddy wagon. Standing in line in front of me was my friend we called Uncle Don. Don knew everyone in the neighborhood, and everyone in the neighborhood knew Don. He even knew the police officer at the door of the paddy wagon. The officer spoke first. He looked at Don and said, "What the fuck are you doing here?" That was all it took. The officer posted at the door looked us over and said, "Get out of here." We quickly left.

Late the next afternoon, I packed my belongings, said my goodbyes, and drove off for Colorado. I felt just as I had in Vietnam almost a year earlier during the rocket attack. I had dodged a bullet last night, but this time I could head back to school and a future.

As I drove west toward Colorado, I thought about last night's events. I couldn't believe our luck. Now I was driving back to Colorado Springs, where that type of circus was off the table. It seemed that I had two lives, one at college and one back in my ever-changing Chicago neighborhood. My Chicago life was tumultuous, footloose, and full of characters and adventures that even the best playwrights would have trouble conjuring. Risk was part of any late-night outing. Even on hot, lazy afternoons I could find conversation at the Joker Pub. Life at college was a bit staid and didn't have the spontaneity or color of my Chicago neighborhood, but I couldn't wait to get back to school.

The one part of my city life in Chicago that ran against the everyday neighborhood norm was my interest in the arts. As hard as I tried, I could not get any of my friends or acquaintances to join me at the

Art Institute of Chicago for an afternoon of looking at paintings. I tried often but soon realized that most of my neighborhood friends' knowledge of art stopped with the large Picasso statue in downtown Chicago. The statue, at least to me, was a large, abstract head made of rusting iron. It sat, and still sits, in the heart of Chicago just in front of City Hall. Everyone knew of the statue because of all the news coverage about it. Mike Royko, the famous Chicago columnist, wrote an article in 1967 discussing it's unveiling. Royko's column was one of two mandatory barroom reads; the other was the sports pages.

Summer afternoons in a Chicago neighborhood bar were much different from summer evenings. For one thing, during the afternoon, the jukebox was usually quiet. There were fewer patrons in the bar, and they were older than the evening crowd. Afternoon conversation revolved around baseball, either the White Sox or the Cubs. In the Joker Pub, the conversation was usually about the Cubs. After a ball game was picked apart and discussed, there was usually a bit of silence, and then someone would ask, "Hey, did you read Royko's column?"

Mike Royko's column about the Picasso statue was published on August 16, 1967, in the *Chicago Daily News*, and it got everyone's attention. I heard barroom arguments about the Picasso statue years after Royko's article was published. After listening to a barroom tirade about "modern art" and the "waste of money spent on the Picasso"—there was no "waste of money" because the statue was a gift from Picasso to the city of Chicago—I would always pose this question, "Have you ever gone downtown to see it?" Most times the answer was no. A few people told me they had driven by it on the way to work or had walked past it on the way to shop at Marshall Field's department store, but few if any people took the time to figure it out, Mike Royko included.

Driving west from Chicago to Colorado Springs was a long journey. The drive was more than a thousand miles, and in my non–air-conditioned Volkswagen during late August, it was always uncomfortable. This time I decided to try a shortcut. After studying a cross-country road map, I found a southerly dip in Interstate 80 near the town of Lexington, on the far west plains of Nebraska. From Lexington I could drive south on Highway 283 into Kansas and then take a diagonal road southwest to the town of Colby, Kansas, where I could pick up Interstate 70. It would take me west and south of Denver and closer to Colorado Springs. This shortcut might shave twenty-five miles off my trip. I decided to try it. I had a sleeping bag with me, and as the sun set after my first day of driving, I stopped at a public park and slept next to my car under the stars. The park had running water and toilet facilities, and it was free.

I started my drive early the next day and continued west on Highway 80 until I reached the cutoff at Lexington. Then I drove south toward Colby, Kansas. At Colby I pulled into a gas station and filled my tank and bought a soda. I began a conversation with a young girl who was standing outside the gas station with a white-haired old man. They were both holding bags of groceries. The girl looked about seventeen years old and she was gorgeous. As we talked, she asked me if I was driving west and if so could I please give her and her grandfather a ride out of Colby, just a few miles west of town. I said sure, and they climbed into my car. The girl was wearing a white sundress, and it wasn't until she stepped into the front seat of the car that I noticed she was shoeless. She had no makeup on her face or nail polish on her fingers or toes. Her grandfather wore a white shirt under well-worn denim bib overalls. He had dusty, brown high-top shoes laced to the top and he wore a brimmed straw hat. He didn't say a word.

From the time the girl got into my car until the moment she got out, she talked. She gave me a full explanation of her life. She told me that she had had a row with her mother and was now living with her grandfather. She went on to say that her grandfather needed help cooking and keeping up his house, so, she said, "This was a good arrangement." They didn't own a car, so each day they walked to town for groceries. We drove slowly through town and then west on Highway 24. She pointed to an intersection and asked me to pull over. I stopped the car and continued to listen as she went on about her life.

She rode a Trailways bus from the Panhandle of Texas. She said the bus ride took almost the entire day because of the many stops at the small towns along the way. I loved listening to her soft Texas accent. Her voice was not a high-pitched girly voice but rather deep and smooth and slow with an even meter.

After thanking me, the girl and her grandfather walked toward a small trailer park just off the highway. She held her grandfather's hand as they crossed the road, and then she turned, smiled, and waved to me. This small bit of conversation and companionship was the highlight of my journey.

I continued driving west on Interstate 70. At the town of Limon, Colorado, I turned southwest for the last leg to Colorado Springs. As I turned off the interstate, I was slowed by a convoy of farm vehicles. At one point, I thought of passing them, but there were too many vehicles, and I didn't want to get stuck in the middle. After creeping down Highway 24 for a sluggish fifteen minutes, the farm implement convoy turned off the road and into a field. This maneuver was painfully slow. A long line of cars with me in the lead came to a dead stop as each farm vehicle made a sharp left turn into the oncoming lane of traffic and then slowly entered the field. By the time the road was clear, I was an impatient basket case ready to drive cross-country to get past them. Between my long conversation in Colby, Kansas, and this convoy of slowpoke farm vehicles, I lost the time I would have saved with my well-planned shortcut.

My first sight of Pikes Peak was confirmation that my trip was almost over. As I rolled my car onto the Colorado College campus, the sun was setting behind the Colorado Rockies. I opened the door of my Volkswagen and felt the cool Colorado air and realized I needed a jacket. The evening air of Colorado doesn't hold the heat as the humid Chicago evenings do. I walked to the Hub, our campus coffeehouse. I was looking for a familiar face and a place to spend the night. I scanned the bulletin board for any available apartments or housing opportunities. Some students made sure they had their housing set up for the fall semester before they left campus for summer break. I, on the other hand, waited until I arrived back on campus, knowing that there would always be someone in need of a roommate. There was a payphone in the Hub; I used it to call a friend. He lived in a house not far from campus; I hoped he might offer me a few nights on his sofa. Luckily, he was home and my request was granted.

My small, green Volkswagen held everything I needed for my upcoming school year. It was packed with books, clothes, shoes, and a pair of winter boots. I would use my car as a closet until I found a permanent home.

✳ ✳ ✳

My classes that fall included an English literature class taught by Lewis Horn. We read an eclectic group of books. There were the unabridged versions of Homer's *The Iliad* and *The Odyssey*, along with Emily Bronte's *Wuthering Heights* and Charles Dickens's *Bleak House*. Night after night, *The Iliad* and *The Odyssey* kept me buried at a corner desk at the library.

I also had a class on Southeast Asian studies taught by Frank Tucker. Professor Tucker's class was in Palmer Hall and started at 8:00 a.m. I was usually the first to arrive, and because of my tour in Vietnam, I had a strong interest in his lectures. At times, Professor Tucker would attempt to crack a joke. The problem was that at 8:00 a.m., students were often late to his class, sleepy, and bored with his monotone voice. I was usually the only one who laughed at his jokes. Accordingly, he liked me and began looking at me as he delivered his jokes. I never disappointed him; I always laughed.

There was one time when his class laughed, but I didn't. We were invited to Professor Tucker's house for a "meet and greet the professor" gathering. He served coffee and soft drinks and gave us a tour of his home. He was very proud of one room that held seashells he and his wife had collected over the years. The shells were displayed on a large sheet of plywood. I decided to get a closer look at one shell sitting toward the back of the plywood. I outstretched my arm and put my weight on the edge of the plywood and began to lean over. The plywood tipped down, and shells began spilling onto the floor. I think only a few broke, but Professor Tucker never invited the class back to his house.

I had two art classes that fall, both at the Colorado Springs Fine Arts Center, a Depression-era building constructed of gray concrete. The building held galleries, an auditorium, and a small library that opened on to an exquisite courtyard; there were classrooms on the second floor. Colorado College's art department housed its faculty offices in this building. The painting studio, a large, open space with high ceilings, had a concrete floor painted battleship gray. There were frosted clear story windows on the north side of the room and a pair of French doors opened west onto a small balcony with a drop-dead view of Pikes Peak. I loved working in that room.

I had two painting teachers—Bernard Arnest and James Trissel. A young Jack Edwards taught sculpture, but my favorite professor that semester was Mary Chenoweth, the print teacher.

Mary was a free spirit and seemed to thoroughly enjoy teaching. She also was a painter and she painted large expressionist works; one work, an abstract painting of a motorcycle rider, was hanging in the campus library. Not to end with painting, she also carved a set of double doors from sugar pine for the Broadmoor Community Church in Colorado Springs. Perhaps it was her seemingly complete satisfaction with her life that motivated the class. Her demeanor let all her students work without worrying about making a mistake. Mary had a staccato teaching voice, and at times she was hard to follow. There was a large printing press in the middle of her classroom. The press had a big red wheel four feet across with a wooden turning handle. As the wheel moved, a copper plate was pressed between two large steel rollers, pushing damp rag paper onto the ink-filled plates. I was intrigued by it and could not wait to learn to use it.

Professor Arnest was a man close to retirement. He painted beautiful landscapes and told me that he had been an army war artist in Europe in World War II. During the Great Depression, he had painted a WPA mural in a Texas post office. Professor Arnest was affable, and we got on well. The most difficult painting assignment given to me by Professor Arnest was the abstraction of a Pieter Bruegel painting. Like so many novice painters, I viewed abstract art as a puzzle. I knew it was good because I was told it was good, and every major museum in the world displayed abstract works prominently. But as a young painting student, I didn't understand it. Professor Arnest helped me.

A few days after school began, I found and rented a small room on the second floor of a house on Tejon Street, just a block from campus. It was a narrow room positioned in the back of the house. It suited me because I only needed the room to sleep. Most of my time was spent on campus and in the library. I also was rehired by the Saga Food service, working once again in the Kappa Sigma kitchen during the dinner hour. Between my studies, my work, and new friends, I was able to put aside the nightmare of Vietnam, but the war memories would never leave me.

If there was a perfect tonic for moving on from my year in Vietnam, I unwittingly found it at Colorado College. The school's setting at the foot of Pikes Pike was exquisite. The students at Colorado College were open and accepting. The professors were always responsive to the students, and they were available at all times.

I graduated from Colorado College in May 1972. My parents and my sister, Irene, drove out from Chicago and attended my graduation on a beautiful sunny day. My brother, Dan, was working and was unable to attend. I was the first in our family to graduate from college.

Appendix A

THE TET
OFFENSIVE

There were two monumental battles fought in Vietnam during the twentieth century. These two battles changed the course of history of three countries: Vietnam, France, and the United States.

The first of these battles occurred in the spring of 1954; it lasted only fifty-six days. This battle cost France its jewel of the orient, French Indochina.

The second major battle, fought in 1968, was launched on Tet, the Vietnamese lunar new year. It was always to be remembered by that name, the Tet Offensive.

Over three centuries and with little difficulty, the major European powers carved up the undeveloped world. From the Americas to Africa and Asia, the Europeans (and, to a much lesser extent, the United States) occupied, set up shop, and began to extract the wealth from these poorer countries.

In the mid 1880s the French claimed Vietnam as one of their conquests, and with two other contiguous kingdoms, they changed the name of Vietnam to French Indochina. This new French state consisted of Laos, Cambodia, and Vietnam. Indochina was France's "Pearl of the Orient." The French had close to one hundred years of relative calm in Indochina. Rubber trees were planted and fueled the growth of Saigon and Hanoi, the two major cities of Vietnam.

Saigon, now Ho Chi Minh City, is located on the far southeastern edge of Vietnam and sits about 40 miles inland from the South China Sea. The French engineers built a series of government buildings, wide streets, and canals to feed the commerce of Indochina. European-manufactured goods poured in and the fruit of Indochina poured out. Seagoing vessels made their way up the Sông Nhá Bé River, then into its tributary, the Saigon River. Here on the docks of Saigon they unloaded goods from Europe, especially France, then, in turn, they picked up rubber and exotic tropical wood for the return trip.

World War II changed everything for the French. Germany invaded France and the Japanese invaded French Indochina. During the Japanese occupation of Vietnam, a small resistance movement developed around a group of Vietnamese nationalists. With some help from the United States, this group waged a guerilla war against the new colonial master in Vietnam: Japan. The Vietnamese nationalists, led by Ho Chi Minh, began to taste a small bit of freedom.

Although the end of World War II brought defeat to Japan, it also brought the French back to Indochina. The French made a mad dash to reclaim their Pearl of the Orient. They were not about to lose ninety years of investment. France had the guns, the planes, and an experienced army to keep any pesky independent-minded nationalists in line.

However, after World War II another problem developed for the French in Indochina: Ho Chi Minh and his top general, Vo Nguyen Giap. After years of battling the Japanese in the jungles of Vietnam, these two insurgents had a well-trained, experienced militia, named the Viet Minh. Ho Chi Minh was not about to have the French return without a fight.

In 1954, after eight years of guerilla warfare between France and the Viet Minh, the convincing loss for the French came at the battle of Dien Bien Phu, ending May 7, 1954. In a splendid display of military overconfidence, the French sent fifteen-thousand seasoned troops into the lush Muong Thanh Valley adjacent to Laos. Through stealth and experience, the French were quickly surrounded by an army of fifty-thousand Vietnamese Communists. Then, beginning in March, 1954, the French forces were bombarded with artillery and overrun with human wave assaults.

The French were crushed, and they were finished in Southeast Asia.

After defeating the French in Indochina, a new dilemma faced Ho Chi Minh and his dream of an independent Vietnam. His problem this time was politics and the Western world's fear of Communism. Ho Chi Minh was about to set up a new government in Vietnam and align himself with two world Marxists powers: Mao Tse-tung of China and Nikita Khrushchev of the USSR. Vietnam was about to become a Communist state, an anathema to the United States and free Europe.

Soon after the French loss in Indochina, the United Nations held the 1954 Geneva Accords to put a final end to the war between France and Vietnam and settle the borders. Ho Chi Minh watched in horror as his country was cut in half. With a nod from the Soviet Union and China, there was to be a North Vietnam under Communist rule and a South Vietnam ruled by a new democracy. Ho Chi Minh was betrayed by his two patrons, China and the USSR. Ho Chi Minh wanted all of Vietnam, but only got half.

During the 1950s and 1960s, the United States found itself in a protracted Cold War with the Soviet Union. It watched the

Soviets crush short-lived freedom movements in Hungary, Poland, and Czechoslovakia. Like dominoes, country after country fell to Communism. Then, right at its doorstep, Cuba was swept up in a revolution. Cuba's Fidel Castro set his country's course as a Soviet satellite state. A real fear rose up in every American one October day in 1962: the Cuban Missile Crisis. The Soviet Union began building military bases in Cuba and launch pads for intermediate and long-range nuclear missiles. President John Kennedy, in an effort to stop this threat, faced down the USSR using gun boats and a blockade of Cuban ports.

The Cuban missile crisis brought the United States and the USSR to the brink of nuclear war. From this frightening episode, a collective fear of Communism gripped the United States. This fear opened the door for Presidents Kennedy and Johnson to send increasing numbers of American troops into the Republic of South Vietnam to prevent another domino from falling to the North Vietnamese Communists.

By January 1, 1968, the United States had well over 500,000 soldiers in Vietnam. The word out of the Johnson White House was this: "There is a light at the end of the tunnel." Most Americans took those words to mean that a win in Vietnam was at hand.

Every evening news station in the United States reported to the American public an enemy taking enormous losses. The national news with Walter Cronkite showed all of us the weekly body count. The body count was the scorecard for the American public. The weekly body count was the number of Americans killed versus the number of North Vietnamese and Viet Cong killed. The numbers were astonishing. Week after week, month after month, thousands upon thousands of the enemy were reported killed. Based on these huge numbers, it was obvious to us all that the United States was winning. I remember watching this count on our black-and-white television set. Like a football match, there were two boxes. One box showed us the Communist losses, and the other box showed the American losses.

General Vo Nguyen Giap, the architect of the defeat of the French forces at Dien Bien Phu, developed a plan to finally put an end to the South Vietnamese government and unite South Vietnam with North Vietnam. In a daring, no-holds-barred attack, the general planned to surprise the Americans and the South Vietnamese Army by attacking and overwhelming them with over eighty thousand troops. His plan was labeled the Tet Offensive.

On January 31, 1968, in a coordinated countrywide, all-out attack, a combination of North Vietnamese regulars and Viet Cong guerillas assaulted almost every major base and city in South Vietnam. In the capital city of Saigon, the Communist forces penetrated the United States embassy grounds and the huge American air base, Tan Son Nhut. They fought their way into the Chinese section of Saigon, Cho Lon, and held it for over a week; they attacked the ancient city of Huế and held it for over a month. By all accounts, the Tet Offensive lasted for over nine months, and strategy after strategy was used in a continuous push to defeat the Americans and their allies, the South Vietnamese.

In the end, the Americans soundly won the Tet Offensive, but the political battle at home was lost. A skeptical public could not understand how an ostensibly beaten enemy could mount such a broad-based attack. A kink in the armor of the White House appeared and Lyndon Johnson did not run for reelection in 1968. The mood of America changed, and thinking adults who once supported the war now had second thoughts. The writing was on the wall, and the new president, Nixon, was left with the job of getting the United States out of Vietnam. Like the French, the extraction was an ugly process, as

President Nixon pushed, shoved, and bombed the North Vietnamese to the "peace table."

My story begins on the eve of the Tet Offensive as I left McChord Air Force Base in the state of Washington for a place in Vietnam called Cam Ranh Bay.

ACKNOWLEDGMENTS

I wish to thank the following people who helped me with this memoir:

Scot Barker, who read my first draft and urged me to publish.

Maggie Duffy, my first editor who gave her time correcting my many spelling errors.

Chris Newman, my second editor who sat with me for hours at the library going over each word.

Chris Montgomery, who took the time out of her life to read this memoir and give me direction.

Chuck Guest, my close friend who gave me encouragement.

Bob Gorman, who gave me sound advice.

Dian Adam, who read and gave me many good comments.

John Todd, my army friend who sent me pictures of the battery.

Roger and Liza Hein, my dear friends.

Julia Lynch, a close family friend who offered her many suggestions.

Carol Hibbert, my Canadian friend who read my manuscript and offered ideas.

Also, Bob Swegle who went over the book with me in Carmel, California during a two-day visit.

Also, thank you Paula Dettrich for your wise suggestions.

Also a thank you to my able editor from Inkwater Press, Holly Tri.

And lastly my three daughters. Rose, who read, reread, and detailed many of my slip ups. Hannah, who gave me her strong encouragement to publish. And Margaret, who read many of my early chapters, gave me new ideas and much support to finish this book. Thanks to you all, love Dad. Lastly, a thank you to my late wife, Peg Duffy.